Media education

Media education

Unesco

Editor: Zaghloul Morsy

The designations employed and the presentation of material throughout this publication do not imply the expression of any opinion whatsoever on the part of Unesco concerning the legal status of any country, territory, city or area or of its authorities, or concerning the delimitation of its frontiers or boundaries.

The authors are responsible for the choice and the presentation of the facts contained in this book and for the opinions expressed therein, which are not necessarily those of Unesco and do not commit the Organization.

Published in 1984 by the United Nations Educational,
Scientific and Cultural Organization,
7 place de Fontenoy, 75700 Paris
Typeset by AUP Typesetters (Glasgow) Ltd, United Kingdom
Printed by Presses Universitaires de France, Vêndome, France

ISBN 92-3-102204-0
French edition: 92-3-202204-4

© Unesco 1984
Printed in France

Preface

Education is, of course, not an isolated subsystem, closed in exclusively on its internal components; it is influenced by many processes that bring change to societies and to knowledge. Identifying such trends, which are often buried in the hurly-burly of daily information, and deciding how they can contribute to the development of education is a priority task for the planners and decision-makers of national research bodies and of those regional or international organizations for which education is an institutional field of competence. Working out the long-term implications of the trends and fitting them into educational policy and programmes undoubtedly helps to bring existing society and current knowledge closer, and to enable school curricula to catch up with the evolution of knowledge. Among the trends that have emerged in recent years, one is ineluctable: the requirement that education should take a different view of the mass communication media, take account in its content of the constantly swelling volume of messages they convey, and learn how to turn media techniques and technology to its own advantage.

    The steadily increasing influence of communication and information and the omnipresence of communication media in daily life have only very recently made people aware of the positive aspects, and the sometimes mischievous effects, of this state of affairs both for individuals and for society. Modern man

Preface

is enmeshed in a tight web of messages and information, of all kinds and of diverse origins, which he does not always manage to control. The press, radio, television, the cinema, posters, and so forth, are not mere vehicles of communication. They constitute a real environment; they condition thought and very often determine behaviour. It seems increasingly plain that education systems will have to be clearly defined in the face of these phenomena and their development, which is patently going to continue and to go deeper. How can education utilize, exploit and master the countless messages and items of information disseminated by the media and make them truly educational while at the same time doing its part, where necessary, to counteract any adverse influence they may have on children's and adolescents' outlook and behaviour. This is admittedly a complex question, but one that deserves attention now that we are fairly and squarely in the communication society in which our children live and will continue to live without so far having been prepared for it.

Of course, educational institutions are already using such media as radio, television and multimedia systems, and doing so more and more often; but neither the problem nor the challenge lies there.

The problem is that, all over the world, there coexist two sources of information and knowledge for the child and the adolescent. There is the traditional school, that of writing and books, with its separate subjects organized in stages from one class and one level to the next; facing it, round about and all-pervading, is the 'parallel school' of the media, whose techniques, operation, modes of presentation and even content are completely different from those of the school and which subject the intelligence, the emotions and the moral character to a substantial influence that is not always in keeping with the aims pursued by education.

Despite the efforts, which have been made here and there, and of which the reader will appreciate seeing some examples later on, the connection between the information received through the mass media and the training given in school remains tenuous, if *not non-existent or even contradictory. The fact is that the coexistence of the two institutions is hardly peaceful: the fight is on, openly or beneath the surface, and is anything but even-handed inasmuch as the media, through their power, their economic, financial and technological weight, and the extent of their dissemination and impact, place the school on the defensive and very often feed its anxiety. The school, for its part, feigns ignorance of the media's specific language and blinks away the evident fact that the knowledge, the values of intelligence and sensibility instilled in the child by his teacher through the spoken word, the blackboard and reading are but an islet in the flood of information and demands for attention, in the form of sounds and images, to which the child is subjected on leaving the classroom.*

It would doubtless be expecting too much of the media, omnipresent and everywhere triumphant, to relinquish their power and adjust to the school; neither should too much hope be placed in families' ability to arouse their children's awareness; only the school is theoretically and practically capable of conceiving and playing this role. Is it not predestined to be the place where this information—not to be confused with knowledge—is made coherent, since the school is the depository of the critical spirit? Is not the school responsible for devising the learning process—since there is no knowledge unless the information is structured as a conceptual whole that can be learnt only in stages? Is it not the school which possesses cultural legitimacy and which, in any case, mirrors its own brightness when required to teach lucidity to the children in its charge? In a word, the school alone is capable of constructing the conceptual and interpretative codes with which information can be mastered and integrated. Even so, it will have to come down from its ivory tower, give up some of its privileges, and make its structures, methods and conception of school curricula and subjects more flexible. Faced with such a challenge, the school must adapt, reform itself and move out into the world, or else resign itself to representing in the long run, no more than an optional and marginal place and knowledge in the midst of a training and an outlook on life that are drawn from another source—the media—which is held to be the only one that is modern, true and full of promise.

No one denies the need to learn to read, and to read critically. Why then should we disregard the need to learn to watch and listen just as vigilantly? The training of the mind should be supplemented by education of the imagination. The best way to train children and adolescents in this new mode of communication, then, is to teach them to handle its language, to read and write it. It is important, therefore, that young people should be taught the proper use of communication and the media.

This trend—this requirement— has been dubbed 'initiation in mass communication media', 'educommunication' or, somewhat boldly, 'media education'; this last was defined by the International Film and Television Council (IFTC) in 1973 in terms that still seem to hold true:

the study, teaching and learning of modern methods of communication and expression considered to be part of a specific and autonomous discipline in pedagogical theory and practice as opposed to their use as teaching and learning auxiliaries in other areas of knowledge, such as mathematics, science and geography.

This definition was appropriately completed and strengthened by an expert meeting convened at Unesco (Paris, September 1979), which took the view that the concept of media education covered

all ways of studying, learning and teaching at all levels (primary, secondary, higher, adult education, lifelong education) and in all circumstances, the history, creativity, use and evaluation of media as practical and technical arts, as well as the place occupied by media in society, their social impact, the implication of media communication, participation, modification of the mode of perception they bring about, the role of creative work and access to media.

Thus the problem and the challenge are clear. To tackle them, new relations should be built up between education and the media in order to work out and bring up to date a rational plan of action and a balanced complementarity between the two institutions in the educational field. Thought should be given, more systematically than in the past, to the ways and means of combining organically and harmoniously the objectives, activities, productions and methods of implementation both of education and of contemporary communication technologies.

In this 'negotiation' the media's assets are—apart from the power of the messages and culture that they disseminate on a massive scale every day—their emotional content, their accessibility, their ability to arouse interest instantly, the pleasure they give and the freshening effect they could have on education. On the other hand, reservations of two kinds are felt regarding their introduction into educational practice. First, any overture to the media should not be made at the cost of a schism between educated countries (which means the industralized countries) and peoples who are being conditioned (which means the developing countries, whatever the length of their tradition in the fields of education and culture). On this point, moreover, reflection and action should be particularly cautious in the non-industralized countries since imported media are also bearers of values and forms that are far from neutral and not always in harmony with the requirement of cultural identity, the development of endogenous culture or historical methods of passing on knowledge. Other reservations concern the material conditions to be met, the teacher-training to be provided, the psychological disturbances to be avoided and, it must be said, a renewal of education which is believable but not yet fully guaranteed.

There are, therefore, questions to be asked: what should be the roles of educators and 'communicators' respectively? What sections of the public should be given priority for media education within the formal education system and as a component of lifelong education? How should the content of media education be defined for each society in the light of its socio-cultural and technological development? How should media education be integrated with general education? On the teaching level, is there any incongruity and, if so, how much incongruity between the modes of presentation and assimilation of the content disseminated by the media, particularly television, and those of the scholastic institution (effort, memorizing, retention, gradual acquisition of knowledge, competition, evaluation, examination)? How can a culture that has to be conquered and one that is given away free be combined and complement each other harmoniously?

In this consideration of the balance to be struck between the methods and contents specific to each of the two institutions, it is clear that an essential function of education systems should be to reduce to order the mass of information disseminated by the communication networks, since it is characteristic of education to refer to a system of values, to methods that teach how to pick out what is essential—in short, teaching how to learn. To achieve this, however, the school would be compelled to consider new learning strategies for a form of 'knowledge' that had already been acquired elsewhere by the learner; this would entail a veritable revolution in teaching, for such a learning process would no longer be conducted along theoretical lines laid down according to pre-established targets, but on the basis of the pupils' actual experience.

As to content: should new, separate curricula be drawn up— that is to say, should specific curricula be introduced dealing with the media, or should processes and methods facilitating the retrieval, appropriation, processing and systematization of available information be integrated into the general curriculum? Furthermore, is it better to work out a general curriculum applicable to all media and independent of each of them individually, or to assemble different curricula tailored to each medium in accordance with specific objectives?

Whatever approach is adopted, at least two conditions must be met in order to introduce the media into the scholastic institution: technological maintenance (space, hardware, upkeep, etc.) and suitable preparation of the teachers (all or just some?) to provide them in an integrated manner with a technical initiation and teacher training.

All these questions remain open, and in the contributions making up this collection the reader will find champions and exponents of every approach. Furthermore, in a field as new as media education, the only proper course at this stage is to refrain from pontificating in any way.

In choosing the theme of this collection and assembling the texts to be included, we make no claim to lay down standards or to cover the entire field of a problem whose complexity, recent emergence and multiple interferences and ramifications we have underlined. Speaking only of Prospects, *it seems to us that the thought and experience that have accumulated in recent years and that reflect the efforts of the entire international community allow us, if not to glimpse the main lines of a synthesis, then at least to spot some important trends of action and a highly promising vitality.*

Readers of Prospects *will find here some articles which they may have read in the review, this time grouped together, linked up and supplemented by a number of hitherto unpublished contributions. In addition to the men and women associated with decision-making on the expansion and renewal of education, administrators and planners in national departments, those in charge of programmes and methods, inspectors and trainers of teachers and activities organizers, directors of innovative institutions, leaders of pedagogic research teams, producers of educational materials, and persons and institutions in charge of educational co-operation programmes, we believe that this volume should also be of interest to specialists in communication and media problems at all levels, comparative education specialists, educational sociologists and, to be sure, parents and educational trade-union leaders. In short, it will be of interest to all those who, whether they be educators or not, are aware that education is not just teaching, and who intend to take the broadest possible look at what is being thought and done in the field of media education in the world today.*

In 1972 the International Commission on the Development of Education established by Unesco carried out a survey of the situation of and prospects for education around the world for the coming decades. This was the Edgar Faure Report published under the title Learning to Be. *In the MacBride Report* Many Voices, One World, *published in 1980, the International*

Preface

Commission for the Study of Communication Problems, also established by Unesco, highlighted the importance of the contribution which communication could make to education, and drew attention to the increasingly numerous reciprocal relationships in existence between communication and education. In the years to come, all those who are keenly concerned with the problems of education and communication and are aware of their interdependence will be seeking to build bridges between the two reports and to institute a practical, operational symbiosis between the two cultures—that of the school and that of the media—each with its own individuality and without order of precedence.

The Editor, *Prospects*

Contents

Media challenges

17 Media systems and educational systems *Abraham Moles*
44 Mass media and the school: Descartes or McLuhan? *Pierre Schaeffer*

Information and knowledge

75 Communication and education *Henri Dieuzeide*
84 Mass communication education *Ana Maria Sandi*
97 The two worlds of today's learners *Donald P. Ely*

Re-appraising teaching and learning strategies

113 Learning, understanding, and communication media *Mircea Malitza*
127 The information explosion and optimizing the educational process *Yuri Babansky*
148 Theoretical issues and practical possibilities *Len Masterman*
166 New tasks for teacher training *Ferenc Genzwein*

Integrated approaches

181 Norway: critical consciousness and effective communication *Asle Gire Dahl*

200 The Canton of Fribourg: media education from primary through secondary school *Gérald Berger*
219 Finland: reducing informational and cultural inequality *Sirkka Minkkinen and Kaarle Nordenstreng*
236 Austria: theory and practice of media education *Thomas A. Bauer*

Focuses on impact and experiment

251 Journalism and pedagogy *Gaspare Barbiellini Amidei*
260 Brazil: the press in school *Dymas Joseph*
277 Cuba: an introduction to radio broadcasting *Renaldo Infante Urivazo*
292 Japan: television for young children *Takashi Sakamoto*
304 France: educating young television viewers *Évelyne Pierre*
319 The United States: visual literacy *Howard Hitchens*

Third world: images and reality

331 Do mass media reach the masses? The Indian experience *G. N. S. Raghavan*
348 Mass media and the transmission of values *Rita Cruise O'Brien*
361 Transnational advertising and education in the developing countries *Rafael Roncagliolo and Noreene Z. Janus*

A tentative conclusion

379 Education and the mass media: where they differ, where they converge *Michel Souchon*

401 **About the authors**

Media challenges

Media systems and educational systems

Abraham Moles

One of the problems preoccupying all international cultural organizations, and especially Unesco, is the impact which the new systems of communication will soon be having on the process of education, which is explicitly set down in Unesco's Constitution as one of the fundamental human needs, but whose very nature is being challenged.

The act of communicating, of relating individuals at different points in space or time through recording or writing, is not a fixed and stable process in which only minor improvements are possible; if it were the task of an international organization would be only to find out the most suitable ways of using communication for educational or cultural purposes.

On the contrary, the past ten years have witnessed several considerable changes in the nature of this communication process and hence in its role; we shall mention three of these changes.

The emergence of new media systems

First, those forms of communication which are 'socialized'—i.e. bound up with a social system of whatever form, and which thereby transcend the individual face-to-face relationship—

were, until a few years ago, reduced to all intents and purposes to mass communication (the mass media), because, among other reasons, the mass media broadcast the same message to a large number of individual or collective recipients from a single source. This process is the equivalent in communication terms of the volume production of goods in industry, the media making it possible to turn out messages in a great many copies and thus to reduce the unit cost of communication, dividing it by a factor representing the number of copies. Radio, television or the press cut by a factor of thousands or millions the production cost of a news or publicity item, thus incidentally making it possible to produce a more finished item of higher basic quality, and to 'address' or 'dispatch' it to a great many individuals scattered over a wide area.

Since the founding of organizations such as Unesco, the Council of Europe and the Organization for Economic Cooperation and Development (OECD), in the development of education and culture emphasis has inevitably been placed on the systematic exploitation of the mass media for those organizations' own purposes, namely, improving the educational or cultural level of their Member States. The problems involved have been the role first of radio and later of television in education, the publication policies of the various countries and the difficulties encountered by those countries and the optimum strategy for relaying to the greatest possible number the most accessible and most useful messages possible, in order to modify the minimum intellectual equipment of each individual recipient in such a way as to enable him to make the best possible use of his environment, i.e. to give him a 'culture'.

Although the age of the mass media is not past—far from it—other forms of telecommunication, also made possible by technology, have now to be taken into account in any analysis of the relations of the individual, no longer with his immediate environment alone, but with people far away who have something or other to offer him, if only by virtue of their own special experience. This is the emergence of interpersonal media or, more generally, of modes of communication in which certain individuals select others from the range of choice offered by society in order to exchange a communication, to communicate what they like, when they like, how they like, making use of the means which technological progress has made available. The simplest examples are mail and the telephone, banal instances which have nothing new about them, but which have in fact been hitherto almost entirely overlooked by the major educational and cultural institutions, which have regarded them as personally convenient amenities, elements of the quality of life, rather than as basic tools of culture or of education.

It seems clear, for technical, political, economic and even ethical reasons, that we should revise our judgement on this matter and take heed of the mounting importance of interpersonal communications as heralding a challenge to the 'totalitarian' role of the mass media. The international organizations should therefore give thought to this new aspect of the matter.

The second phenomenon to consider is the emergence of the practical role of communication through time, or rather of what Cloutier has called the 'self-media'—communication from oneself to oneself over a period time—of the personal document or recording. The only important form of this known in the past was the written form (students' notes, contracts, archives, private diaries, business papers), but communication from self to self through time gave rise, at the end of the nineteenth century, to a development of an anecdotal type, the souvenir snapshot, a personal record of a very special sort, the possible social role of which was reduced by the vicissitudes of history to the function of a fashionable gadget, giving birth to a major industry, amateur photography.

It is only in the last few years that the tape recorder and especially the videotape recorder have given us an intimation of other ways of regarding the self-media, particularly bearing in mind the fact that there are few appliances the price of which cannot be brought down sharply when economic pressure and the will to develop them have made themselves felt and have met with universal support. We need only mention the tremendous reductions there have been in prices in relation to the facilities being offered to the individual in the case of such extraordinarily complex technological tools as motor cars, transistor radios and television sets.

Such examples illustrate two axioms of a technological society: (a) a technological society is capable of assimilating, producing, putting into service and controlling any technical appliance, however complex it may be—in other words, complexity is no longer an obstacle or an objection to the production of technical appliances of any kind; (b) a technological society is also able to place such appliances at the disposal of a very wide public, at least if there is a sufficiently steady and strong public demand to create a market and to justify the corresponding development and marketing efforts required.

Cars and television are now normal features of the way of life of people the world over, even those who do not own them.

Since the role of international organizations necessarily involves a certain amount of forward looking, they should learn from these developments and ask themselves what will be the future role of the self-media, what role could be played by the recording of speech, sounds and images in the sphere of everyday life whereby, so to speak, the individual sends himself a message (which he could also send to others), thus storing up in an artificial memory a whole series of stimuli from his previous experience of life, without having any longer to rely on the simple symbolic processes of writing or drawing. These latter processes required a certain type of initiation and skill and a certain investment, which did not show immediate returns during the individual's as-yet unproductive youth—a sufficiently serious problem to have provided education with one of its main aims, the fight against illiteracy. In learning to write, one mastered a procedure which was rudimentary, but applicable everywhere, in almost any circumstances, for the purpose of exchanging messages both with oneself and with others, and thereby of retaining the mental and symbolic forms of past experience.

We always tend to underestimate the cost, in intellectual, temporal and moral terms, of writing. It represents in fact a considerable investment which only certain societies have been able to afford for each of their members in terms of time allotted to education. How many people who 'can read and write' actually do no more than make notes, a few signs and elementary calculations, and decipher newspaper headlines or the names of shops? An analysis of the day-to-day habits of broad social categories even in the so-called developed countries (agricultural and factory workers), even in Western societies, reveals the cost of writing, and shows how rare it is for the written word to be used spontaneously, a fact which contrasts with the proliferation of administrative or social archives and of temples of culture which are so seldom visited by the man in the street. In other words, writing, although the only truly widespread of the self-media, remains, despite its success in various civilizations, a luxury article for the human brain; if only because of the investment which it entails at the outset—learning to read and write. It thus stands in contrast to other types of imaginable self-media or documents, which, although based upon a more complex and costly, but duly socialized, basic technology, recommend themselves as being much easier to use, much more natural, as many observations made by Unesco experts in a wide variety of countries have shown.

A third and last basic change in the world of the media is the emergence of communicational affluence, more as an ideal than as a reality, but as an ideal in the direction of which there is a broad movement. Communicational affluence means a break, initiated by technology, with the fundamental law of proxemics according to which the individual takes a keener interest in those things, people and events which are closer to him in space or time and of which he is therefore more aware. All human societies are organized on the basis of the principle that what is far away is necessarily less important than what is close at hand. Although some of them, the technological societies, have made substantial readjustments to their scales of measurement of nearness and distance, such changes of scale have not really challenged this basic idea. Whether one is dealing with transport or communication, something will always be near and something else far away, and access to the latter is more difficult and costly than access to the former.

Only recently, and under the pressure of certain very specific needs (space exploration and the safety and maintenance of technical plant) has the idea of 'communicational affluence' taken concrete shape in people's minds: the idea that it is possible for someone to get into contact with anybody, anywhere, without feeling that the idea of distance interferes with this contact as a negative factor polarizing his field of representation and interaction. In other words, it is something new under the sun that the concept of communicational affluence should be able to call in question the immutable law of proxemics.

So things are changing in the world of the media. The media can no longer be considered as synonymous with the mass media, leaving correspondence, the telephone and conversation to private life. More specifically, the videotape-recorder, the satellite, the video-telephone, the photocopier and the data bank are all inventions which have to be reckoned with.

This is certainly not a short-term project. While one may accept the fact that the totalitarian domination of the mass media over the individual's time budget is no longer to be taken for granted, it will quite obviously continue for a long time to come, and it will go on playing a determining role, particularly in developing societies, whose problem often seems to be that they will use any available means to pull themselves up to the technological level they consider ideal.

Among the interpersonal media, the postal and telephone networks, soon to be followed, perhaps, by the telex machine, systems of liaison between terminals and computer, and the tele-reproduction of documents, are gradually spinning across the planet a new web the true implications of which we have not yet fully grasped; it is arguable that it is precisely the role of major organizations such as Unesco to perform the task of integrating human thought. Such organizations, transcending the limited aims of a particular nation, aspire to guide the course of progress towards certain goals regarded as desirable (education and culture) and are by virtue of that function compelled to engage in futurology. What is the possible or probable significance of a particular development in the light of a number of new or even foreseeable discoveries or concepts? What short-term activity must be undertaken here and now with a view to encouraging or controlling some of these 'long-term images' constructed by futurology? It has often been said that the developing countries could legitimately hope to avoid some of the wrong turnings, false starts and errors that have occurred in the evolution of developed countries which have been unable to escape the constraints of their history and the intractable nature of their own circumstances.

New media systems and education

Our task is to outline some of the implications of the emergence, from these new media systems, of the very idea of possible communicational affluence and a conceivable break with the law of proxemics, and in particular their implications for education.

CULTURE AND EDUCATION

We shall here make a rough distinction between the two terms 'education' and 'culture'. Culture, in its widest sense, means the entire artificial environment which man creates by acting on the external world: it includes tools, machinery and works of so-called art, but it also includes the tools of thought—words, concepts, mental techniques, algorithms and know-how. Culture, then, is the residue of past experience in the memory, either that of the individual (personal culture) or the collective memory of society as manifested in its libraries, museums, institutes or academies—residues or traces left by the totality of previous experience.

In precisely the same way, individual culture is all a person's past experience (in the sense of the German *Erfahrung*): everything which has remained in the person's mind in a usable form. This is one of the basic components of our image of the world at any given moment, combining with our immediate perceptions in our field of consciousness to determine our subsequent behaviour. Culture is the accumulated residue of all that we have assimilated, understood and absorbed in our past and which becomes a factor in our present, conflicting or combining with our current perception of the external world.

Of all the processes which incorporate the past in the present, special prominence should be given to what is known as education. This is a process specially devised by human beings to influence other human beings, especially when they are young and hence easier to influence for better or for worse. Education includes acquisition of the skills needed to drive a car or ride a bicycle, absorption of the values simultaneously plugged by advertising and propounded by politics or, more simply, the knowledge of the multiplication table, English grammar or moral values which is supposed to be provided by the school curriculum.

In short, culture is the deposit left in our minds, and education is the interpersonal or social process for determining the composition of that deposit. This extremely general definition is much broader than the stricter definitions usually laid down by the various national ministries of education or culture. It suggests that there may be several types of education, corresponding to the nature of the processes which bring about this sedimentation, which is at the same time a mental tool and a form of mental sclerosis. One might, for example, distinguish between psycho-motor education— leaning how to open a door, hold a pen, drive a car or type— and more 'intellectual' education—learning to recognize letters and figures, words or formulae, symbols or codes, and adapting to situations or conjuring up the past by reading or looking at a document, i.e. by communication with the historic or aesthetic past through symbols or images.

CONCENTRATED EDUCATION AND SELF-EDUCATION

These are already well-established categories and we need refer to them only in passing, but one of the distinctions which concerns us results from the very ecology of the media systems and their distribution in space and time, to which we referred earlier. Basically, we shall distinguish between two types of education in considering the process of the acquisition of 'culture', whatever that culture may be.

The first, which fits the most usual definition of education, is the system concentrated in space and time, or more simply, what used to be meant by 'school' or 'university': essentially a concentration of human beings in space and in time for a definite purpose, employing a form of learning more or less systematized on the basis of that individual embodiment of the mass media, the teacher, who is a source of intellectual knowledge (or even 'corporal' knowledge, for example the gymnastics teacher). The teacher sprays his knowledge over a number of receptive, or at any rate recipient individuals, the process being limited by material factors, greater or lesser possibilities of feedback and the principles of optimization of cost-effectiveness. The purpose of all this is to lay down a particular sediment in the mind of these recipients, who are mobilized, that is, brought in from all over a given area, town or village, at a given moment, and then immobilized at a particular point of concentration in space, that is, the classroom, for a fixed period. Concentration in space and in time in the school or place of instruction is justified by reference to the principles of the division of labour (the concept of the specialized educator), of maximum receptivity (utilization of the period of childhood or adolescence) and of optimization of cost-effectiveness (dividing the cost of providing the teacher by the number of receivers that he is capable of reaching in sufficiently favourable conditions). Table 1 gives some idea of such types of evaluation, as they may reasonably be calculated for the purpose of assessing educational cost.

This spatio-temporal concentration is, however, a constraint on the life of individuals. It is time taken out of their time budget; from a certain hour to a certain hour they are herded together in the school or university, travelling across the town, or, in more general terms, across a given area. This element of constraint, emphasized by writers of children's fiction who talk of the delights of playing truant on a sunny day in May, is expressed in another way by parents in lower-income groups, who see it as removal from the production unit, for varying periods, of a number of its members.

The constraint was not felt so sharply in an older world where the very notion of a time budget was unknown, and where time and space seemed to be unlimited resources since the flow of life was little affected by the amount of space or time available to the community. Then, the main obstacle to building a school was the cost of the social labour that had to be deducted from the resources of the community, but it was certainly not the number of square yards of space which the school would take up in the area nor the time that it would take up in the lives of those who had to attend it. To be precise, the loss of active time entailed by time spent in training or education was felt to be marginal, not central, by all sectors of the population, except for certain poor classes in the nineteenth century.

We shall contrast this type of education concentrated in space and time with the very broad and still little explored concept of self-education, that is, the acquisition of responses, knowledge or values that is, theoretically, unconnected with a particular point in space or time. The individual lives and builds up experience of life; this experience leaves behind a sediment the richness of which depends on how often the experience has been repeated in different circumstances, how often the same patterns have been seen against different backgrounds. All this is incorporated into the memory as a totality with a greater or lesser degree of structure, a patchwork or 'mosaic' culture. It is certainly, therefore, an educational process in the broad sense of education defined above.

In fact, education in this sense is synonymous with life; self-teaching is one aspect of the process of living. Yet our minds, brought up with the traditional categories of the schoolmen and by Comenius, who invented the image of the school and can almost be said to have invented its mythology, have the greatest difficulty in acknowledging as a specific educational mechanism this process of deposition of sediment by the stream of life which we call self-education. It is something which has been brought to our attention only recently.

The growing interest in this matter results partly from the criticisms levelled at traditional concepts of schooling and from various attempts, some more speculative than others, to produce alternatives, such as Illich's school without walls, the open university and the university of the air; but also simply from a new awareness of the role of the mass media in the daily development of our culture, especially television, whose sudden impact has done more to change the structure of daily life in twenty years than schools had succeeded in doing in ten centuries.

ORIGINAL FEATURES OF SELF-EDUCATION

The time has come to take a look at this self-educational aspect of daily life, which is fully acknowledged by psychologists but goes unrecognized by the institutional systems, since it is by definition the antithesis of any kind of institution. However, various factors help to mute this conflict which, for the sake of clarity, we have shown as existing in principle between educational systems concentrated in space and time and self-educational processes—which constitute a sort of compound interest from the business of living, which can in theory occur at any point along the individual's trajectory in life and are the traces left by the stimuli which assail him in his passage along that trajectory (see Figure 1). Other traces are left by the individual's encounters with certain places at certain times—to

TABLE 1. Cost of producing an intellectual (in French francs)[1]

	Cost of biological maintenance	Instruction for a group of twenty	Social productivity foregone	Investments in equipment and premises	Total
Period of life at primary school (10 years)	600 per month	1 teacher at 1,500	No production possible		
TOTAL	72,000	9,000		1,000	82,000
Period of life at secondary school (8 years)	1,000 per month	5 teachers at 1,600: $5 \times 1,600 \over 20$ = 400 per month	Apprenticed for 4 years at at 5,000 per normal working year		
TOTAL	96,000	32,000	20,000	2,000	150,000

	1,000 per month	10 teachers at 2,000	No ordinary work	Practical sciences (engineer, etc.)
Period of life at university (5 years)				
TOTAL	60,000	60,000	50,000	10,000 (theory course 2,000)
				180,000 (182,000)
Period of training during working life (research workers, managerial, etc., personnel) (5 years)	1,500 per month	3 teachers at 2,000 for a group of 5	Compensation (half-time work)	
TOTAL	90,000	25,000	25,000	3,000
GRAND TOTAL	318,000	126,000	95,000	16,000
				143,000
				555,000

Subsistence = 318,000   Training = 237,000

1. For the sake of comparison, an ordinary IBM 360 computer costs 1 million francs.

take a very simple example, a man regularly returning to his place in front of the television set which is a fixture in his home. Here the problem is that of getting the message across to the man, which is what is meant by programming.

In fact, the question hardly arises in this form but must be dealt with scientifically, by means of a statistical analysis of all the stimuli encountered along the individual's trajectory and classification of their content. Self-education will include the memory of a particular television or radio production and the

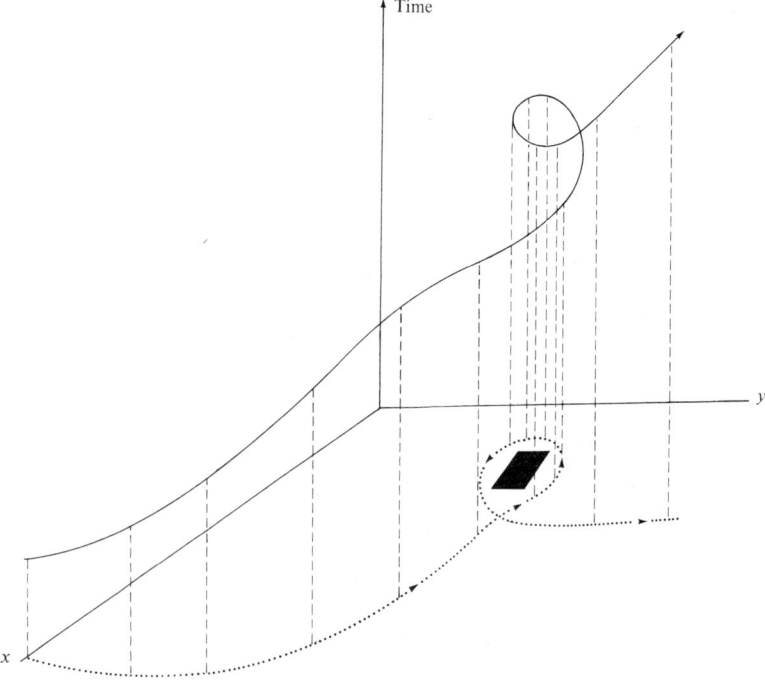

FIG. 1. The 'line of the universe' or the trajectory of the life of the individual. Each individual circulates in space, represented here by two dimensions x, y, where there is a trajectory shown by a dotted line, for example on the plan of the town considered as the preferred area of displacement of the individual. This trajectory is traversed as a function of time, and we shall call the line in the space x, y, t, the line of the universe of the individual.

reading of a particular newspaper and it will above all be influenced by the density and repetition of such stimuli, producing an integrated pattern in the memory which separates fleeting memories from deliberate or enforced memorization. One might say that the individual describes a trajectory through a vast labyrinth of space and time—a four-dimensional labyrinth which is showered at certain points with streams of stimuli, impressions and messages of varying density. Self-education is the net result on our mental structure of various instances when these influences have impinged upon it from disparate sources.

This observation leads us to restrict somewhat the meaning of the term self-education. It is not enough that all living experience should theoretically be a component of our mental equipment. It is also necessary that it should be sufficiently intense, sufficiently dense and often enough repeated. If this is not the case, self-education is only a new word for something already familiar. On the other hand, if human society, duly equipped with advanced technology, feels capable of taking control of and modulating the flow of these stimuli—initially by detecting them and locating them along the trajectory of the individual's life, by analysing their frequency or rate of repetition, and by artificially increasing their density at certain points along the line, or perhaps even by programming them statistically—then the idea of self-education no longer implies simply the residue left by experience but a blueprint for a process which, while still imposing no constraints in space or time, leaves imprints on the individual mind corresponding to a range of educational content judged to be desirable. It is, therefore, a fundamental new process of education which must be taken into account by the authorities.

Programming of the self-education field

This is where modifications in the media systems come in. Hitherto, our knowledge of daily and individual life has been hampered by the complexity of the data: Who does what? When? Where is he? How many times does he pass a particular street corner plastered with advertising posters, a particular television screen showing a particular programme, or a newsstand displaying particular photographs? This is a personal matter, private in the strong sense of the term, and our statistical grasp of random phenomena has not hitherto been advanced enough to provide us with a usable quantitative picture of it. However, the trend in urban life towards mass phenomena has not been accompanied by an enrichment of the variety of human behaviour. On the contrary, human behaviour has become restricted and standardized; to point out its growing tendency towards uniformity has become a cliché.

A great many people doing the same thing—a great many citizens watching the same television programme in their suburban boxes—this is one of the phenomena which sociologists vie with each other in deploring. They discover constants in people's time budgets and regularities in their behaviour patterns and their interactions with the media. We see patterns of life emerging in which the individual, while believing himself free, in fact follows an almost predetermined path from point to point in space at given times—the regular ebb and flow of commuters being a prime example. The individual obeys statistical laws which are just as strict as those which governed the labourers' return from the fields at sunset. Nowadays, in the cabled society, we are better able to chart the interactions between individuals and messages, in terms of laws which, though they seem to have no binding force—everyone feels free—are in fact obeyed by all.

In other words, we can see the possibility emerging of programming the field of self-education, and we shall consider that problem. Let us suppose a certain programme of knowledge, reasoning values and intellectual or sensory tools to be desirable. Then:
1. How can this programme be cut up to form a sort of 'basic

text', consisting of educational units all of which should, in society's view, be assimilated within a reasonable margin of error by all its members or by a certain proportion—also specified—thereof?
2. Knowing the trajectories of all individual members of this society, in space and in time, how should all the various fragments of the basic text be set forth? How many times must they be repeated, related to one another, etc., in time and space so as to form definite sequences such that more than x per cent of society is both subjected to all of them and, bearing in mind the processes of perception, assimilation and forgetting, retains a sufficient proportion of them? This would be the theoretical form of what might be termed 'programming of the field of self-education'. Let us note in passing that this form of technical description will be familiar to certain of the 'persuaders' of modern society, particularly advertisers and propagandists who do in fact try to instil into the general public, by means of random repetitions of disparate elements and fragmentary messages, a whole set of values, not always contradictory, which are intended to accumulate to form a complete philosophy, seldom worked out in detail, often facile and alienating, but which already exerts a considerable influence in the consumer society.

The problem which concerns us is the interaction of this process with the new media systems. Various tools of reasoning should help us to solve it, such as the possibility of educational integration of all the existing sources of message—press, radio, television, cinema, posters, news-stands, shop-windows and transport, which are all mass stimuli present in society and which are strewn across our individual paths through life. Today, they are still mostly discontinuous, uncorrelated and anarchic. In the last half-century, they have assumed a decisive importance compared with educational processes concentrated in space and time; to that extent they have helped to create what we have called a mosaic culture, the culture in which every member of an overdeveloped society is obliged to live, bombarded by disparate messages, some contradicting others, as he moves about within his life-space.

CULTURAL PROGRAMMES AND THE PROGRAMMING
OF SELF-EDUCATION

In order to understand why Western society has remained so strongly attached to institutions which it can see for itself are outdated, it is advisable to seek the origins of this attachment as they are to be found in the very fabric of Western civilization. Only an analysis of the reasons which make us cling to outdated programmes of education will enable us to challenge those programmes.

Traditionally curricula are subject-based. The history of these subjects goes back to the Middle Ages (the quadrivium, the type of curriculum proposed by Rabelais, etc.) culminating in the humanist image—an image which, even today, is still at the centre of much of our thinking and on the basis of which proliferation rapidly gathered momentum. The proliferation is due partly to the development of technical education (a corollary of the development of technology itself) which, fascinated by the status of the humanist, has always striven to win the latter's acceptance; and partly to a confusion between 'knowledge' and 'disciplines' (a discipline demonstrates how to learn, and implies strictness, effort and constraint; knowledge, on the contrary, is an accumulation in the memory).

Auguste Comte's classification is a linear classification, obeying the principle of the subordination of one discipline to another. This is the basis of Comte's well-known model, which plainly demonstrates that, if one wants to study chemistry, one must first study mathematics, physics, etc. (see Fig. 2(a)).

The type of classification suggested by Ampère is a tree, which later gave rise to the decimal classification system invented in the United States by Dewey. In this system, each initial field is subdivided into a number of branches of knowledge, which in turn are subdivided into a number of others, and so on. Thus, as one moves up the tree from the

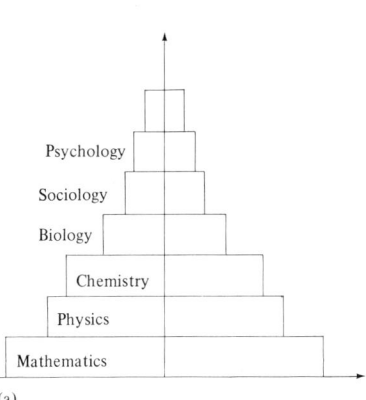

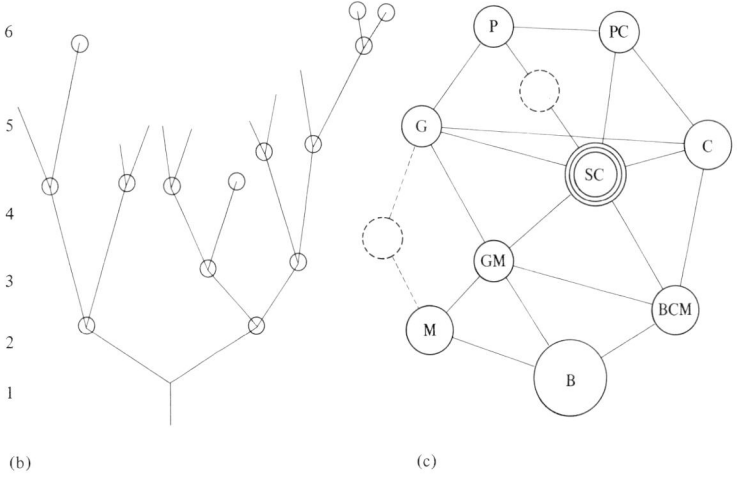

FIG. 2(a) Comte's linear classification; (b) Ampère's branching classification; and (c) a knowledge network.

common trunk towards the top, the number of branches increases by an *a priori* geometrical progression. The further the individual moves along a path of knowledge, the more he must explore all its byways and, consequently, his own capacities. As the latter are limited, a point comes where the total amount of knowledge to be acquired is too much for the individual, who can no longer grasp it all, and this is certainly what we can see happening nowadays. This system makes him aspire to identify with the complete social model which, by definition, transcends each of its component individuals (see Fig. 2(b)).

The foregoing two types of classification have led to the currently accepted classifications of knowledge, which are based on a network-type system (see Fig. 2(c)).

If there already exist two established fields of knowledge a new field is formed at their intersection. In other words, if a series of such fields exists, it is always possible to define, arbitrarily, the existence of a new field based on a combination of two or more already postulated. The result is an unlimited proliferation, not, be it said, due to some sort of epistemological frenzy, but to the very nature of scientific development.

HOW CAN AN INDIVIDUAL BUILD UP A CULTURE OF HIS OWN IN SUCH A SYSTEM?

He may first of all adopt a sampling procedure, proportional in scale to his capacity for absorption and assimilation of items of information. At this stage, in a well-planned programme, he will tend to choose crossroads areas from this universe of knowledge, that is, those areas towards which, according to our suggested schema, the greatest number of branches converge, or those which overlap with the greatest possible number of other fields of knowledge. This is the method currently used, not so much by the individual as by the authorities which impose it on him, and it should be replaced. It has three main faults: first, the nature of the samples proposed (whether chosen by the individual, as is the case at university level, or by the public authorities, as is the case in general and technical education); next, the undergrowth of sub-branches of knowledge which are constantly sprouting out of autonomous bodies of knowledge; lastly, as emphasized above, the confusion between branches of knowledge and disciplines, constantly deplored by many educationists but never fundamentally refuted. It should also be remembered that the term 'discipline' has more to do with intellectual gymnastics and an aptitude for working within constraints than with the accumulation of knowledge.

Thanks to the rise of the interpersonal media and the self-media and to the dissemination of message-stimuli within the social field regularly trodden by individuals, the new media society opens up a whole new range of approach roads to knowledge, quite unlike what was available in the past. This is one of the problems facing the educational system—how can it take these new processes in hand?

How education might take these processes in hand

SITUATIONS, TIME BUDGET
AND THE TREND TOWARDS MASS SOCIETY

Precise studies of the individual's situation in relation to his environment have already been widely undertaken. What is the individual's trajectory in the social field? At what points in time does he stay for a shorter or longer period in a given place? Is there a constant or probable spatio-temporal pattern? Initially, such studies involve statistical analysis of the programme or timetable of various classes of individuals correlated with their probable movements. This is already a familiar idea, but so far it has never been considered as a determining factor in an educational process. Whereas traditional education was able to bring together in a classroom or university lecture room certain individuals of a given age and to keep them to an inflexible timetable, the new society has to consider the problem from a much more sophisticated point of view, and in particular to investigate slack time and 'porous' time, including the in-between times in life—time spent in transit, waiting at railway stations or public transport terminals, and on the variously well-defined travel paths in the town centre—all of which have been totally neglected by educators hitherto. This statistical approach to the whole of life contrasts strongly with the rigidity of the systems of concentrated education which have given education its traditional image down to the present day.

INTERFACE STRATEGY

In order to obtain better data, it is also advisable to conduct a careful typological study of the interfaces of communication, as they are coming to be called; that is, that small part of the virtual sphere of contact between the individual and the world (the *Merkwelt* of von Uexküll) through which images, sounds and signs reach the self from the great outside world.

We can make a rough list of these interfaces: the television screen, the telephone receiver, the loudspeaker, the small luminous screen of Skinner's box, the dark auditorium of the cinema, the coloured poster—these are just a few, particularly common in modern life, and one might add the printed page of a book, the tutor's tête-à-tête with his pupil as handed down to us from antiquity, or the situation of the teacher on the dais explaining what he knows with chalk and talk to forty individuals, attentive or otherwise, cooped up in a classroom. Each of these interfaces of communications, now supplemented by the video-tape recorder, photography and many other devices, has its own peculiar characteristics, whatever the means of producing the images, sounds or signs. It is attractive or dull, one-way or potentially two-way, sometimes occupying the individual's entire field of attention and virtually excluding peripheral vision (the cinema screen, for example), and sometimes being one item among others in the environment (the poster or the television screen). It may monopolize the attention or allow it to wander, be personal or anonymous, oblige the individual to remain at a particular point in space (the telephone receiver, or the earphones of someone listening to music on hi-fi at night), or it may allow him to move about. These are a few of the characteristics emerging from a brief analysis of what might be called the phenomenology of interfaces.

Partial studies on this subject are already available, but the data we have are not sufficiently systematic and comparable. It should be emphasized that, as we suggested above, this is much more a phenomenology of interfaces—zones of contact between the individual and the world—than a phenomenology of the media themselves which takes account of the whole process, including the source of information and the means of supplying it.

One question which, in various forms, is now facing most people responsible for organizing education on a wide scale is which interface to choose for which target public, and for which type of mental activity or transmission of knowledge. If the aim is to offer the Mato Grosso peasant a number of rules and recommendations for protecting crops against vermin or for irrigation, to suggest tricks of the trade or to explain the administrative formalities involved in applying for assistance, which type of contact should be chosen? The television screen in the corner café, leaflets distributed and stuffed into pockets, a chat from a leader of opinion from the next village, a lecture by an agricultural expert, or a programme on the transistor radio? Which of these will ensure that the largest possible number of people grasp the message and, where possible, act on it? This is a problem of education and universal communication: Which interface, for whom, to transmit what?

What is new about the situation today is, primarily, the way that new media systems have developed over the past few years, some of which will in fact become accessible both to the Brazilian peasant and to the city-dweller in Rome. Also new is the fragmentation of social life into numerous enclosed spaces, scattered at random in the flux of life but obedient to knowable laws of large numbers.

CONCEPTS OF COHERENCE AND COMPLEXITY

The third major tool for studying or analysing the adaptation of media or interfaces to types of content is a systematic effort, scarcely begun by communication theory, to find the metrical or descriptive features of those types of content which one wishes to incorporate into messages and to transmit, through the media, to individuals. Some ideas are already taken for granted in this field.

These include the complexity or quantity of information contained in a message; the redundancy of this message, or more simply its intelligibility; concepts borrowed from the theory of form, such as the idea of pregnancy or attraction, or those suggested by content analysis, such as human interest, degree of involvement or contingent relationships.

These major ideas taken from the psychology of perception are enough to provide us with a whole range of intellectual tools with which to give a description of a message in general terms. The study of self-education will, however, devote special attention to factors such as the internal coherence of content, for which communicologists propose theoretical units of measurement (a concept of an ordered spectrum), but which it is often easier to assess directly by empirical comparisons.

The idea of the internal coherence of a basic text which must be assimilated by the memory and culture of a number of people is an essential one. It is what distinguishes the aggregate of various known facts, all of them interesting or useful (a great many minor technological facts or data from daily life provide examples: the mains voltage is 220; margarine melts at a higher temperature than butter; glass melts at $800°C$; $\pi = 3.14$; diamond is harder than iron), from structured knowledge in which every component of the basic message is linked, by a shorter or longer chain of logical constraints of varying strength, to every other component of the 'discourse' which one wishes to transmit and imprint on the memory. It is also that which separates what we have called a 'mosaic culture' from a 'creative culture', and is relevant to all imaginable realms of thought.

The idea of coherence relates to the level of creative activity: creativity involving unconnected or weakly connected elements in literature, art or science, must be contrasted with the creation of 'profound' integratory ideas implying long chains of thought. Mathematics or the general theory of physics are commonly taken as examples of the latter type of creativity, but it is also applicable in a great many fields, since intellectual coherence increases with generality and abstraction. The idea of coherence applies to the reading of texts, the acquisition of knowledge at school, the difference between enumeration and classification, etc. Generally speaking, the existence of logical constraints as a rule for the ordering of the elements of discourse tends to result in a degree of redundancy, a reduction in complexity (and hence in the quantity of information), and finally to an increase in intelligibility when this coherence links elements not too far removed from one another.

At this level coherence therefore makes such discourse more accessible and easier to retain. But the human mind has a relatively limited deductive faculty which varies considerably according to culture and social level, and it must be considered as fairly impervious to the long chains of coherent logico-deductive reasoning which form the basis of the system of scientific knowledge. The edifice of 'science' seems, in this case, to be largely an intellectual luxury.

However, if we wish to live in a universe regulated by scientific thought, we must, in fact, acquire a minimum of coherence of discourse; it is this structuring of the field of knowledge which transforms a mosaic culture into an effective culture, leading the way from erudition to creation and from the magical to the systematic. Naturally, therefore, the principal efforts of modern education must be brought to bear on this factor, and it is in the light of this factor that we shall examine the aptitude of the various media systems to convey and imprint on the minds of receivers either messages or modes of behaviour having a greater or lesser degree of coherence. As Stuart Hall observes, there are behavioural systems just as there are systems of knowledge, and education is never merely a black box.

The mass media, with their structure and their hard-to-achieve coincidence with the trajectory of the individual in space-time, have enjoyed an increasingly exclusive sway in the past fifty years and have been instrumental in reducing the internal coherence (at long range) of the messages retained. For example, the chopping up of the universe of what is representable on commercial television into seven-minute sections interspersed with advertising spots which interrupt the flow of the main programme helps to preclude any dramatic action or philosophical argument that does not fit neatly into a seven-minute slot; vast areas rightfully belonging to scientific or technical culture are thereby excluded.

In short, one way of studying interfaces or media in relation to content is to ask how far they are capable of conveying messages that have a certain amount of internal coherence and homogeneity, that is, in which one component determines (or at least evokes) another component situated at a specific distance; theorists of culture call this 'coherence distance'.

On the whole, the self-education field, by its very structure, appears to have a very low degree of coherence because it is the result of fragmentary stimuli distributed along a trajectory which varies from individual to individual. It offers fragments and particular aspects, but from the outset it disperses them to form a heterogeneous mosaic. At this stage and indeed, looking more to the future than to the present, one is justified in wondering whether this process is as essential as it appears to be in television programmes, or whether, on the contrary, the stability of people's habits in relation to things may provide an opening for certain types of semi-random *programming*, which are quite conceivable in theory but of which we have comparatively few examples.

Finally, the self-media, of which the notebook has long

been the classic example and which, thanks to electronics, are now assuming sophisticated forms, suggest the possibility of achieving and developing *continuity* within the mind which can thus contemplate a reflection of itself or of its earlier activity. They raise the question of the self-media's contribution to the internal cohesion of the incoming flow of knowledge.

One final question will arise at the level of interpersonal communications and their role in relation to what one may call knowledge. If education, instead of being a highly specific and concentrated process, with an unchallenged claim to a fixed portion of the time budget, tended to blend once more with all the circumstances of daily life, it would recover some of the features of immediate learning, not involving any schooling, which the tribe or old-fashioned village used to offer its young members.

In an electronic society of communicational affluence, distance would no longer count and everything could become accessible to anyone, anywhere, any time. To what extent does such a society hold out the prospect of a new education, which, instead of being a set of take-it-or-leave-it packages, would be a network of interests comprising everyday intellectual activity? This is one of the questions which the new media systems raise for the educational system, and the examination of this question falls within Unesco's field of competence.

Mass media and the school: Descartes or McLuhan?

Pierre Schaeffer

The French Minister of Education stated not long ago: 'The difficulties being encountered by schools are not specific to them: rather, they express the consequences of a general value crisis.'[1] The same can be said of the mass media: sometimes we regard them as a passive reflection of our current uneasy state, while at other times we accuse them of playing a prominent part in the 'crisis of civilization'. Let us acknowledge that we have a habit of looking at both schools and the media through two distinct sets of lenses, while they do the same with each other.

We must still decide what we mean by the terms 'mass media' or 'information media'. Are we referring to means of communication in the operational sense, or to the content of what is communicated? Depending on which meaning is adopted, there are two quite different approaches.

If the media are only means of communication in the operational sense, we can follow Descartes in regarding them as serving the content; in that case, they are subordinate to educational objectives. At once, however, we encounter McLuhan's riposte, 'The medium is the message.' We should undoubtedly be well advised not to overlook this paradox.

If, however, 'media' means the mass media, our task, as both Descartes and McLuhan would surely agree, is to situate schools within a world of radio and television, which soon will be a world of computer technology as well.

The term 'content of education' is disconcerting too. In a school context, presumably it is to be differentiated from the procedures involved, that is, the methodology of teaching; the reference is to the programme itself, the subject-matter. To distinguish a 'content', however, leaves us perplexed with regard to the 'container'. The container can only be the school itself—the school as an institution, as a system, and as an ideology. In a school context also, is it not relevant to say that 'the medium is the message'? How can the two components of the school media nexus be asymmetrically handled, given radio and television in the sense of McLuhan's analysis, and the schools' seeking to walk in the way of Descartes?

If we wish to be Cartesian, let us be consistently Cartesian. What does the word 'content' suggest if not that the schools' acknowledged mission is teaching rather than education? Teaching, in the last analysis, is concerned only with the content of the material taught; it is identifiable with the information which it is desired to convey. Education, in contrast, cannot be regarded as restricted to a 'table of contents'; it is concerned with 'how' rather than 'what'. Whatever the curriculum, education is a matter of how to learn: selecting what is essential, exercising the critical faculty, intuition and judgement, learning how to learn. In other words, the training of the mind presupposes the training of the character, a choice of values, and a concomitant stimulation of the emotions.

Historical overview

THE GROWTH OF KNOWLEDGE

Our contemporary society takes pride in the fact that the number of scientists now living is as great as the total produced by humanity over the millennia. This statistical datum is both arrogant and tendentious; it reveals the mentality of the 'advanced' nations. Looking at the matter differently, it would be possible to make another sort of count of the 'wise men' of former ages and less 'advanced' parts of the world. In that case it is by no means certain that the outcome would be favourable to the twentieth century.

In the words of Stéphane Hessel, 'Knowledge in the sense of wisdom, in the sense of a kind of ingenious respect for and effort to sustain myths, has now been replaced by a 'scientific mentality' which has been admirably described by Jacques Monod in *Le hasard et la nécessité*. This mentality knows neither boundaries nor fear, and finds within itself its own ethical justification.' Here knowledge is identified with the concept of science, a term which is etymologically related to a Greek word meaning 'to cut' or 'to cut off', indicating how science constitutes itself by means of a series of cutting-off operations in an experimental procedure which defines its approach. An experimenter always gives himself power, and knowledge comes to him in the form of new power. But while all this is quite clear as far as the material sciences are concerned, it is hopelessly confused in the case of what are termed the human sciences, and the result is a twofold barrier: experimenting is forbidden, and standardization is impossible.

Knowledge, then, is growing in a situation of severe unbalance between knowledge about the universe, that is to say power over things, the little knowledge that exists about man, and the absence of will which finds its outlet in politics. Presumably it will be agreed that even the humblest school is located, as it were almost clandestinely, somewhere on this broad and all-too-clearly visible horizon.

Possibly by way of compensation, we can point to the quasi-exponential growth of 'efficacious' fields of knowledge, while in order to make room for these in overcrowded programmes, there has been a corresponding decline in the disciplines of considered thought, literary expression, the accomplishments, and poor ineffectual philosophy, to say nothing of religious experience, which is also isolated by a 'specific' form of segregation.

We shall be concerned in this discussion only with 'official' knowledge, that is quoted on the university 'stock exchange', not out of personal conviction but out of deference to the consensus, and also because that type of knowledge really is synonymous with power: it conditions both individuals and communities, confers prestige and status on various cultures, differentiates social classes, and lends power to more or less developed countries.

This knowledge, which is power, also prompts dissatisfaction with inequality between individuals, classes, races, nations and continents. Accordingly, because of the compensating myth of equality, we find demands for knowledge to be more equitably distributed, for those who have lagged behind to be allowed to catch up, and for large-scale solutions to be sought wherever this is made necessary, as it really is in places, by threats to survival.

This summary presentation shows how formidably complex and how profoundly paradoxical the issue of access to the content of contemporary knowledge really is. Greater speed is needed, but at the same time the laggards must catch up; quality is essential, but so is quantity; cultural unity is desirable yet fields of specialization must continue to proliferate.

We shall not attempt to consider this gigantic problem and the crises it causes. We refer to it here only to highlight what has been perceived as a parallel, offsetting, as it were, the providential form of progress—progress in the field of the mass media.

Let us simply confine ourselves to considering the various remedies which appeared at one time to have come to hand for each of the various ills of scientific knowledge. Severe lag, it was thought, could be corrected by basic education, the effect of which could be multiplied through the immensely powerful vehicles of radio and television broadcasting and perhaps satellites as well. At the other end of the scale, at the very summit of scientific knowledge, inadequate human memory could be supplemented by data banks, with the processing power of computers reinforced by a worldwide data communication network. In this way the same satellites could carry in their multiple and divergent circuits both the highest and the lowest levels.

Between these extremes, they could also carry a full range of circuits suitable for all cultural gradations, taking into account local needs, population dispersion, and even inadequate teaching personnel. From a distance, then, the multiplier effect of broadcasting appeared to be an ideal answer to an economic and social problem which was crucial in the case of the most underdeveloped countries. Even if a price had to be paid in terms of greater centralization, ordinary common sense seemed to suggest that an audio-visual programme, carefully prepared by a number of specialists and disseminated via the broadcasting media, would be more efficient and have a greater impact than the long and costly business of training all the teachers required to cover every area.

PARALLEL FLIGHT: THE WORLD OF LEARNING AND THE WORLD OF MEDIA

We should not be blind to everything but the disappointing outcome of all this. It did seem possible, in theory at any rate, to resolve certain problems of the transmission and distribution of knowledge through the operational tools of the media. More to the point is the fact that this 'best of all possible worlds', utopian though it may be, has been neither suitably approached nor seriously researched. The upshot has been a sort of parallel flight, like the flight of two galaxies, both expanding and simultaneously repelling each other. It is obvious that virtually everywhere on earth, regardless of the disparity of the resources involved, both schools and the media have sought to grow, each institution along its own lines, with its own style, public, personnel, mission and financing. It is striking to observe to what extent the two have remained separate and alien entities in the course of the twentieth century, and to what extent the example of the developed countries has been a determining factor. In these countries, to be sure, certain radio and television broadcasting organizations, claiming a monopoly of the field, have proclaimed objectives virtually identical with those of schools: 'to inform, educate and entertain'. It is natural enough that these two institutions, with such similar general aims, should have striven to achieve, if not complementarity, at least originality, each on its own side.

As far as the mass media were concerned, information was contemporary, while the schools' area of interest lay in records of the past. Education in the true sense, which the schools appeared to have neglected for some time, was taken up again in the more immediate context of the current scene by way of 'exposure to the world'. With regard to entertainment, as we have repeatedly been told, this could serve a 'cultural' function, provided it was of suitably high quality; indeed, it might be more effective in this sense than many an earnest lecture.

The human community thus found itself attended by the schools on one hand and the media on the other, in the role of a father and a mother, as it were, with the former assuming the masculine function of providing training, while the latter undertook the feminine role of gathering to its bosom information from the entire universe. As a rule, the male parent took charge of the children. Accordingly, the adult population, reduced in a sense to the status of children themselves, turned to 'Mother Television' to escape from their cares, to fill the void of their leisure time, and to watch light-heartedly while the festivities of the 'global village' took place before their eyes.

THE DOMINANT MODEL

When the time came to provide the developing countries with broadcasting facilities, other options appeared to be available, and would have been justified not only by educational factors but also by other factors having to do with health, agriculture, economic situation and the like. In the event, while enclaves were organized in the nascent media with a view to serving these needs directly, they were treated as poor relations, preference being given to programmes of the type popular in the industrialized countries. We may add that, in order to be really effective, basic radio broadcasting designed to serve a country's economic and social needs, as well as agriculture and public health, would have had to be supported by a local infrastructure, that is, not only receivers (transistor radios had not yet been invented) but local agents capable of making use of very modest means such as simple home-made sets running off storage batteries or powered by a bicycle-mounted generator. It is extraordinary to find that preference was given to other types of broadcasting aimed at a different audience, the already privileged élite; it is also extraordinary to find television being developed in its turn, despite its cost, and despite the fact that it has encountered the same type of obstacles, to the detriment of radio. Television has been pursued while the use of a potentially more suitable and a less costly radio broadcasting system has been neglected.

Some comments are in order at this point:

With reference to a hierarchy of needs in the developing nations, there is a sort of dominant model favouring the adoption of the most advanced techniques and the most elaborate programming in imitation of the developed nations.

The reverse may be said of the developed countries with reference to the 'sub-population' in the schools. For want of an adequate supply of suitable receivers, for want of local storage and trained and motivated personnel, these populations are not being reached and the broadcasting media are proving to be ineffectual and irrelevant.

One factor strengthening resistance to change is the development of a 'quarrel between the Ancients and the Moderns', as depicted by the conflict between McLuhan's 'galaxies'; crudely put, it is a matter of text versus pictures.

In practice, the rivalry comes to be expressed in institutional terms, and through the institutions in question brings professional groups into confrontation.

Lastly, these professionals divide along different lines in accordance with the selection of vehicles which is a predominant element in any educational strategy.

It thus appears, not only as a matter of debate but in reality, that there is a constant confrontation (beyond institutions and functions) between different techniques and budgets all of which are playing their own game. No one takes the trouble to develop the co-operation that is so essential between ideas and men, between institutions and networks, and even between different kinds of equipment.

EDUCATIONAL TELEVISION

Thus the two communities which we have designated 'the world of learning' and 'the world of the media', while brandishing similar slogans, refuse to treat each other hospitably, although they do borrow from each other, and each is willing to let the other have whatever unappetizing gristly bits it may have left over. In the eyes of the schools, the mass media were a foreign body, but also a corporate body, and as such represented competition. Hence the prolonged period of refusal to recognize even the existence of the media, or at any rate to admit that they had any 'cultural value'.

However, a forward-looking component of the teaching profession which wished to be able to compete on equal terms and not get left behind, and which was impelled by a highly original sense of mission, came to stand out from the mass as a sort of 'irregu-force', a hybrid form, as it were, displaying characteristics of both institutions inasmuch as it made use of the broadcasting facilities of the one to disseminate the 'content' of the other. This group, the pioneers of educational television, ran the risk of being disowned by those of their colleagues who had remained within the mainstream tradition of either schools or media. This in summary is what happened in France at any rate.

The experiment will undoubtedly be repeated elsewhere, wherever wide-scale distribution is associated with elementary-level education. The same miscalculation, made out of concern for what is in reality a false economy, will recur, the matter of human and material infrastructure will be overlooked again, and all because of the same simplistic assumption about the broadcasting vehicle, which is the predominant element in the system!

AUDIO-VISUAL DIFFUSION

Audio-visual diffusion, that is, radio and television broadcasting, is slowly emerging from a long period characterized by severe confusion and contradictions, with too many messages competing for inadequate channel space. Yet, in this flood of pictures and sound, what a barrage of recriminations is heard: poverty of contents; confusion of style and monotony of programmes; a frantic search for the average viewer or listener which is not really satisfactory to anyone concerned; the number of viewing or listening hours rising but production declining; budget constantly expanding and consistently inadequate to cover expenses; employees as the source and the victims of disruption, shuttling between strikes and unemployment, etc. While these are generalized phenomena (economic crisis, employment problems and the like), the same features characterize the audio-visual diffusion sector in the poorer nations, where different causes have produced similar effects.

However, major additional resources which have appeared or are on the point of appearing will serve to broaden this field of activity, despite the fact that it is so visibly limited by the width of the broadcasting spectrum, with its scarcity of wavelengths, its overcrowded time-slots, its off-peak hours, etc.

With regard to the area with which we are concerned here, the crucial development is the gigantic pincer movement that is currently threatening broadcasting networks, and will undoubtedly throw the field of broadcasting into disarray in regard to its practices, its monopolies, its legislation—in a word—its policy. At both ends of the horizon, at ground level and at the altitude of stationary orbit, the dust of small-scale transmitters and the hail of satellites are about to invade us and possibly inflict further pollution upon us.

Once again we see that it is apparently the vehicle which is the predominant factor in determining the system of the near future. Decision-makers are free to follow or not to follow hasty assessments that are quantitative in nature; it is up to them to introduce a social and educational dimension—in a word, to refuse to respond with blind obedience to the determinism of the vehicle. In other words, what is needed are types of content that are appropriate in terms of the vehicles involved, and lastly, correlation between vehicle, production and storage.

A MEANS OF EMERGING FROM THE MIDDLE AGES: AUDIO-VISUAL STOCK ACCUMULATION

In view of the difficulty of obtaining access to audio-visual production, or at any rate that production which appears as the essential counterpart of printed documents, we must conclude that the only possible hope for the future in this area, as also in the case of textual material, lies in storing and making available audio-visual products that are increasingly relevant and selective. These messages will be neither broadcast programmes nor films, but documentary elements to be inserted, as required, at the local level. The availability of these badly needed content materials is, of course, closely bound up with the types of storage media employed, the prototypes of which at present are the videotape and the audio-visual record. Apart from the technological effort called for by the variety of equipment involved, a powerful braking effect has been exerted both by dissemination systems and by a paradoxical lack of any expression of need in this area. Here we find the explanation of another paradox, namely the absence of quality and competition in the production of suitable audio-visual documents covering the main fields of knowledge.

Let us recapitulate these three points:

Existing systems, notably radio and television broadcasting organizations, are concerned with day-to-day events, concentrating on the facile and sensational, and seeking to reach a mass audience. Consequently, their production is unusable or even non-existent from the educational point of view.

The 'storage media' have yet to be standardized, and new launching will be a tricky operation, more especially since the sole sources of supply are the cinema and television.

Lastly, a special type of author/producer is needed to fill the dual role of teacher and film-producer, a role which is not encouraged by either of the institutions (university or television) or by any area of commerce, except for very rare cases of publishing and broadcasting firms bold enough to see in such a venture a chance, albeit slim, of long-term development.

Thus storage that is barely possible is awaiting a content that is barely probable. The audio-visual medium is still languishing in the Middle Ages in the world of incunabula.

A HISTORICAL ANACHRONISM

Clearly, then, educational television could have developed differently if the educational institutions of the advanced countries had possessed the means of production or at least of storage. Similarly, if adequate infrastructures for reception had existed in developing countries, it is likely that the media networks might have been able to balance better and more rationally the entertainment of the few with the basic education of the greatest number. It is quite evident that the mass media have imposed a kind of historical anachronism by the very nature of their content, originally based on a newspaper model (broad, one-way distribution of ephemeral, trivial or sensational information).

One would really need to recapitulate the history of technology in order to establish at what point it imposed an illogical development from which the entire world will take decades to recover. If it is to do so, it must reshuffle the conflicting phases of this development. To persuade ourselves of this, it is enough to imagine that transistor radios were invented first, and that the use of wavelengths required only a small amount of energy. Nothing would then have prevented, at least in theory, the 'Marconi galaxy' from developing according to the 'Gutenberg model' with smaller output and reciprocity of transmission and reception. In particular, if the tools of production at our disposal, such as tape-recorders, lightweight video-recorders, portable video units and small, low-cost transmitters, had come before the tall towers and the high kilowattages of the medium, and long wavelengths, the face of the world might have been transformed. Not merely the schools but the entire twentieth-century world would probably have taken on another appearance.

This comment is not made as an attempt to rewrite history, but rather to draw attention to the very simple fact that while this 'historical overlapping' will obviously have to cease, the problem is far from being resolved at the moment. The proof of this is in the extraordinary rivalry of the systems, the now political conflict between the small and the big stations, and the clear pedagogical dilemma between the activities involved in production and the passivity associated with reception.

To summarize, history has shown us the astonishing headlong rush of two parallel societies as well as the ill-will existing in their dealings with each other. In contrast to educational television (that hybrid already briefly mentioned), it remains for us to describe its feared and envied rival: the famous 'parallel school', as well as the audio-visual media, the stakes for which this unevenly matched battle was joined. In other words, were educators who were vaguely inspired by educational television in fact responding to the attractions of audio-visual media, or were they engaging in a battle against the other institution? Through educational television were they attacking the medium or the broadcasting vehicle? It was being said at the time that ours was going to be a civilization based on the image. Was it fitting then for educators to turn away from this? A few of them, newly inspired, went over to the image while the majority denigrated it. Even if educational television was rejected or inadequate, was it not justified by its spin-off, by the introduction to audio-visual media that it gave to those same educators despite itself?

First crucial aspect: the media society

THE VISUAL CIVILIZATION

This well-worn subject has been the traditional stumbling block between 'media' and 'content'. On the one hand it provides a premise with regard to the mode of culture, and on the other it provokes a pedagogical discussion on the image as a vehicle for content.

To restrict ourselves to the prosaic, that is, the second point, it could be observed that the image has functioned in human culture in the same way as language and that in this respect it is not especially contemporary. As for its influence on content, we will not engage in subtleties. We hope to remain within the bounds of common sense in suggesting that the image best suits the descriptive disciplines in the same way as sound has been helpful for the learning of languages. On the other hand, the more we move towards reflection and abstraction, whether it be in the domain of the exact sciences or that of philosophical and legal concepts, we must no doubt leave description behind. These are very basic remarks which we must doubtless go beyond to recall the high pedagogical value of a constant interchange between the concrete and the abstract, the picture and the idea, the facts and the pattern.

Thus we rid ourselves of a false ideological problem and an illusory basic discussion of the image, in order to reveal the two real problems of audio-visual equipment and audio-visual systems.

By audio-visual equipment we mean sound-and-image machines, films and video, the use of which must be paid for at its real price, both economic and technological. That is to say that, beyond the required investments and training, we must also recognize the related problems and complications, the mixture of speed and ponderousness of this equipment. By audio-visual systems, we mean the large production and distribution units such as are imposed on the schools from without through the media of films and television.

THE MEANS ARE LACKING

However simple the operation of equipment may be, its utilization is far from satisfactory. There is a kind of general clumsiness due to negligence through lack of training, and in particular of supervision through lack of maintenance technicians and operators. In short, the equipment is doubly despised: at one moment its influence is feared, while at another it is considered inconvenient and complicated. It complicates teaching methods by its fanciness, its unpredictable breakdowns, its mistakes.

Finally, even when working well, it imposes unavoidable restrictions. Images and sounds cannot be flicked through like a book; they impose their own delays in real time, and short of producing images oneself, which is a whole field of competence to be acquired, one generally relies on images from elsewhere, unfolded at the speed of a film show, which are subject to criticism because they cannot be stopped or reread.

These drawbacks certainly exist and are not exactly intrinsic to the technology, since, in place of the film which cannot be reversed, the video recording can be stopped, played back, edited and corrected. While there may be complaints about videotape reels, we can look forward to the videodisc with immediate access to every image, able to be played backwards or forwards at will.

Thus, one of our conclusions is that it is necessary to replace fundamental discussions on the image with a more careful, pragmatic approach; for example:
We must avoid setting up between text and image (the same can

be said for sound) a pointless rivalry, a struggle where one must exclude the other, but rather aim at a complementary relationship to be constantly revised and adjusted.

We must renounce, if not all semiological ambition, at least all useless talk about the image, in favour of a practical approach. That is to say we should encourage instruction in 'reading' and 'writing' the image as much as we do the application of this practice to some or other part of the content which requires it as a matter of course.

THE PARALLEL SCHOOL

A completely different debate revolves around systems (the machinery of the mass media in contrast to audio-visual equipment). While the latter can be incorporated in educational institutions and gradually mastered, as we have just shown, the former exert their influence outside the school and have long enjoyed the prestige of an exclusive novelty. We know that McLuhan went as far as to say that when the child left the television screen to go to school he could only regress. Many educators will reject this with indignation and a matching riposte, claiming that television is incapable of disciplining the minds of the young (when it does not actually corrupt them with models of violence, weakness and stupidity), and that school is an antidote.

We agree that it is necessary to introduce some order into the undiscriminating and, indeed, television-ruined minds of the young. But we hesitate somewhat in preferring the step-by-step conceptual approach to global imagery. We cannot conceive of an educational philosophy which does not bring together these two extremes, these two poles of rationality. We also wish, at this point, to expand the debate by calling not only on Husserl and phenomenology, but also on the Gestaltists and what is known about the perception of shapes. Normal human functioning (more so among children than among adults) favours the immediate perception of wholes, this being motivated or inspired by intentionality. It is only subsequently that we analyse and rationalize. Why then should we complain of an avalanche of images and messages which provide an abundance of visual material, the very thing so often lacking in schools?

With all the time wasted in schools on descriptive lectures, which are so rarely retained, and which are furthermore so simplistic (whether they concern history, geography or natural sciences), how can we not wish for blanket impregnation, even if it entails establishing intellectual order afterwards? So, instead of maintaining that the harmful effects of television must first of all be undone, why not allow that the concrete approach is already half-established, even if it needs to be rectified?

Several comments are necessary, then, on the 'proper use of the parallel school'. They are in answer to the usual criticisms.

The disparateness of television programmes and the lack of balance between fiction and reality, quality and mediocrity, literary and non-scientific content, etc. This means, of course, that the school should have supplementary images at its disposal.

The scattering of images in time and the impossibility of inserting them in a curriculum. That is true, but children will remember a programme of several months ago when recall material is available to them; this leads to the following point, by far the most important.

The flood of unrecoverable images. This is the essential point, which when coupled with the former brings out the need for storage in every educational institution. This storage, after some time, will balance the general effect of the messages, and a local film library will serve to complement and counterbalance the daily programmes.

THE JUNGLE

These practical remarks only partly answer the major objection: impregnation by the media leads to the famous 'culture mosaic' defined by Abraham Moles.

We have just shown certain ways of differentiating this flood of images and refashioning it into a more coherent whole. We must admit, however, that there will remain an enormous residue, not only of unusuable programmes, but also of undesirable ones. This, we think, is where we must adopt a definite position regarding the essential role of the school. The school can very well give advice on good viewing habits, which will not necessarily be heeded any more than that given by the head of family. Why then not make the best of a bad job and incorporate this residue in the teaching scheme?

Our arguments are as follows:

Since children generally prefer to watch adult programmes, such viewing cannot be ignored.

After all, this viewing, however premature, provides a look at society, such as it is; and if programmes are considered bad, it is not just the fault of the programme directors, because they are merely providing the public with the diet it wants.

In short, whether we like it or not, the media mirrors the very society in which the child finds itself. Is it the task of the school to criticize what takes place in reality, or to arrange it so that the child lives artificially in an abstract, aseptic world?

This is what we choose to call the 'jungle', referring to the deprived continents which have, at any rate, provided the means for man's survival for thousands of years.

The schools of Africa, Papua, India, from the Wild West to Mowgli's jungle, were not concerned with programmed education and semiological discussions; rather their programmes consisted of teaching how to survive, and semiology was not just a question of speech but of signs in the sky and on the ground, of tracks and warnings of danger. It is hardly a metaphor to situate the modern child in a new 'jungle' with which he must learn to cope. From the clouded window of his pigeon-hole, he sees a jungle in all directions. In preference to the so-called 'culture mosaic', for which the reference will soon be put in order by the computer, we favour another diagnosis and prescribe for the schools the task of the critique of values, rather than the role of restoring conceptual order.

There is no simple answer, so we will not be so presumptuous as to suggest one. It is most probable that the 'critique of values' will henceforth be more important in schools than the discourse on concepts. It is obvious that the existence of schools is based on common sense as much as on knowledge. But perhaps schools should no longer be alone in taking responsibility for such an unfinished and hesitant education. Many children experience elsewhere another educational environment with complementary activities that are freer and less obstructed by the educational bureaucracy. We cannot ask everything of the school, nor bank knowledge alone.

Second crucial aspect: the computerized society

COMPUTER SCIENCE

If humour were appropriate here, we could say that trouble never comes singly. We mean by this that computer science and technology, from which we expect such progress, can also bring disappointments or result in no clear advantage, as with the 'Marconi galaxy'. Finally, since computer science appears to be an adaptation of logic and a permutation of concepts, so with the resources of a super-language (or a sub-language?) we can say with Aesop that it could be the best as well as the worst of things. In any case we have still to define the variety of its applications in the field that concerns us. First, it is clearly a relatively new subject-matter in the field of knowledge, and radically new where its applications are concerned. Secondly, even for someone with no knowledge of computer theory, it is sufficient to know how to use a program to be able to use a computer as a data-processing machine, that is, for storing, classifying and collating data. In other words, the effects of computerization on education are vital and resemble the automation of industry. Finally, it is in fact an *ideology*, or at least the expression of a trend which consists in replacing man by a machine that will perform better (for particular tasks), or be more competent (for a given area of knowledge) or heuristic (having an artificial intelligence which is better developed, at least in certain areas).

This brief chapter suggests the need for a deeper study.[2] Can the computer be considered one of the mass media? Yes, it probably can, but only on the strength of a questionable extension of the definition. Our civilization, which is privileged to possess complex machines, likes to mix everything together in order to achieve the highest development of its systems.

TELEMATICS

This hybrid is in fact obtained by the interconnection of telecommunication devices with computers.

To summarize, we would venture to predict a revolution which will affect intellectual work as profoundly as the Industrial Revolution altered the physical nature of work. We can thus reckon on a complete shape-up of the functions of learning ahead of that of the content of knowledge. Education can only be transformed by it, and triply so, in its curricula, its methods and its aims.

Even more so than in the case of the mass media, whose influence on teaching has been minimal, the influence of computer technology promises to be vital. At present, it is willingly used in an auxiliary capacity, but it threatens to become master as well as servant.

What was, in fact, the target of education in our uncomputerized civilization? In theory, it was to provide each individual with knowledge in a given area, where he had a specific task to perform. Beyond this competence, which corresponded in general to a profession or trade, each individual was to receive general cultural training. Every citizen of contemporary civilization received primary education which met the vital economic, political and social daily requirements of being able to read and write, in other words, to communicate.

Having thus roughly summarized the three objectives of

any education, let us consider what could become of them in a world of telematics.

At the primary level, while admitting the archaic necessity for reading and writing (but what is the point of arithmetic?), we must include the need to use everyday machines: pocket calculators, automatic devices, terminals, etc. A part of primary education should henceforth be concerned with training the disabled in the skilful use of artificial limbs.

At the secondary level, one will need to become proficient in processing information and interrogating data banks. In short, this is the ideal of polytechnical ability, since after secondary education one will be able, in theory, to handle the most far-removed subjects. Every good graduate of secondary education will of necessity be a qualified programmer.

Finally, given the exponential growth of knowledge in all areas, the essential thing will be to *maintain data banks* and to familiarize specialists with their use. We can then see two possibilities, according to whether the task in question is more conceptual or manual. In the first case, intelligent machines will help the specialist; in the other, robots will carry out tasks better than the worker, who will nevertheless be assigned some sort of supervisory role.

One might thus predict, to the satisfaction of all, an extensive 'withering away' of 'teacher power', a shortening of studies, a lightening of curricula, a reduction of budgets, perhaps even the abolition of the universities, unless the theses produced there should prove useful for data banks; only a supreme computer could be the judge of that!

While these ideas may appear exaggerated (as they are), it cannot be denied that they reveal ideological inspiration as well as the emergence of certain symptoms.

PARALLEL POWER (A PROGNOSIS FOR THE COMPUTERIZED SOCIETY)

It is in the framework of society as a whole that it is appropriate to attempt a prognosis, even one restricted to education. It would be opting for the improbable to imagine that things will remain as they are as far as the content is concerned, with the new technology just functioning as an auxiliary.

Knowledge-power

While we would willingly take up the question of the quality of knowledge in a computerized society, and of a possible decline in quality in favour of quantity, it should be said straight away that knowledge is becoming increasingly likely to coincide with power, no longer as a development of the mind, but as a deliberate delegation of power to intelligent machines.

There are two reasons for this hypothesis. One is by analogy with the Industrial Revolution during which, in fact, the transfer of muscular strength to machines (allied with a growth of knowledge, of course) completely changed the power relations and the rule of the strongest in the world. The other reason is intrinsic: once data have been gathered and combinatory power acquired, it will scarcely be possible (for the governing class) to make choices outside the domain of a decision-making industry to which it is already committed.

The power of computer technology

The importance of computer technology as a discipline and as an institution for its industries and its workers will become decisive and will be identified with the very machinery of political, social, economic and financial power. Proof of this is to be seen in the fact that it was initially adopted for military purposes and that we rely on computers for offensive and defensive nuclear weapons as well as for space operations.

The hierarchy of knowledge

There will be a dual hierarchy according to whether one has access through competence or assignment to one or other pole of the knowledge-power pair.

In effect, while some people operate the computers, others will make use of them. Access to data and to the higher rungs of computer potential will become more and more limited, for legal as well as practical reasons. The potential for knowledge will inevitably be accompanied by an increasing degree of secrecy: knowledge-power will be hierarchical.

On the other hand, knowledge held by computers could become the supreme knowledge, since, not content with processing data, they will want to manipulate and develop them, and it will doubtless be they alone who will be able to manage the interfacing of the multiple and advanced specializations that result. There will then be few persons capable of keeping up with the machine that they invented and programmed, even, and especially, if the machine interrogates them in return on human functioning.[3]

We shall limit ourselves to pointing out the scarcity of real experts and, among them in turn, those with sufficient intelligence, honesty and sensitivity (qualities rarely found together) to ensure follow-up and control. We imagine that the situation will be identical in all the areas of advanced technical research, and that we shall witness a kind of tearing apart of the fabric of knowledge, which will be most alarming. While it is true that there are more and more scientists, fewer and fewer of them attain the higher levels of synthesis.

Contradictions and solutions

THE POWER OF EDUCATORS—AUTHORITY OR BANKRUPTCY?

In an archaic society (and the early twentieth century seems such to us) communications are sparse and carried out physically, areas are clearly defined and everyone has his place therein, even if it appears unjust to him. Demands are of a rational kind and are negotiated on the basis of social consensus. This consensus recognizes competence and merit, and thus an implicit process of selection and an accepted line of transmission of knowledge and skills. Conflicts due to social injustice are not aimed directly at these values, rather the contrary. The provision of equal cultural opportunity and access to skills are sought for the greatest number in a more democratic recruitment process, which thus comes up against two kinds of obstacle. One is inevitable, since justice done to the greatest number (or less injustice) leads to a harsher selection which will vest educators with increased power. If one fails to recognize the first obstacle, which is alas an objective one, one will discover a second, either subjective or ideological, denying selection and refusing transmission.

Accordingly, university authorities who had considered themselves, often in good faith, to be educating for a better, egalitarian world without constraints, found themselves under fire in the name of these very principles.

Internal and external factors which probably accelerated this crisis culminated ten years ago, in Europe at any rate. Within higher education the greater demand for courses providing more and more extensive and diversified knowledge fitted badly with employment opportunities, since, in contrast to the archaic society which required numerous middle-level skills, the advanced society required a large number of ordinary operatives to perform tasks remotely supervised by decision-makers or technocratic élites.

CONTENT—FOR WHOM AND WHY?

Does the problem of content in education consist only of finding a place for what comes from elsewhere, of incorporating the media, of explaining them, even going so far as to use audio-visual media in the schools? Should we not fundamentally review not only the content but also the purpose of education in today's world?

So far, even if we haven't managed it, we have at least tried to incorporate, to adjust, to arrange everything that is desirable. But is this, after all, really possible and worth while? Could not an analysis of the media be applied in its turn to schools? Schools appear plethoric, bloated, adding subjects to the curriculum as television adds programmes. The so-called culture-mosaic of the Marconi kind seems to influence the educational culture of the Gutenberg variety, not by media pressure but by the same kind of social pressure to which the media are subject.

On the one hand, then, we have an accumulation of subjects, on the other, a massive average public. On one side modern developments and a proliferation of knowledge, on the other a cultural tradition and a desirable unity of mind. In short, just as a programme manager of a television channel, supposedly culturally oriented, will mix opera with a western, serious news with a piece of nonsense, the president's speech with those of other personalities, so will a curriculum planner be guided in his selection on 'proportioning' of content by considerations of style and concern for good form, constantly torn between the wolves of modernity and the guardians of tradition.

This is why we are so bothered by the term 'content' which we are dragging like a ball and chain throughout these reflections. It is not that we have refused to discuss it, as one is certainly needed for a curriculum, but for whom and why?

We could cause surprise or even criticism by such a vigorous line of argument. That is because we are touching here on the very myth of universal progress, which has hitherto been invoked as unlimited and unfailing. We imagine that the twentieth century will pose, in all areas, the question of limits, and that this cruel question goes right to the heart of the debate on content, and this at the very moment when the mass media seem to be offering themselves in an almost limitless profusion.

TOWARDS A NEW CONTENT SCHEME

Thus, our truly surprising conclusion would be that the media society requires schools fundamentally to alter their teaching structure. Since a child is attached to an over-informed world (apparently) and is threatened by the 'jungle'; since the adolescent is ill at ease in it, and rebels against it with some semblance of justification; since the student stagnates there with an all-consuming sense of futility; how can we maintain these primary, secondary and tertiary gradations as if the times had not profoundly changed, as if we still had the time to lay on, layer upon layer, the fragile varnish of a knowledge so ill-adapted to its environment?

We consider, for example, that the distinction between primary, secondary and tertiary, while remaining useful for denoting progression in knowledge and ability, reflects outmoded institutions rather than reality. We would suggest rather that the selection or 'proportioning of content' should be effected at each stage according to the same three directions or criteria: (a) the needs of communication (universal literacy); (b) the development of the mind (in the spirit of the continuing development of the individual); and (c) preparing the student for the contingent requirements of work, taking into account both his talents and environmental factors.

While the media seem well adapted to handle many kinds of content, their intervention will be much more effective if it is governed by these three criteria. Instead of false problems, or a false relationship between content and media, we will be posing a worthwhile problem and a pertinent question if we consider the correlation between all the media and each of the three directions: communication, intellectual training and competence.

ADAPTATION OF NEW MEDIA TO NEW CONTENT

Since we reject the idea of a practical conclusion which would consist of fallacious, detailed suggestions, we prefer to describe the ideal situation, in precise terms, as a technological whole, having its own dynamics and answering the general bankruptcy with an original virtue, best described as autogenous or self-produced. We thus formulate two working hypotheses which, we are well aware, do not correspond at all to established usage.

One of these hypotheses has just been formulated: for the content of each of the three levels of education, it proposes a functional scheme of which the three main objectives are communication, intellectual training and competence.

The other hypothesis results from our criticism of the media being dominated by institutionalized power, that is, coagulation of content and vehicle with the whole constituting an institution, for example educational television. We thus envisage a complete reworking of the systems. This working hypothesis would have no chance of success if we could not count, over the next ten years, on two powerful trends which will 'put the squeeze on' existing media systems. We are talking about micro- and mega-vehicles: the micro-installations of individual production and distribution and the megasystem of satellites.

This project differs considerably from the preceding systems in what it presupposes (which is perfectly probable and possible): a satellite channel entirely devoted to the needs of national education. In contrast to educational television, this satellite, even though providing direct transmissions, would not be aimed at the consumer as such, but at institutional groups, not just those concerned with school, but also those having to do with life-long education (local centres, firms, etc.). Used in this way, the satellite channel would permit the transmission day and might of such a large volume of messages, that it would probably outstrip at the beginning the capacity for production of educational material. We could take advantage of this shortfall to establish stocks of film, or rather of film sequences borrowed from international documentary and feature-film repositories and for which we envisage a supporting role in the cultural field. Eventually the satellite would be used just to transmit educational material.

If it has been clearly understood that we are regarding the satellite here in its role as carrier, and that it is in no way an educational institution, but simply a means of facilitating exchanges between educators, consumers and producers, it will be clear that the essence of the project is to help local groups regain their initiative and independence on the strength of the service provided to them by the satellite and, more generally, the developments to be anticipated in telematics.

AN ESSENTIAL STRUCTURE: LOCAL AUDIO-VISUAL CENTRES

The organization of microcentres clearly depends on the level and scale of education, and on local aims and finance. We suspect that most primary schools have difficulty in finding the means to acquire visual equipment, but why should not sound be adequate for them to start with, since it is so well suited to the first steps in language? As for films, why not rely on the 'parallel school'? In Europe, for example, it would be unusual for one or another of the channels not to transmit, at least once a week, a programme which could be used as a cultural aid. Finally, several primary schools could share a common audio-visual centre adapted to their needs. Such a system is clearly essential for basic education in developing countries, which are obliged to strike a balance between too general a transmission service and too specialized local resources.

Flight and fight

Thus, in the face of the threat of the 'parallel school' and audio-visual 'corruption', we advise advance rather than withdrawal. Fight evil with evil and with its own weapons. It must be admitted that it is asking a lot of teachers not only to overcome their adversary but to beat him on his own ground. Where is the strength and the inspiration to come from, and how can the means be found?

Finally, let us return to a problem mentioned above which is of a totally different kind since it consists of seeking a spiritual dimension, moral inspiration and a will for civilization in a world obsessed by technology. The example of the media is alas much more than just an object lesson. It reveals the world as it is, and as it threatens more and more to become.

We have made so bold as to tell educators that, without neglecting their humble list of responsibilities, they should add another one to it: that their role is not only to transmit scraps of knowledge but to draw attention to a broader horizon or, if there is only jungle ahead, to blaze a trail through it. 'By what right?' it will again be protested. The 'neutral', apolitical school, concerned with nothing but the syllabus and the famous content, is certainly reassuring. But is it possible to talk about the media without being critical and, to a certain extent, political?

There is a fine line drawn between neutrality and indifference, between values and tolerance. Any adult who abuses his power to effect propaganda which exceeds his mandate is blameworthy. But any educator shrinking from contact with a student when a question of value arises is shirking his duty. For his behaviour is like what we witness in the media: the accomplice of a false 'transparency', of one-way communication, of the theatrical device.

Science is proffered in the absence of morality or collective wisdom. And so the schools are reduced to the same doubts and confusion as the rest of society. What good is knowledge, if such poor use is made of it? What is the point of atomic power when loaded nuclear silos hold us in terror? What good is culture when we return to the Middle Ages with tortures to which are added our brilliant contemporary innovations: concentration camps, racial exodus, psychiatric asylums? Did our history classes not teach us to hate injustice and violence, to support the martyr against the executioner? What good will come, then, in today's absurd world, of technological promises and telematic sophistication? To escape the problems, will we have access to machines wiser still than they are intelligent?

What is the attitude of schools, situated, as they are, on the fringe of this scenario? Should they applaud, or penetrate boldly into the wings, revealing the hoax and denouncing the prompter? How could they do this, subject as they are to political power, to their own organs and to collective fantasies? Are they not, first and foremost, the buffer between the generations, subject to a provisional role, a waiting game, having nothing more than a child-minding function?

Hence, the title of this section airs two problems at once: that of content materials, which is much too ordinary, and that of values, which is much too original. If schools could cope with the problem of values, why not society as a whole? Or do schools have a special mandate to deal with it? Not really, not in so many words, but we always expect a little more of schools. Yes, the world in its confusion continues to expect schools to do what it cannot do itself: provide an 'education', it says, that goes beyond 'instruction' to 'bring out the best' as the etymology suggests. This explains the strange behaviour of schools everywhere and under all regimes, their strategy of alternating 'flight and fight'.

Notes

1. *Revue des deux mondes* (Paris), June 1979.
2. To be perfectly categoric, let us state that the impact of the media on education is negligible compared with that of computers, not only on education but on the functions of knowledge and the divisions of human activity.
3. Artificial intelligence poses problems of this kind in the apparently fringe areas of artistic and especially musical creation. The incredible nonsense that has been going on for a good twenty years now in the field of music and computers matches the presumptuousness of the doctrinaires.

Information
and knowledge

Communication and education

Henri Dieuzeide

The rapid extension of the various forms of mass communication (especially audio-visual communication, together with the more general use of informatics) seems to bring education a new dimension.

Communication was quick to develop its new vectors (press, radio, television) in most countries at a time when education was emerging as an aspiration of all categories of the population and the ideas of democratization of education, lifelong education, and equality of opportunity were becoming widespread. The two phenomena inevitably came into relation with each other: communication is seen as bringing about an 'educational environment', wresting from the school its monopoly of education, getting the school to use modern forms of communication for its own purposes. Finally, communication, by becoming a subject of education, may very well evolve new forms.

The ever increasing volume of information with which the public is swamped and, above all, the extension of the dissemination of information, especially by radio and television, to new social or geographical categories, have given the impression that anyone at all could come into direct contact with the very sources of knowledge, that social distances and professional secrets no longer exist.

The young have been particularly appreciative of this opportunity of direct and effortless access to an adult world previously closed to them. In Europe a 10-year-old spends, on average, twenty-four hours a week looking at television, that is, as much time as in school. In the United States today an average 16-year-old has spent at least 15,000 hours of his life watching television.

This sudden extension of communication was first of all analysed in terms of 'effects' or 'impact' and the direct influence of the ever increasing stimulation on individuals and groups, and there was talk of the 'educational action of the media' on cognitive development or behaviour, using mechanistic terms of psychology. Today, with a more subtle analysis, the impact of communication is considered only in the most obvious aspect of a wider series of transformations due to gradual changes in the human environment. Research shows that the influences of technology are in fact differentiated in accordance with the psychological, intellectual, social and cultural conditions of the individuals exposed to them. From this point of view, interpretation of the non-formal educational action of the media is undergoing the same changes as thinking on education: emphasis is laid on the role of interpersonal relations and the influence of values common to the group, on long-term effects and on the fact that we know little about them as yet. Interest is moving from the transmitter to the receiver. The question is not so much what the message does to the individual or the group as what the individual or the group does with the message.

The all-pervasive character of communication is but the sign of the advent of a new environment. Ideas such as the 'civilization of visual media', the 'alternative school', the 'computerized society', the 'global village', indicate awareness of the fact that the technological environment is creating a permanent means of presenting or proliferating information and gaining access to knowledge. There has been talk of the emergence of a new man whom this new environment could in varying degrees fashion from day to day as regards his emotional context and his habits of reasoning, his critical attitudes and imagination, his technical skills and his behaviour.

Is this new man conscious of being so? It has to be acknowledged that young people are now normally accustomed to handling a whole series of miniature electronic devices that have become a part of everyday life, tape- and cassette-recorders or pocket calculators. We adults have been brought up to make distinctions between functions (television, computer, telephone) and do not readily perceive the connections that electronic developments have now made between these formerly incompatible functions—the television screen becoming a computer terminal, a notice-board, and a video play-deck as well as conveying film images, the pocket calculator becoming a clock and the radio making the morning coffee.

Here ought we not see how the child, caught up in a technological environment imposed on it by the adult world, has now built his own ecological niche? It is no longer in school, which should be the place for reflection and the passing on of knowledge, that he gets to know about the basic concepts common to our technological universe—*real time*, for instance, which indicates autonomous transmission, or the controlling of a process while it is going on; *memory*, a magnetic trace of data; *program*, which now exists in all domestic automation and which corresponds to an ordered sequence of acts.

Knowledge presented in this way, in abundance and day by day, has a 'mosaic' pattern that no longer fits into the traditional intellectual categories. Emphasis tends to be laid on the heterogeneous and even chaotic nature of the information presented, the priority given to the dissemination of superficial or sensational information of ephemeral interest, increasing the 'noise' to the detriment of the actual message. Emphasis is laid, too, on the fact that it is imposed on the user, who has the feeling of undergoing this environment rather than exploring or controlling it. In so far as the education of the individual is concerned, the incoherence is probably less important than the constraint. Mass communication tends to reinforce common symbolic systems, to enrich, re-express and reinterpret them. In doing so, it flattens out the individuality of groups and builds up stereotypes. It seems to bring about a kind of intellectual standardization. There is nothing, however, to justify us in thinking that this tendency towards standardization, which is a feature of most communication industries today, is inexorable. Communication refers us back to education: how can the consumers of information (and also the communicators) gradually be educated to use in a positive and imaginative way these immense new resources put every day at their disposal? Will education be equal to the task of preparing people to take on communication, while still preserving their own personalities and creative abilities?

The question is an urgent one, since in nearly all societies the school must share its monopoly of education with the institutions responsible for communication. This shared responsibility is often claimed by the communicators themselves. It is sometimes established by statute—for example, in the triad 'inform, educate, entertain' frequently invoked by broadcasting organizations. This situation and the growing presence of communication in most societies, raise the question of the reappraisal of the functions of the school and perhaps even, to some extent, those of the family. Up until the beginning of this century, even in industrial societies, the school was the first source of knowledge and the educator was its patented distributor through the spoken and printed word. Knowledge of the world and mastery of the skills enabling one to be integrated into it were obtainable from the school alone, and the role of the family was to strengthen and supplement this function. Gradually new sources of information, cinema and radio, television and soon telematics* have come to upset, contradict and sometimes replace the traditional information sources of the school and the family environment.

Today, in most societies, the two systems are either covertly

---

* From the French neologism, *télématique*, meaning transmission of data over a distance.—Ed.

or openly competing with one another—not without creating contradictions and even major difficulties for individual consciences that are unconsciously subjected to this competition, particularly in the case of the very young.

The educational institution, based on values of order and method, curriculum, personal effort and concentration, and competition, is now opposed by a system of mass communication, geared to the topical, to the surprise element exalting world disorder, to facility and hedonistic values. Is there any way to reduce this competition, implicit or explicit, the waste of resources and talent that it has entailed for thirty or forty years in the rich countries? Can the countries that have only limited resources be spared this problem?

Finding solutions is not easy: sharing of responsibility between education and communication can take very different forms. Some pragmatists hold that the communication media should purvey contemporary knowledge while education should be responsible for passing on the heritage accumulated by tradition. For the technocrats, the school should concern itself with the most effective social knowledge, the promotion and dignity of the individual, the economic efficiency of nations, while communication should serve for recreation and entertainment, but also for international exchanges and understanding. For many people who are concerned to preserve traditional values, the school should provide a protective haven of silence, meditation, intellectual exercise and personal integration, in contrast to the proliferation and hubbub of communication. Yet many educationists would consider that the prime function of the educational institutions, henceforth, should be to put in order the 'knowledge' disseminated at random by the communication networks; the education systems would put forward systems of values and methods enabling the essentials to be picked out, helping to identify the positive aspects, to relate the main facts concerning material already acquired elsewhere—in short, teaching how to understand and how to learn.

So far, there does not seem to have been any systematic

thinking on policy with regard to such a redistribution of functions between education and communication, the two systems still tending in most countries to ignore one another; any negotiation has been on minor questions or in marginal fields that do not call the prerogatives into question (school television, children's cinema). Pierre Schaeffer has called this 'the sharing out of the cheap cuts'.

It is obvious that any genuine effort of integration would necessitate both a reconversion of all teaching staff to new tasks, and a real awareness on the part of communicators of the problems involved in education.

The need for this basic change should not lead us to underestimate the attempts already made to enlist communication in the service of education. Since the school is a 'communication society', it is gradually tending to submit most of the modern forms of communication to its own purposes in a selective, deliberate way: by using communication systems as they stand in order to provide the usual audiences of these systems with information of educational value (family education programmes, functional literacy teaching, health and hygiene etc.); by utilizing the same communication systems to introduce new components into formal educational activities (school's radio, television and films); by relaying the functions of a traditional system by transferring the educational tasks to a communication system (in particular teaching of remote or handicapped pupils by radio and television); and even, on occasion, by reorganizing the structure, methods and processes of education (as, for instance, in self-teaching ventures and teaching laboratories based particularly on the use of informatics).

Owing to the number of different media (films, records, audio-visual montages, radio, television, video-tapes, video-records, portable television sets, computers, microprocessors), owing to the number of types and levels of education involved (literacy teaching, adult education, rural development, pre-primary, primary and secondary education, technical and vocational education, higher and post-graduate education), owing to the differences in the extent to which the media are used (continuously, regularly, partially, occasionally) and owing to the situations in which they are used (in a group, with or without a teacher, for home study), there are several thousand combinations in the use of communication technologies that have been developed with varying success.

Experience today shows that the major educational campaigns by the media have often been too optimistic, the educators having underestimated the difficulties, the complications and the unwieldiness of production and facilities. Where the information environment was poorest, it has taken more readily to educational communication—for example, radio in rural areas. Today, renewed interest is to be noted on the part of educators in the use of less cumbersome technical means of stocking and distributing—local radio transmitters, video-cassettes, lightweight or portable videotape-recorders—which can be handled more easily and better adapted to local needs. However, the absence of any coherent cultural policy and the rigidity of educational strategies in most countries reduce the possibilities of massive, systematic applications of the media to major educational tasks.

What does seem possible, on the other hand, and is desired by most societies in view of the increasing importance of communication, is the new responsibility of teaching everyone the proper use of communication; the more so since the family, in most cases, has shown itself ill-prepared to face up to its sudden expansion. What is required is a more critical education that can point to the dangers of pseudo-knowledge from audio-visual sources and the illusion of the power of information. It is a question of freeing the individual from the fascination exercised by technology, making him less receptive and more exacting, more aware. It now seems to be recognized that any improvement in the standards of the press and of radio and television programmes is dependent on this training of individual and collective discernment.

There are already many forms of education for the appropriate consumption of communication. Some are essentially concerned with the individual consumption of information as a product, others with the encouragement of the creative use of communication seen mainly as a social process. In the context of better consumption of the product, the last few years have brought about a development in the use of newspapers in schools as texts for study, the teaching of the rudiments of visual communication and the screen arts, showing how to appreciate and judge messages, to read the author's intentions, to distinguish the real and the imaginary, to organize and select. In some cases it is the content of the audio-visual culture itself (films, television), that is used as a reference for teaching purposes. Sometimes, even, communication provides the basis for a school exercise: production of filmed synopses or cartoon montages. This amounts to an introduction to communication as a process.

Communication is no longer the monopoly of communicators. Inaugurated in earlier times with the school newspaper and printing shop, this 'participatory' approach is now leading many schools, clubs or youth movements to have pupils handle portable television or 8-mm movie cameras and even to dialogue with mini-computers.

In this way, educators are taking their place at the heart of the popular Utopia of a convivial society in which everyone can be at the same time a producer and a consumer of information, as part of a group.

This proliferation of initiatives has not yet found its way into coherent educational strategies, and much remains to be done in this field. Some maintain that communication technologies and their use should be a new subject of study, even if this means increasing compartmentalization. Others maintain that it is within each subject in general education as it now exists that the pupil must gradually learn to master the media, despite the possible danger of forcing into the school a culture that it may be unable to assimilate. But for the time being, neither the audio-visual media nor data processing are sufficiently well established within educational institutions to become an everyday concern there. This makes it clear that the time has come for a more systematic exchange of information, experiences and ideas, within the international community, in a field where the causes are as difficult to control as the effects are decisive. It has become obvious that neither policies nor methods of education, neither initial or in-service training of teachers nor educational research, can henceforth ignore the new set of problems arising from the confrontation between education and communication. And the poorer countries are affected even less than the others, inasmuch as their very poverty leaves them directly exposed to the corrosive effects of this information explosion that is going to shake the end of the century.

Mass communication education

Ana Maria Sandi

Mass communication: a challenge

Twentieth-century educators have been challenged by a fierce and irresistible competition: their pupils are overwhelmed by the information transmitted by mass media. When compared with television programmes, films, comics, coloured pictures in magazines and science-fiction pocket books, the lessons or the maths and grammar exercises seem dull and constraining.

Nowadays, parents and teachers are trying hard to break the magic of images and sounds and to send their children back to homework.

There are families who avoid buying a television set in order to maintain their 'cultural purity'. The selective attitude that operates in relation to printed matter is readily abandoned as soon as the television programme is involved.

The power of mass communication and the fact that it may play either a positive or a negative role in individual and social development have caused many people to view its new dimensions with both mistrust and apprehension.

The obsolescence of the printed word was announced, regretfully, with the outset of the video culture; however, world book production has almost doubled in the past ten years.

On the other hand, specialists in information have established that a twenty-minute television news programme corresponds roughtly to three columns of newspaper text. Going even further in the demonstration of audio-visual inefficiency, it may be added that the television programme was in fact based on printed texts such as agency news, notes, summaries, written syntheses. However, any such discussion overlooks the astonishing properties of the moving images, the impact that images from far-off, unknown places may have.

The mass-communication phenomenon is here, developing in all its complexity and variety of forms, and future forecasts indicate an even greater expansion, largely due to new technological advances.

In the 1990s the specialists are expecting a large-scale expansion of video-cassette systems, which are going to invade the world market as the record player did some time ago.

Cable and inter-regional television and communication satellites are also booming. At present over eighty communication satellites are in orbit; they ensure the retransmission both of phone calls and of television programmes, thus making it possible for a large part of the world population to be directly involved in major events at the very moment of their occurrence. A typical satellite programme may be beamed around the globe in nine-tenths of a second.

The developed countries are said to be undergoing a transition toward the post-industrial phase of development, towards the informational society and the informational economy, based on an infinitely renewable resource: information.

In this type of society, according to Lars Ingelstam, the citizen must be able to deal with information in order to survive.[1]

On the other hand, many developing countries are simultaneously developing their industry and their information and communication capabilities, in an attempt to have an equal share in the information process of the modern world.[2]

There are striking disparities between rural and urban areas: the rural population is submitted to urban-oriented communications and information.

The problem is therefore related not only to the actual channels and effective methods of communication, but also to the content of the material to be communicated and to the relevance or irrelevance of the latter for the masses receiving it. The misuse of mass media for commercial purposes, for obtaining large profits by broadcasting advertisements, is unfortunately characteristic of a large part of the information network.

Finally, disparities are further increased by such problems as accessibility and the ability to interpret, understand and utilize the information received. Among the factors hampering the development of the press as an effective mode of communication in the developing countries, U. Ahamed enumerates 'the high rate of illiteracy, the number of languages spoken, the lack of printing presses, the high cost of imported newsprint, the poor telecommunications facilities for transmission of news and the slow and poor rural communication between the few cities and towns and the larger rural areas'.[3]

The social, cultural and economic development of a country depends to a great extent upon its way of responding to and utilizing mass communication.

Soedjatmoko defines the learning capacity of a nation as the 'collective capacity to generate, to ingest, to reach out for and to utilize a vast amount of new and relevant information'.[4]

Education is one of the fields that could fully make use of the increased possibilities of information and knowledge.

The conflicts between the education system and mass communication are often dealt with; their potential for complementarity and co-operation is mentioned far less often. And this is a time when television has been called, with reason, the children's 'early window' on the world.[5]

Promising attempts exist: an interesting programme called 'Success in Reading', which has been tried in some schools, consists in a system of teaching reading and writing by using newspapers and magazines instead of the classical first-grade handbook.[6] Children, attracted by the use of interesting things they will deal with the rest of their lives, are prompted to obtain better results in learning.

The general picture seems, however, to reflect antagonistic relations and interests rather than co-operative tendencies.

The contrast has been theorized about by educators, and thus the mass media have emerged in an unfavourable light. On the one hand, in organized, formalized school education, knowledge forms a coherent, ordered system. On the other hand, mass communication transmits simple, disconnected, scattered information. At one extreme is the utmost economy, optimization in the sense of the minimum of signs used for a maximum of message; at the other extreme is redundancy, superposition, wastage. At one end is science with its paraphernalia; at the other, amateurism and superficiality.

Nevertheless, if we were to analyse the sources of the knowledge used by our children, the balance would be strongly unfavourable to the school.

The quantity of information

It is a well known fact that the information that incessantly surrounds us also acts upon us.

Scientists such as H. von Foerster insist upon the enriching character of the 'noise' when it is introduced in self-organizing systems characterized by a sufficiently high degree of redundancy and reliability.[7]

But our main interest in the education process is knowledge. The essential difference between information and knowledge is the fact that the latter is endowed with meaning. The fact that either 'it is raining' or 'the weather is fine' provides information. It may eventually be measured. In this case, if the two situations are equally probable, we have what specialists call a 'bit' of information.

Specialists in information theory are especially interested in the quantitative aspect of information. Starting from the idea that the essence of information is to make a choice, the measure chosen for the quantity of information is conceived so that the more the possibilities of choice, the larger the quantity of information provided. If n possibilities exist the quantity of information, I, should be an increasing function of n. The chosen function, owing to reasons connected with its properties, was the logarithm: $I = \log n$.

A more refined measure allows for analysis of the cases in which the possibilities are not equally probable. In this case, the lower the probability of an event, the more surprised we are when it actually occurs.

Learning processes may seem at first sight to be governed by a decrease of entropy. In the case of a question permitting more than one possible answer, the entropy is initially maximum (the answers being equally probable). In the process of learning, the incorrect answers are eliminated, while the probability of the correct ones is increased and consequently the entropy decreases.

The dialectics seem to be more intricate, including both stages of increase and decrease of entropy. Unlearning implies an increase of entropy, and any anti-entropic evolution in a system implies an entropic evolution in the frame of a larger system.

However, the information transmitted by mass media is neither pure, isolated from a certain context, nor value-free, as considered in quantitative studies. And educators are interested exactly in the meaning and value of the information.

Let us remember the childhood game in which a chain of children whisper the same word from ear to ear; to the players' delight, the final version is often completely different from what had been initially transmitted. The problem is that very often things distinctly and plainly expressed at emission are wrongly understood at reception.

The measure of the quantity of information is of no help in such situations.

Context

Influenced by the dominant logical positivist school, we are used to defining sense (and therefore meaning) by making reference to a system of rules defining correctness. The knowledge provided by the education system is stored in the logical blocks of theories and disciplines; it has a meaning determined by its place in the system of inferences (deductive in the ideal case of the theoretical sciences or inductive in the empirical sciences). But the logical criterion, which is so exclusivist and an enemy of any exogeneous considerations and which also overlooks the contributions of psychology and sociology, is strongly challenged nowadays.

We are in a period of ample reconsideration of the psycho-social component of knowledge.

The sense (the meaning) is given by the context, and the context also helps the process of strengthening accumulated knowledge and memory recall. The context may be considered 'a collective term for all those events which tell the organism among what set of alternatives he must make his next choice'.[8]

In this respect, mass media are a fantastic source of a large variety of contexts, which logical and systematic learning sweeps aside as impurities.

Formal education transmits schematized, arranged, ordered knowledge, while the large mass media sources provide knowledge as it is elaborated, taken out from the production process even before the latter is completed. Knowledge is provided within the framework of real problems, not in the narrow one of disciplines.

It is true that the systematic presentation mode in school has the advantage of being economical. However, this should be viewed cautiously, and a margin should be left for the diffused communication provided by mass media.

Values

On the other hand, the information transmitted by the mass media is not value-free; it emerges filtered and interpreted through the value systems, offering a specific image of reality. In fact, the transmission of information implies a selective judgement reflecting a specific scale of values. This is also true for all distortions reflected by over- or underemphasizing news, the presentation of isolated or incomplete statements, omissions, creating unfounded fears, etc.

The fact that in a children's magazine there is an image alongside the following problem: 'how many possibilities are there for a little girl and two boys to sit together in a car, given that only the boys can drive?' is certainly the reflection of a specific value system.

Learning may proceed within the framework of a value system, by a process of detection of error and correction leading to the improvement of answers. This is single-loop learning; in its framework the values and the norms that lie at the core of the whole process are not questioned.

In double-loop learning,[9] the value system itself is challenged. Within its framework weights are modified and new priorities or even entirely new values emerge.

Value-laden and contextual information transmitted by mass media continually offers the potential for both types of learning.

Restructuring

The activation of this potential requires an active attitude from the learner. Some authors consider that information is not received, but constituted.[10]

Everyone is familiar with a situation in which a radio is on, but we fail to hear what is transmitted because our attention is concentrated on some other activity. Moreover, the messages transmitted are not always clear and specific, but vague and ambiguous. An active attitude of inquiry and reflexive inquiry aimed at attaining the specification and the clarification of information as well as its completion and simplification is necessary.

Knowledge does not accumulate in a desert; it is inserted in mental schemata belonging to a general thinking framework created in time on the basis of the contextual structure and of past experience.

Specialists in artificial intelligence lately have been paying particular attention to these knowledge structures. M. Minsky calls them frames:

a structure of data used for representing a stereotype situation, for instance a type of room or a child's birthday party. To each frame, indications of various nature are attached: some of them regarding the way of utilizing the frame, others on what we could expect further, others on what should be done in case the previsions are not confirmed.[11]

On the philosophical plane these structures represent a *Weltanschauung*, the images we may have about reality.

K. Boulding makes distinctions among three possible situations on confrontation with a message: (a) ignoring the message (unaffected images); (b) modification of images by a routine procedure; and (c) revolutionary change of the images (the message reaches the support structure).[12]

Similarly, in learning, information may produce simple modifications of the probabilities to choose one answer from a given set of answers and/or it may have a more complex effect, generating restructuring at the level of the general thinking framework, translated by modifications of the set of answers itself (for instance by the creative addition of new possible answers). The restructuring capacity is specific to living organisms, the autopoietic systems that in a given physical space do not lose their physical identity (and do not, therefore, modify their organization) as a consequence of the permanent renewal of matter and of the restructurings that occur through learning and development.

As against these systems, in another type of dynamic system, an allopoietic one, the organizations are maintained the same as long as the product of their functioning, differing from themselves, does not change.[13]

In this process, a central place is undoubtedly played by

motivation, but the role played by learning to learn may also be added.

This presupposes learning about the previous contexts of learning, learning to restructure, learning how and when to apply single-loop or double-loop learning.

Learning to learn implies reflecting on previous contexts of learning in which you learned or failed to learn, trying to identify the situations and the modalities favourable to learning.

This second-order learning, or deutero-learning as Bateson calls it,[14] leads to saving the time and effort implied by the usual first-order learning.

Learning processes between school and mass media

The two criteria for achieving learning advocated by the report to the Club of Rome[15] are participation and anticipation. Let us see how they are satisfied by formal education (schools) and the mass media.

Mass communication is generally blamed for the creation of a passive attitude of reception and simple additive accumulation of knowledge. Unfortunately, many of the classical pedagogical forms are also non-participative (without roles, based on reception, absence from choice and decisions).

As regards the roles, the mass media are a real guide, a permanent introduction, to the world of adult actors, generating models, aspirations and endeavours.

The unidirectional relationship of the unique transmitter and listener audiences tends to be changed, owing to innovations in tele-data processing that offer the possibility of dialogue and interaction.

Cable television allows for direct and immediate capturing of the audience response. The communication satellites enable the organization of meetings such as tele-conferences in which famous scientists at great distances may be interviewed or involved in discussions.

As regards anticipation, it is obvious that the mass media are more imaginative, capable of future prospections based on scenarios that capture the interest of children and youth. They may present the latest discoveries and suppositions, while the curriculum and the schoolbooks are strikingly poor, as far as anticipation is concerned.

School education may, however, contribute to a better understanding of the information transmitted by the mass media and to the formation of the capacity for critical judgement by continuous debates and discussions.

Educational television and radio programmes and scientific programmes are among the first that may be coupled into the educational process. It is recommended that pupils read certain books in addition to classwork—why not also that they watch certain television programmes and films? The latter may represent a bibliography as useful as the books.

In Romania, a successful television programme that has been maintained for many years is a scientific programme: the tele-encyclopaedia. It is watched by pupils, parents and teachers alike. In school, however, there is hardly any reference to the extremely interesting issues presented in this programme.

A very successful serial all over the world was conceived by a scientist, J. Bronowski. Science presented in a personal, captivating vision aroused prolonged and controversial debates but generally not in school. Discussions in class of articles, programmes or films may contribute to establishing connections, interpreting the things that were read or seen, getting full awareness of the value system and of the proposed vision of the world. At the same time, the teacher could stimulate interest for programmes and journals in an educative context.

The interest in watching the scientific-educative programmes is enhanced if they are presented under the form of competitions in front of audiences. These should not be competitions of memorization but rather of deduction, imagination, creative thinking. The simple questions must be completed with the commentaries of specialists and experts in different fields.

Another modality is a television programme such as the one called 'Do You Have Another Question?' in which a group of specialists answers questions regarding a specific problem; the questions are put directly through on the telephone, which is placed in the studio from which the programme is broadcast.

Another scientific television serial, 'Connections', conceived in a very lively manner by the British journalist James Burke, is watched with great interest not so much for the information displayed as for the fact that it helps establish connections and explain the way in which science and society have advanced in close correlation over the years. This is a good example of a modern, well-achieved programme making people think, involving them and thus breaking the pattern of passive reception.

Under the conditions of the information revolution, the young should become 'media literate', learning to learn useful things.[16]

A process of learning to utilize communication contrasts with the tendency to be used.

Flexible curricula are already including communication courses. In the first grade of a school there are already three types of courses: sciences (mathematics, languages), arts (music, drawing, manual work) and library. Thus quite small children become familiar with the great variety of information and knowledge that may derive from books and journals other than schoolbooks. The obvious attraction of the illustrated storybook facilitates and hastens the pupils' contact with the new environment, creating from the beginning the aptitude to work and become informed in an independent way.

Education in watching, in reading (including fast reading) may be achieved by utilizing both formal and non-formal means. The training of children in utilizing mass media communication has proved to be particularly efficient when the pupils are effectively involved in the process of editing a magazine, producing a radio or television programme or shooting a documentary film. Ample evidence in this respect has been provided by the results obtained by school cineclubs or the audiences drawn by youth programmes edited and presented by pupils.

Two conclusions may be formulated: in the first place, all authors, script-writers, cartoonists, producers of advertisements and editors should assume the responsibility of being educators. Awareness of participation in the learning processes of society should determine the exigency towards the released information and the modalities used, ensuring also an efficient feedback from the public.

A way (which does not fall into the category of technical performance) to enhance the role of public opinion in the control of mass communication and of the information process is to ensure its presence in the management of the institutions involved in this process.

Secondly, all teachers and the other persons involved in the educative system should cultivate the high standards of those who receive the information transmitted by mass media. They should feel like real authors and script-writers for the pupils and the adults, directors in permanent education.

As H. de Jouvenel remarks, 'the development of everybody's capacity to think, understand, criticize, undertake is more important than the transmission of information and knowledge'.[17]

Notes

1. Lars Ingelstam, *Feudalism or Democracy? Communications at the Crossroads*, paper presented at the World Future Studies Federation (WFSF) meeting in Cairo, 16–19 September 1978.
2. The Fifth Conference of the Heads of States of the Non-Aligned Countries in Sri Lanka in 1976 stated that a new international order in the field of mass communication is as vital as the new international economic order.

3. Uvais Ahamed, *Communication, Cultural Identity in Our Interdependent World*, paper presented at the WFSF conference, Cairo, September 1978.
4. Soedjatmoko, *The Future and the Learning Capacity of Nations: The Role of Communications*, paper presented at the Annual Meeting of the International Institute of Communications, Dubrovnik, September 1978.
5. R. M. Liebert, J. M. Neale, E. S. Davidson, *The Early Window: Effects of Television on Children and Youth*, New York, Pergamon Press, 1973.
6. *Newsweek*, 24 September 1979.
7. H. von Foerster, 'On Self-organizing Systems and Their Environments', in Yovitz and Cameron, *Self-organizing Systems*, London, Pergamon Press, 1960.
8. Gregory Bateson, *Steps to an Ecology of Mind*, New York, Ballantine Books, 1974.
9. The terms of single-loop and double-loop learning are used for organizational learning in C. Argyris and D. Schön, *Organisational Learning: a Theory of Action Perspective*, Reading, Mass., Addison-Wesley, 1978.
10. Valeriu Ceauşu, *Cunoasterea psihologică si condiţia incertidutinii* [Psychological Knowledge and the Uncertainty Condition], Bucharest, Militară, 1978.
11. P. Winston (ed.), *The Psychology of Computer Vision*, New York, McGraw-Hill, 1975.
12. K. Boulding, *The Image*, Ann Arbor, Mich., University of Michigan Press, 1956.
13. H. Maturana, 'Strategies cognitives', in *L'unité de l'homme*, Paris, Éditions du Seuil, 1974.
14. Bateson, op. cit.
15. J. Botkin, M. Elmardjra, M. Malitza, *No Limits to Learning: How to Bridge the Human Gap*, Pergamon Press, 1979.
16. Jim Dator, *Identity, Culture and Communication Future*, paper presented at the WFSF conference, Cairo, September 1978.
17. H. de Jouvenel, *Quelle question pour demain?*, paper presented at the Unesco seminar on the perspectives of educational development, Paris, 1978.

The two worlds of today's learners

Donald P. Ely

One of the major anthropological discoveries of the last decade was the Tasaday tribe in the hills of Mindanao in the Philippines. The interest generated by that discovery was based on the isolation of the tribe from society. To find a group of people who had lived in isolation for an estimated 2,000 years was so unusual that care was taken to preserve the separation of the tribe from the remainder of society lest some contamination destroy the uniqueness of their situation.

Isolation is an ever-decreasing phenomenon in our world. The pervasiveness of communication and transportation technologies virtually ensures movement of people and ideas. It is rare that a person is immune from daily messages by radio and, to a lesser extent, newspapers and television. Where the more glamorous medium of television is not available, pressures by the public and visions of modernity by their leaders hasten to bring electronic images to the people. The demand for television is often great enough to give it political priority over running water and sewage disposal systems.

The Tasadays are unique because they were removed from the mainstream of society. This example highlights the contrast between a group of about 100 people and the rest of the world, which is totally immersed in the technological age. Global communication systems provide information and entertainment to national and international audiences. Today, even rural people in remote areas press the transistor radio to their ear and become part of a world beyond their own village.

The pervasive influence of mass media

The ubiquitous nature of communication media in nearly every nation has brought about a significant increase in the amount of information available and a significant decrease in the time in which a message moves from a source to thousands of receivers. Add to the usual broadcast media those of print, film and recordings, and we begin to sense the extent to which every person in every part of the world has access to audio and visual stimuli.

It is with thoughts of a media-saturated society that McLuhan comments on the way in which media are reshaping and restructuring patterns of social interdependence in almost every aspect of life except education:

There is a world of difference between the modern home environment of integrated electric information and the classroom. Today's television child is attuned to up-to-the-minute 'adult' news—inflation, rioting, war, taxes, crime, bathing beauties—and is bewildered when he enters the nineteenth-century environment that still characterizes the educational establishment where information is scarce but ordered and structured by fragmented, classified patterns, subjects and schedules.[1]

The separation of schools from society

The paradox is that in the midst of a global communications revolution, schools can remain aloof, rigid and unchanging. In societies that have embraced new communication technologies, the tendency is for those technologies to permeate every sector of that society. However, schools have remained walled off from the society of which they are an integral part. This separateness can be observed not only in advanced technical societies but also in developing nations, which have 'succeeded in multiplying indefinitely existing monopolistic forms of conventional education, based on the historic, rigid models of the West, thus heading rapidly toward economic disaster and social bankruptcy'.[2]

Schools will increase their irrelevance as long as they remain separate from the society from which they derive support. Adults who missed earlier opportunities for advanced schooling or who want to gain new competencies are seeking alternative means to achieve their educational goals. Many of the new approaches of open learning[3] and distance education use communication technologies as major elements of instruction. Younger learners, however, do not have choices when they pursue their education.

Dieuzeide states the basic problem when he says that 'education remains the only major human activity in which technology may not increase man's potential. Voices rise to denounce the strange and pernicious paradox whereby the educational institution is required to change the world without any concession that it must itself be transformed'.[4]

For the past fifty years visionary educators have attempted to bring the schools into the mainstream of society by introducing a variety of media into the classroom. As each new medium was introduced and tried by brave innovators, it was usually treated as an experiment whereby the medium substituted for other stimuli. It was usually additive; that is, almost no changes in the basic instructional process were made nor was the role of the teacher substantially changed. Those new media that were adopted, such as the overhead projector and audio-tape recorders, did not bring about any major changes in classroom procedures. Enthusiasm about new teaching methods among school administrators or among the learners themselves has had very little effect on the ultimate users—the teachers.

The classroom ritual

Historically, classroom teaching has been highly ritualized, and any major change is perceived as an invasion of sacred territory. Hovan points out that 'Ritualization in teaching is flexible enough to permit idiosyncrasies of personal style, arrangement of the daily schedule, police methods, pacing, etc., but major characteristics of ritual tend to be invariant'.[5] Two invariants to which Hoban refers are teacher control of the teaching-testing-grading-reward-punishment processes and face-to-face interaction with students. Any substantial reduction of the teacher's dominant status or major change in the interpersonal teacher-learner communication is likely to elicit some teacher hostility and resistance. Such resistance is likely to continue as long as the teacher perceives any medium as a replacement of teacher performance or as requiring a change from accepted norms of teacher behaviour.

A problem of change

Most theories of innovation hold that the individuals who will be responsible for installing and maintaining any innovation must be a part of the trial-and-adoption process. An innovation that originates outside the system or proceeds from the top down in a hierarchical structure is unlikely to succeed. The problem, therefore, is not one of how to bring media into education settings but how to bring about educational change. An innovation, such as the use of communication technology in education, should be as compatible as possible with the cultural values of teachers who use it. Innovation should not be presented so as to threaten the teacher's self-esteem or to jeopardize a teacher's position in relation to professional peers.[6] Faure et al. point to the key role of teachers:

The essential problem ... is to combat routine, arouse public interest and, above all, to have ... teachers co-operate in their undertaking.

This latter condition is indispensable, not only in order to tranquillize susceptibilities among certain sections of the population, but in particular because the use of new technologies in education requires them to be integrated into the educational system.[7]

The acceptance and use of communication media in teaching are probably easy innovations when compared to more fundamental changes that must be brought about if we are to harness the ever increasing influence of media on children when they are outside the schools.

The influence of television

The most dramatic influence on children is brought about by exposure to television. Authorities in the field of television research[8] regard television as an agent of socialization and acculturation equal to family and peer influence. Forbes points out that

in times past the elders of each society communicated to the next generation through legends and myths their picture of how the world functions—who holds power, who are the aggressors, who are the victims, what are the appropriate patterns of social interaction, where one might expect danger, and where one might be able to trust and feel secure. Now TV brings to all children its own myths and legends, its own picture of how the world functions.[9]

In areas where television is inaccessible, radio performs many of the same influential functions. Advertising in many formats, and local cinemas introduce people, ideas, products and actions that would otherwise never be known by the young. These experiences are brought to schools, where they are usually considered to be irrelevant, and teachers generally continue to do what they have done in the past. Postman describes the irony of the new student facing the traditional educational system. He says that schools are dealing with a different type of student now, one moulded by 'the electronic media, with the emphasis on visual imagery, immediacy, non-linearity, and fragmentation'.[10] Today's learners do not fit into the traditional classroom with its emphasis on 'sequence, social order, hierarchy, continuity, and deferred pleasure'. It is this type of young person with new ideas and attitudes who helps to bring about the failure of some of the most intelligent and dedicated teachers.

The influence of computers

The information age, as the current epoch has been called, is based upon computers which store, manipulate, and retrieve information in almost every sector of society in the developed countries of the world. They are invading the developing nations as well. Some children see them in schools but more see them in video games, arcades, toys and home appliances. Computers are embraced by children much more rapidly and with less suspicion than by adults. Once again, technology outside the school has become firmly established before schools have recognized the potential for learning. But the scene is changing.

The development of microcomputers has become the dominant educational innovation of the 1980s. In the United States alone, the number of personal computers available for instructional use in the public schools tripled between 1980 and 1982. Students had access to more than 120,000 computers in the schools in the spring of 1982.[11] National commitments to bring computers into the schools have been made in the United Kingdom, France, and the Netherlands, and other nations seem to be following rapidly. Cautious observers warn that rapid and unquestioned adoption of computers in schools may bring about repetition of the blind acceptance of television technology by some educators when it was introduced in the 1960s. Such nay-sayers may be the advocates of separation of school and society. If they are successful, the two worlds may continue to move further apart.

New roles for teachers

If some headway is to be made in creating a rapprochement between experiences gained outside the classroom and learning within the school environment, teachers will have to learn how to use the media to enrich learning and to ease the transition from school to contemporary society. The introduction of electronic media into the teaching-learning process is not necessarily the key to bringing the media into the mainstream of education. It is in teacher recognition of the influence that radio, television, computers, recordings, cinema, billboards and advertising media have on the students who come to their classrooms. It is in teacher understanding of the media content and context. It is in day-to-day teaching efforts and long-range curriculum planning that teachers can incorporate ideas, examples and personalities from outside the classroom into concerns inside the learning environment. Media should become an integral part of the instructional plan. They should be used as motivational tools that arouse and sustain interest but do not compromise substantive efforts. They can also be used to present content.

The suggestion of bringing the classroom and the world closer together is not new. Comenius, Pestalozzi, Froebel and Dewey were advocates of such an approach. Contemporary interpretations of their philosophies would undoubtedly call for a closer relationship between media influences and classroom learning. While teachers may endorse such an approach in principle, it is difficult to implement, and for some, the very idea appears to be a compromise because popular entertainment media are being introduced in an academic atmosphere. Some teachers may feel that essential knowledge and skills are not being learned if electronic communications media enter the classroom.

A new literacy for a new time

In addressing this concern, one must remember that the issue is not to adopt one approach and completely eliminate the other;

it is how to define a literate person in today's world. The nature and level of literacy may differ from village to village and from rural to urban areas. Literacy, as it is used here, goes beyond the normal interpretation—the ability to read and write. A literate person today is one who is able to understand, interpret and use myriad stimuli that are present in a given environment. Written and spoken language, music, sounds, still and moving pictures, natural objects and actions are some of the stimuli that affect people and hence need to be understood, interpreted and used. Schools often limit teaching to the traditional skills of reading and writing, with some time spent in observation. Such a limited approach is not sufficient for students who live in a much more sophisticated world that requires a type of literacy beyond basic primary-school knowledge and skills. Two new facets related to the concept of literacy are visual and computer literacy.

The visual literacy movement

Since the early 1970s there has been a growing interest in visual literacy among some educators in North America. Whether visual literacy, media literacy, or visual communication is the best label, the concept needs to be considered an essential element of today's curriculum everywhere in the world. As educators consider a broader definition of literacy, it should include the study of symbols, message carriers, non-verbal language, communication channels and effects on human behaviour. The National Conference on Visual Literacy,[12] an organization in North America, suggests the essence of a definition:

When a person has developed a set of visual abilities through seeing and sensory experiences, and when they are able to discriminate and interpret visual actions, objects, patterns and symbols in the environment, then they are becoming visually literate. It is through the creative use of these abilities that a visually literate person is able to comprehend and communicate. An appreciation of the visual skills of others will lead to greater enjoyment of visual communication.[13]

Programmes in visual literacy have been established in many primary and secondary schools in North America.[14] Australian educators are planning and experimenting with 'mental imagery'[15] and 'media studies':

'Media studies' refers to mass media communication, e.g. film, television, newspapers and radio, and the way they affect us. It is the exploration of communication through our senses and the development of our perceptions and skills in communicating by utilizing media tools. The primary concern of media studies is with concepts, not media tools.[16]

A major training programme for adults in North America is Television Awareness Training. The goal for individuals who follow this approximately twenty-hour course is 'to become more aware of how we use TV, what the teaching messages are and how we can make changes that seem appropriate'.[17] The curriculum approaches the study of television from the viewpoint of human values. Another example is the five-session inservice course for teachers, 'Visual Learning', which has been prepared by the New York State Education Department.[18]

Interest in visual symbols is not new. Adelbert Ames, Rudolf Arnheim, Ernst Cassirer, Charles Morris and others have explored the relationships of signs and symbols to human communication. Those efforts continue today in the work of Marshall McLuhan, M. D. Vernon, and Jerome Bruner. Recently visual communicators from India, Iran, Japan and the United States worked as a team at the East-West Center to develop a new visual language to convey complex concepts about interdepencence of nations and peoples, with emphasis on the energy crisis.[19] They reviewed existing international symbols and visual languages, revising and refining 70 of more than 700 images.

And now... computer literacy

There is no accepted definition of computer literacy but the concept of teaching students to understand and to be able to use computers is becoming a dominant movement of the 1980s. Watt[20] catches the essence of most definitions and descriptions by saying that computer literacy is a 'cultural phenomenon which includes the full range of skills, knowledge, understandings, values and relationships necessary to function effectively and comfortably as a citizen of a computer-based society'. Clearly, this definition charts a course for society and the schools to come closer together.

The basic definition of literacy has been distorted in an effort to point up the centrality of computers in the lives of people. Computers are pervasive and, according to even the most conservative observers, are bound to affect the fabric of almost every society. Never before in this century has such a strong effort been made to add new subject matter to the curriculum. Such attempts to integrate computer-related knowledge and skills with school curricula offer modest evidence that the two worlds of today's learners are closer than they have been in the past.

Entertainment versus education

Historically, visual communication has been primarily identified with entertainment and teachers have been reluctant to use examples from entertainment in the classroom. Education and entertainment are actually poles apart. A test of entertainment is immediate pleasure. What is seen or heard may not be remembered. A person usually recognizes entertainment immediately, while the test of education may come soon or many years in the future. Education is memorable; entertainment is written in the sand.[21] Pleasure usually comes from entertainment but education may be pleasurable, painful or painless. Teachers should strive to make learning pleasurable but need not avoid the pain that often comes from disciplined thinking. The most important questions are not 'Is it difficult?' or 'Is it easy?' but 'Is it clear?' and 'Is it relevant?'. 'The enjoyment of an educational experience comes mostly from its clarity and design in exposition and the relevancy of the ideas expressed to the life of the reader, viewer, or listener.'[22] It is not necessary to make learning fun, but it is important to make the teaching-learning process real, lively and challenging. Like life itself, education can be both sweet and sour.

Developing the relationship

Educators need to look anew at the experiences which today's child brings to school. In comparison with learners of a decade ago, today's students are certainly more visually oriented and more aware of the world beyond the home. There is probably a higher level of expectation that the school will build on the experiences and skills already gained prior to formal schooling. Teachers need to be ready to meet that expectation.

Teachers first need to understand the multi-media, electronic world that is so strongly influencing children outside the classroom. That means looking at, listening to and experiencing some of the same events as young people are using. They need to try to understand what is attractive about these sensory stimuli and perhaps determine how to use them to further school objectives.

Teachers need to know what sights and sounds students prefer, what programmes they seek out, what films they see, what activities have a high priority in their lives. Seels has developed a 'Visual Preference Survey' to be used in association with other questioning techniques to determine what learners prefer to see and do outside the school.[23]

Once teachers understand the dynamics of our multimedia electronic world and possess information about the information-rich sophistication of their students, the central problem of transfer must be addressed. How can a teacher transfer the knowledge and attitudes gained outside the classroom to the school setting? Then, in turn, how can the learner transfer newly acquired skills back into the world? The problem of transfer in this case is not a problem of learning but one of motivation.

Motivation

Keller describes several types of motivational problems in classroom settings:

In order to have motivated students, their curiosity must be aroused and sustained; the instruction must be perceived to be relevant to personal values or instrumental to accomplishing desired goals; they must have personal conviction that they will be able to succeed; and the consequence of the learning experience must be consistent with the personal incentives of the learner.[24]

Attempting to relate out-of-school learning to in-school goals must go beyond entertainment and show. Teaching does not have to be dull and uninspired, however. Teachers should learn how to relate the knowledge, skills and attitudes gained in the multimedia world to problems and issues considered in the classroom. Content and quality of learning need not be compromised but, rather, enhanced as learners perceive the relationships between the two worlds they inhabit.

Notes

1. Marshall McLuhan and Quentin Fiore, *The Medium is the Message*, p. 18, New York, Bantam Books, 1967.
2. Henri Dieuzeide, 'Educational Technology for Developing Countries', in David A. Olson (ed.), *Media and Symbols: The Forms of Expression, Communication, and Education*, Chicago, University of Chicago Press, 1974. (73rd Yearbook of the National Society for the Study of Education, Part I.)

3. See Norman MacKenzie, Richmond Postgate and John Scupham, *Open Learning*, Paris, Unesco, 1975.
4. Dieuzeide, op. cit., p. 431.
5. Charles F. Hoban, 'Man, Ritual, the Establishment and Instructional Technology', *Educational Technology*, Vol. VIII, No. 20, 1968, p. 6.
6. Gerald Zaltman and Robert Duncan, *Strategies for Planned Change*, p. 88, New York, Wiley-Interscience, 1977.
7. Edgar Faure, Filipe Herrara, Abdul-Razzak Kaddoura, Henri Lopes, Arthur V. Petrovsky, Majid Rahnema, Frederick Champion Ward, *Learning to Be*, p. xxxv, Paris, Unesco, 1972.
8. See George Gerbner and L. Gross, 'Living with Television: The Violence Profile', *Journal of Communication*, Vol. 25, No. 2, p. 173–99; A. D. Liefer, N. J. Gordon and S. B. Graves, 'Children's Television: More Than Mere Entertainment', *Harvard Educational Review*, Vol. 44, p. 213–45; G. Comstock, S. Chaffer, N. Katzman, M. McCombs, and D. Roberts, *Television and Human Behavior*, New York, Columbia University Press, 1978.
9. Norma Forbes, *Entertainment Television in Rural Alaska: How Will It Affect the School?*, paper presented at the Annual Meeting of the American Educational Research Association, April 1979.
10. Neil Postman, 'Order in the Classroom', *Atlantic Monthly*, September 1979.
11. National Center for Educational Statistics, United States Department of Education, 7 September 1982.
12. Roger B. Fransecky and John L. Debes, *Visual Literacy: A Way to Learn, A Way to Teach*, Washington, D.C., Association for Educational Communication and Technology, 1972.
13. Gillian Sellar, *Project Primedia*, p. 2, Perth, Western Australia Education Department, 1979.
14. Roger B. Fransecky and Roy Ferguson, 'New Ways of Seeing: The Milford Visual Communications Project', *Audiovisual Instruction*, Vol. 18, April, May, June/July, 1973.
15. *Just Imagine... Learning Through Mental Imagery, A Guide for Teachers,* and *Pictures of Ideas: Learning Through Visual Analogies*, Salisbury, South Australia, Visual Education Curriculum Project.
16. Sellar, op. cit., p. 1.
17. Ben Logan (ed.), *Television Awareness Training*, p. 6, New York, Media Action Research Center, 1977.
18. *Visual Learning*, Bureau of Educational Communications, New York State Education Department, Albany, N.Y.
19. 'New Ways to View World Problems,' *East-West Perspectives*, Vol. 1, No. 1, p. 15–22, summer 1979.
20. D. H. Watt, 'Education for Citizenships in a Computer-Based Society',

in R. J. Seidel, A. E. Anderson and B. Hunter (eds.), *Computer Literacy: Issues and Directions for 1985*, New York, Academic Press, 1982.
21. Edgar Dale, 'Education or Entertainment?', *Can You Give the Public What It Wants?*, New York, Cowles Education Corporation, 1967.
22. Dale, op. cit., p. 36.
23. Barbara Seels, 'How to Develop Your Visual Maturity', *Audiovisual Instruction*, Vol. 24, No. 7, 1979, p. 33–5.
24. John M. Keller, 'Motivation and Instructional Design: A Theoretical Perspective', *Journal of Instructional Development*, Vol. 2, No. 4, summer 1979, p. 32.

Re-appraising teaching and learning strategies

Learning, understanding, and communication media

Mircea Malitza

The quest for meaning

Education has always been concerned with the search for meaningful learning which will help the learner to understand while at the same time developing his powers of thought. Meaningful learning is the very opposite of mechanical learning or learning by rote. From the theoretical point of view this is still a highly controversial subject. 'Meaning' is certainly the focus of attention in logic, psychology, and linguistics, but no consensus has yet emerged which might be translated into specific recommendations in the field of education. As regards educational practice, the last few decades have shown a clear decline in meaningful learning in favour of learning by rote. An example is programmed instruction. This has unquestionably brought about a more economical use of resources, speeded up the acquisition of certain types of knowledge and made it possible to assess the learner's progress by computing the percentage of correct answers to multiple choice questions. But programmed learning does not help to measure the learner's understanding of the subject. As I write I have before me the eighty-nine questions designed to test a learner driver's knowledge of the highway code. For each, only one of the three possible answers indicated is correct. Preparation for the test thus requires memorization rather than comprehension. This method is to be found in technical schools, faculties of medicine and departments of higher mathematics, where students learn to design automatic assessment equipment, typically for use with a computer. It is not simply the ease of automatic assessment that has promoted the increased use of programmed instruction, but also the advantages it offers in regard to the progressive structuring of the knowledge to be acquired.

In the technological world of today man is surrounded by machines and automatic devices. The only requirement for coping with these is the mastery of certain instructions. There is no need to have a thorough knowledge of how they are made or of the scientific principles on which they are constructed; and in any case it is neither absolutely necessary, nor always possible, to understand fully how they work. All that we need are certain set patterns for finding our way around our technological universe, for living a normal healthy life, and for participating in social intercourse, which is to a large extent governed by convention. Thus a plea for meaning in no way implies arguing in favour of doing away with the automatic element in learning and cognition, which is essential in any profession or occupation, or decrying quasi-mechanical means of acquiring or assimilating knowledge. But it is none the less legitimate to feel concern over the possibility that meaningful learning may be threatened or even overwhelmed by the vast spread of routine learning in the world today.

The logical machine and context

It may be asked whether the widespread diffusion of the mass media will aggravate the situation by striking a further blow against meaningful learning—which will then have to be rescued—or will on the contrary come to its aid. Before answering this question let us consider the somewhat paradoxical situation that in the past few decades meaningful learning has suffered less from an insufficiently 'scientific' approach to educational content than from exaggerated recourse to scientism, a craze for systematization, and overreliance on deductive reasoning. The exposition of a scientific truth, regarded by teachers as a piece of knowledge ready for transmission, is far from being the same thing as the process of its discovery. The former calls for brevity, clarity, a polished presentation; the latter bears the mark of questioning, hesitation, curiosity, setbacks and the influence of the environment. Teachers clearly prefer to transmit knowledge in ready-made form, without explaining how it has been arrived at. A theorem, demonstrated elegantly and concisely, is taught without any reference to the history of the intellectual trials and errors which led to its establishment. The desire to save time and resources is an important consideration. But there is also a conviction, raised in recent decades to the level of a paradigm, that true science is, like mathematics, essentially axiomatic rather than heuristic. That which is deduced from self-evident truths by a process of ratiocination is held to be more noble and more rigorous than anything in the nature of the sudden inspiration that made Archimedes exclaim 'Eureka!' when he discovered his famous principle of buoyancy.

We shall not dwell here on the consequences of the main formative current in mathematics (and consequently other sciences) which has led to a major reform of the teaching of mathematics in schools, namely the introduction of set theory before the teaching of numeracy. We shall merely note the failure of the attempt by logicians to establish strict rules governing the meaning of a proposition similar to those for determining the truth of a proposition. The meaning of a proposition transcends its purely formal correctness as determined by its conformity to certain rules of logic.

Today it is increasingly recognized that meaning depends on context. The educational corollary of meaningful learning is thus to increase the number of contexts within which concepts, propositions, and knowledge can evolve.

Mircea Malitza

Participation and anticipation as learning criteria

The idea that the sciences are finite entities arranged like objects on shelves, definitively labelled by scientific category and bearing the mark of the general field which has produced them, is in flagrant contradiction with the evolution of the sciences themselves. Even as new subjects are being introduced into school curricula, one can be sure that others are being developed which will either add to or refute truths previously held to be unshakeable. These are the product of a great number of fields, and their precise source is uncertain. A new area for research is growing before our very eyes, the study of the actual cognitive phenomena basic to thought and comprehension. Cognitive science is providing inputs to traditional logic and psychology, linguistics (via semiotics), physiology, educational science and the study of artificial intelligence and computers, whose programmes are now discovering the frontiers of learning and understanding. The speed of developments in artificial intelligence and computer science makes nonsense of the notion that science is static. It is no longer possible to say that the purpose of education is merely to impart knowledge: one should rather emphasize the need to train students to be active participants in the learning process and in the advancement of science.

Meaningful learning is in fact more than merely acquiring the ability to handle contexts; it also involves getting inside a particular context and being caught up in the dynamics of knowledge and science.

We propose to take the two fundamental components of meaningful learning, participation and anticipation.[1] To appreciate that these are vital ingredients of learning one has only to take that most common of the acts of independent thought, decision-making. Throughout one's life one is confronted with choices and the need to decide on a course of action from among several possibilities. Decision is impossible without a value judgement as to the course to be adopted. It is values, that is to say preferences, which govern one's choice. We shall not dwell here on the basis of interest or the social considerations on which value scales are constructed. We shall simply posit that it is participation which is responsible for their formulation and for their retention in one's mind. To adopt a particular course of action it is not enough to assign it a value. It is also necessary to estimate the chances of success, in other words to evaluate its probable outcome. That which shapes and sustains the ability to think in terms of the possible is the faculty of anticipation.

These two criteria help one to find one's way among the many theories advanced about the learning process, and to take up a position in relation to them. We discard from the outset the theory that learners are passive recipients of knowledge. A whole range of meaning separates the ideas of teaching and learning. For the latter it might be preferable to use the term 'active learning', with which participation is very closely linked. Participation implies not only activity, but also the existence of a role to be played. One has only to consider how invention and scientific discovery come about to realize that if the student is to be involved in the process it is necessary to define the part which he himself is called on to play as inventor or discoverer.

From behaviourism to school learning

Yet another argument is to be rejected when we apply the principle of participation to learning theories based on studies of animal learning. For a long time, the subjects used for research into the psychology of animal learning were hand-picked specimens kept in captivity, for example Pavlov's dogs, Thorndike's cats, Skinner's pigeons, Köhler's apes and Lilly's dolphins. Hence the results obtained applied only to animal learning and to particular types of response which recurred with some regularity under specific laboratory conditions. Between 1930 and 1960 virtually every experiment with animal learning gave rise to a new more or less coherent learning theory. By extrapolation these could be applied to certain types of human learning, particularly mechanical ones such as the acquisition of skills until the point that proficiency is reached, various forms of instruction, including programmed instruction, and habit training for children. But the attempt to present them as a general model of human learning failed, due to the social, participatory and conscious nature specific to human learning.

Laboratory research, with all the artificiality of its context, did have the merit of arousing the interest of specialists in learning in general, an interest which in the 1960s manifested itself in studies on school learning. A change took place in the methodology of research. Instead of starting from a particular type of learning behaviour and immediately making an effort to produce a general learning theory therefrom, the approach now used is largely deductive: the usual practice is to choose a conceptual model of the entire process of instruction, to define its variables (including school learning) and to analyse their interrelationship. The subject of the investigation is no longer the 'task' imposed, or the learner's behaviour as such, but its interrelation with the other parts of the instruction process, in particular with the action of the teacher. The value-generating notions of 'context' and 'participation' are built into these models. Most recent research no longer separates the student's activity from that of the teacher, nor the activity of an individual student from that of the social group of students to which he belongs. The most representative authors of this new approach to school learning include Ausubel, Gagné, Taba, Tyler, Galperin, Bruner and Bloom. It is not our intention here to review the various aspects of research into school learning or the major contributions of the above authors. An account of their views would require a comprehensive general study,[2] the need for which is felt by those concerned in practice with school learning the world over, in both the developed and the developing countries. Our observations will be confined to one aspect of their investigations, namely meaningful learning in conjunction with the use of the media.

Ausubel's 'organizers'

The contribution of the media to meaningful learning has not been sufficiently taken into account in research on school learning. Most research seems to centre on text-assisted learning. We are still living in the 'Gutenberg galaxy': reading and the written message continue to dominate education systems in practically all countries of the world. But in view of the obvious fact that the media have developed from being 'aids' into fundamental components of the school learning process, it is high time we gave more attention to media-assisted learning. One example will show how some of the findings obtained with the conceptual models developed for meaningful learning may be applied to the most obvious contributions of the media, namely sound and images.

It was Ausubel who emphasized the fact that human learning is pre-eminently meaningful learning. It was he who in the heyday of behaviourism and neobehaviourism demonstrated that learning is first and foremost a function of the individual's personal experience, of the subjective integration of new data into a body of previously acquired knowledge. In one of his key works he wrote:

The essence of the meaningful learning process... is that symbolically expressed ideas are related in a non-arbitrary and substantive (nonverbatim) fashion to what the learner already knows, namely to some existing relevant aspect of his structure of knowledge.... Irrespective of how much potential meaning may inhere in a particular proposition, if the learner's intention is to memorize it arbitrarily and verbatim (as a series of arbitrarily related words) the learning process must be meaningless.[3]

Unlike environmental psychologists with their emphasis on physical surroundings, Ausubel stresses 'cognitive learning' by the individual. A new piece of knowledge is characterized not so much by the stimuli inherent in it (as the behaviourists would have it) as by its specific relation to the learner's past experience. This individual cognitive experience ('psychological meaning') is a subjective variant of the objective conceptual structure of each subject studied ('logical meaning').

Ausubel identifies three types of meaningful learning: 'representational learning', which consists of learning isolated symbols (words, numbers, letters); 'propositional learning', which concerns the assimilation of propositions along with their logical sense; and 'concept learning', a more advanced type, in which terms become notions which constitute generalizations of a number of anterior meanings and experiences.

Having discussed 'progressive differentiation' and 'integrative reconciliation' as ways of integrating concepts at a lower level into concepts at a higher level (that is to say concepts of a higher order of generality), Ausubel proposes an educational method in which the teacher makes use of 'advance organizers', defined as

introductory material at a higher level of abstraction, generality and inclusiveness than the learning task itself. The function of the organizer is to provide ideational scaffolding for the stable incorporation and retention of the more detailed and differentiated material.[4]

While it is possible to contest Ausubel's argument that it is preferable for concepts to be learned from the higher level downwards, and the doubts he expresses as regards the inductive method, which he considers to be long and laborious, his idea of 'organizers' deserves study. With this method each lesson or learning sequence should be preceded by the presentation of an 'organizer' introducing the student to the context into which he will integrate the new 'curriculum content'. Ausubel limits himself to verbal and written communication, but research has shown that 'organizers' can consist of sounds and images. At Teachers College (Columbia University, New York) films, stories, and demonstrations have all been used as organizers.

Learning, understanding, and communication media

This brings us to the subject of the new and specific role which images can play. Formerly used as accessories in the teaching process, audio-visual aids are now becoming the main instruments, whose purpose it is to present holistic structures to which the learner can meaningfully link new material.

The image as organizer

The role of the image merits being placed on the same level as that of the concept. Taken together or in various combinations, they can function as organizers, each complementing the other's action. The use of organizers in audio-visual form has the following advantages:

1. The subject-matter is presented not in a sequential or analytical manner but as a whole, seen from a general point of view.
2. A maximum of detail can be presented, and any number of 'cues' provided to facilitate meaningful learning.
3. The use of moving images permits diachronic presentation.
4. The presentation of the subject directly, without any intermediary, gives an affective component to the new content, involving not only the individual's cognitive structure but also his socio-affective experience, interests, and motivation.
5. Organizers are suitable for learners of all ages and all types of subject-matter.

Television has so forcibly invaded the lives of schoolchildren that one author, citing the findings of a United States statistical survey to the effect that during the thirteen years of his school life a child spends approximately 15,000 hours looking at television as against only 11,500 hours in the classroom has described television as the 'foreground of education', with school now relegated to the background. The role of television has been lessened by the idea that its purpose is entertainment, not education. It has been justly criticized for its programme content, sometimes described as 'chewing gum for the eye'. It is none the less true that it has gained recognition as an educational instrument. From the standpoint of semiotics, an image is in fact just as much of a symbol as a word. The image is an analogue or representational symbol, while the word is a digital symbol. The image is direct, unique, and specific; the word is abstract, conceptual and translatable. Both enable us to represent aspect of reality, and both can rightly be described as models of reality.

It can be argued that the image requires less effort to assimilate than the word. But it is richer in context. Does it really involve participation? We can affirm that the audio-visual media have been welcomed by children with unprecedented interest and enthusiasm. The absorption with which children are bound up in them, to the exclusion of everything else, suggests intense participation.

It is no longer possible to conceive of the teaching of history without school video equipment, using cassettes to show Greek temples, Roman arenas, Hindu temples, Aztec pyramids, Arab mosques, places where great battles took place, the activities going on in the great cities of the world, or the work of peasants in African or Asian communities. Everything, from life inside a living cell to space travel, has become accessible as an introduction to, or a commentary on, a conceptual synopsis of the written or spoken word. It appears only normal that the widespread dissemination of the video cassette should be followed by the development of an educational video-cassette industry, in the context of new curricula catering not only for schools at all levels, but also for adults and the elderly.

The computer and psychology

The computer is the most advanced of the electronic innovations that are shaping our new world of information. No other machine devised by man has developed so rapidly. Miniaturization, falling costs, increased speed, greater computing and storage capacity, and the profusion of languages and software, place the computer at the very centre of school education. Claims that it can take the place of the teacher, and that the process of instruction can be completely automated, are however exaggerated. The large-scale introduction of computer-assisted instruction requires a large number of teachers to provide guidance in the use of the computer.

As in the case of television, it may be objected that the personal computer has entered the lives of young people via entertainment and games, with their trivial content which sometimes even encourages aggressive attitudes or leanings, for example the 'space war' type of game. But in both cases the attraction exercised is immense. Children learn computer languages as easily as foreign languages, much more quickly and with greater application than adults. It would be absurd to deny the computer's vast educational potential.

The most abstract ideas can be illustrated by the computer, which can display equations in the form of curves, whereas no manual provides such graphic illustrations.

The key question is that of the degree of participation afforded by computer-assisted instruction. If it affords nothing more than programmed instruction, with questions and answers presented in well-established sequences, it is doubtful whether learning of this type is participatory. But where there is a dialogue between man and the machine, the situation is different. The student can take turns to interrogate the computer, and even direct the development of a dialogue. If he can avoid relying exclusively on ready-made programs and can do his own programming, he will achieve a substantially greater degree of participation. By engaging in dialogue with a computer, a student can simulate roles.

It is interesting to note that the advent of the computer has not confirmed the fears of dehumanization to which it initially gave rise. It was categorically argued that any advanced symbiosis of man and the computer would tend to turn man into a robot, developing the automatic thought patterns which are characteristic of the computer. One author, applying a simile taken from computer science to present-day psychology, points out that subjective intentional categories are just as central to artificial intelligence as they are to psychology. The operation of a computer program, like that of the human intelligence, depends on its store of representations of the world and the way in which these representations are compared and transformed. Once behaviour is mediated by representations, intentional categories such as knowledge, belief, error, purpose, and emotion, which artificial intelligence has introduced into its vocabulary, become legitimate.[5]

Teleinformatics and values

The combined use of computers, or information from any source, with remote data transmission facilities, has given rise to powerful information technology networks which are opening up new vistas for the mass media. Access to data banks and major libraries, links with other, more powerful computers, text processing, the communication of written documents by means of personal computers, all provide vast opportunities for education. Schools cannot remain unaffected by this immense potential. There are now practically no limitations to the availability of documentation on a given subject, be it literary or scientific. The possibility of asking a national library for a book or text, consulting an exhaustive bibliography or obtaining a programme for studying a given subject, and the availability of models for solving a series of similar problems, are examples of the new media to which active and creative thought can have recourse.

The information technology revolution has not yet made its full contribution to education. It has demonstrated the attractiveness of its new tools, exhibited its extraordinary performance in fields closely related to education, shown what it can contribute to scientific research, laid the foundations for new areas of creation, broken down the barriers between art and science, even revolutionized music, but it has not yet produced a new paradigm for education.

Learning, understanding, and communication media

Hitherto, discussion of the relationship of the mass media to education has centred on the educational sector that seems specially suited to make use of the mass media, namely lifelong adult education, including informal education. The notion that the school represents formal education, indissolubly linked with classical methods relying on the written word, has impeded the adoption by schools of the rapidly developing new methods of informal education. The informality of the media has been regarded with reserve as implying a departure from rigour, active intelligence, and meaning, which are the hallmarks of a type of education free from the encroachment of sound, images, and information technology.

As we have seen, however, not only is it wrong to consider that the factors that generate meaning, namely context, participation, and anticipation, do not form part of the input of the media, but it is precisely these factors which highlight the media's capability for providing a deeper insight into the content of education.

There are grounds for satisfaction even from the purely theoretical point of view. 'Meaning', rejected by behaviourism as a mentalistic concept used to refer to an intellectual content, is now recognized by the new theories of cognition based on the comparison between artificial intelligence and psychology. One requirement, that of anticipation, is in fact met. Few developments have so fired the imagination as the mass media have done. School textbooks appear dreary when compared with the vast prospects opened up by the new world of information technology. Participation, whose presence as a factor was initially doubted, has now been made possible with the advent of dialogue and the creation of roles.

But optimism should be tempered by one consideration. The information network which opens up such new possibilities of knowledge is nothing more than an artificial world, in fact very much like a school. In simulating reality, it is governed by the models which it uses to represent it. School likewise simulates life, in order to prepare the pupil for life in the real world. The world of information created by the mass media ceases to exist if it becomes closed in on itself. It is in a real environment, *in vivo*, that meaningful values come into play, whatever the preliminary laboratory or *in vitro* training. If it is to be viable, the world of information should meet the same basic requirement as for the school: that of remaining open to inputs from the outside.

Notes

1. James W. Botkin, Mahdi Elmandjra and Mircea Malitza, *No Limits to Learning*, pp. 17–44, Oxford, Pergamon Press, 1979.
2. Two promising contributions can be cited: B. Joyce and M. Weil, *Models of Teaching*, Englewood Cliffs, N.J., Prentice-Hall, 1972; C. Birzea, *Rendre opérationnels les objectifs pédagogiques*, Paris, Presses Universitaires de France, 1979.
3. D. P. Ausubel, *Educational Psychology: A Cognitive View*, pp. 37–38, New York, Holt, Rinehart & Winston, 1968.
4. D. P. Ausubel, *The Psychology of Meaningful Verbal Learning*, p. 29. New York, Grune & Stratton, 1968.
5. Margaret A. Boden, *Minds and Mechanisms: Philosophical Psychology and Computational Models*, p. 308, Ithaca, N.Y., Cornell University Press, 1981.

The information explosion and optimizing the educational process

Yuri Babansky

The information explosion characteristic of our times gives rise to a whole series of complex educational problems. How can the information which must be assimilated by pupils in general secondary schools be selected from the enormous amount of information available? How can the assimilation of this necessary information be ensured during the course of secondary education? What means and methods can be used to ensure the successful processing of new scientific, socio-political and other types of information? How can the unavoidable intensification of teaching be brought about without overburdening pupils and teachers?

To answer these questions it is necessary, firstly, to have special criteria for selecting the fundamentals of sciences; secondly, to substantiate and create a specific system of teaching materials, equipment and methodological means of using scientific information in the teaching process; and thirdly, to be equipped with a theory and with methods for optimizing the teaching process. In other words, the teaching process must be constructed in such a way as to give the maximum possible educational results at a given stage of education. We shall endeavour to do this, relying on the results of previous educational research.

Criteria for selecting educational content

In educational schools in general not all scientific and practical information is assimilated, but only the basic scientific information required to ensure the all-round development of the personality and to enable pupils to undertake active practical work after appropriate training. The process of selecting the fundamentals of science is extremely complicated since one must assess objectively the degree of importance of the information, its value for forecasting purposes, etc. In making such a decision, one should be guided by a set of specific criteria whose application reduces, step by step, the amount of information introduced into the content of school education. The volume and complexity of such information should be the maximum that any age-group can cope with, without being excessive.

The dialectical structural systems approach is the methodological basis for substantiating the system of criteria for selecting the fundamentals of sciences. Such an approach requires all the basic components of scientific information, as well as human relations and activities necessary for life and work in society, to be considered as an integral whole. A structural systems approach calls for the establishment of links between all the components of education and the identification of the most essential and important links among them. Finally, such an approach presupposes the establishment of the indicators which characterize the system as a whole. Specific regular teaching links spring from a structural system analysis.

The regular features of education are essential, for they serve as recurrent links between this process and external processes and conditions, and also between the internal components of the teaching process itself.

From an analysis of external links of the teaching process the following regular features of education may be noted:
1. The educational process is determined by the requirements of society and by prevailing social conditions.

2. The educational process is conditioned by the amount and nature of scientific, cultural and socio-practical information accumulated up to a given time.
3. The educational process is linked with the processes of education, upbringing and development of the personality which make up an integral educational process.
4. The educational process depends on the teaching materials available in schools, on the health standards, the ethical, psychological and aesthetic conditions and on the teaching time available.
5. The educational process depends on pupils' real learning capacities (by age group and individual).

Furthermore, the following regular features of the internal links of the educational process may be mentioned:
1. In the course of education a correlation is to be found between teaching and learning.
2. What is taught and learnt derives from the general purposes of education which in turn are conditioned by social requirements and by pupils' real learning capacities.
3. The content of education depends on its purposes.
4. The methods and means of education depend on its purposes and content.
5. The forms of organizing education are governed by its purposes, content and methods.
6. It is only the interrelationship between all the components of education that ensures the attainment of results corresponding to the objectives set for it.

It follows from the logical links of teaching that the selection of the content of school education is not simply a matter of bringing out the necessary elements of scientific information. Society not only requires that the individual should be provided with scientific information, but also that he should be prepared for social relations and creative activity, that he should be equipped to benefit from the achievements of culture and to maintain contacts with those around him, etc.

When one is aware of the above-mentioned regular features of the educational process, one can be guided by them in formulating the criteria for selecting the content of the fundamentals of science.

The first criterion for selecting the content of education is the integrated reflection in it of society's requirements on the level of modern scientific, production, technical, cultural and socio-political information. The integration criterion guarantees that no social requirements or branches of scientific and practical information will be omitted from the overall content of education. This criterion also guarantees that it is inadmissible for general education to be one-sided or narrow. It is to be seen primarily in the content of the curriculum for general educational establishments, in which all the basic branches of modern science and all the basic spheres of social and production life, culture, art, etc., should find their reflection. The integration criterion presupposes the inclusion in the content of different subjects of all notions, laws, theories and practical skills associated with the field of knowledge concerned, so as to form pupils' cognitive interest, train their intellect, will and emotions and develop socially valuable personal qualities.

But the use of this criterion inevitably leads to the selection of a content of education that is too extensive, although very comprehensive. Another criterion is therefore needed to reduce the amount of information introduced into school education to proportions which the educational process can cope with.

This gives rise to the second criterion: the criterion of ensuring the high scientific and practical value of the content of the fundamentals of sciences. This criterion is applied by a comparative assessment of the value of all the elements of the content of education on the basis of appraisal by experts and the application of rating methods, graphs, etc. As a result, information of a more universal nature is retained in the content of education; information that is absolutely necessary to bring out the essence of the theories, laws and basic concepts of a given science and that is also the most generally recognized and polytechnical and offers the greatest prospects. With such an approach, more specific, complementary, illustrative and factual data and reference materials are excluded from the content of school education, and such information can subsequently be easily complemented by the pupils themselves through recourse to literature and also to the mass media.

The third criterion for selecting the content of education consists in ensuring its conformity with the real learning capacities of schoolchildren of a given age. The use of this criterion reveals which parts of the information contained in the content of school education turn out to be incomprehensible for pupils of a given age. This may be observed from specialized appraisal reports and from an analysis of entrance examinations at institutions of higher learning. A great deal can also be learned from carrying out physiological tests when written tests are being held, for these show which sections of the curriculum are the most difficult to assimilate and which cause pupils excessive fatigue at a given age. This gives grounds for excluding from the curriculum sections which are too difficult for one age-group and for transferring them to a later stage of education.

The fourth criterion consists in ensuring conformity between the volume of educational material and the time available for studying the subject concerned. For this purpose, a laboratory experiment is conducted to record the time needed for the full and conscious assimilation of educational material, and the time spent on studying corresponding topics at school and as homework is also measured. On the one hand, the application of this criterion makes it possible to distribute educational material more rationally between various divisions of the subject. On the other hand, it leads to the study of some divisions of a subject being moved up to a higher class or excluded from the content of school education if there is not sufficient time to deal with them, however useful they may be, bearing in mind that more general aspects of this problem are still to be found in the content of education.

The fifth criterion is the consideration of international experience in establishing the content of education for a given subject. International experience widens the range of experimental verification of the comprehensibility of teaching material, of its scientific value and potential usefulness.

The sixth criterion is the conformity of the content of education with the educational material and methodological possibilities of the modern school. The use of this criterion eliminates the programming of laboratory or practical experiments that cannot be undertaken in the near future due to lack of school equipment. It also takes into account the standard of the teachers' scientific and methodological qualification. Of course, this criterion is very flexible and it should not hold back improvements in the quality of education; rather it should encourage those responsible for organizing public education to improve the educational, material, methodological and teaching staff capacities of education. At every concrete stage this criterion must be taken into account.

The essential feature of this set of criteria is that the application of one criterion after another gradually narrows down the range of educational information in the basic scientific information offered, bringing it closer to the optimum volume.

These criteria may also be applied to the selection of the content of vocational training and further training for school leavers. But in this case the criterion of the value and importance of the content of the nucleus of education should be correlated with the requirements of the sphere of production and vocational activity concerned and with the general demands of society on the individual.

Experience gained in the application of these criteria in working out improved curricula for general secondary schools in the USSR during the late 1970s showed their real practical significance: it made it possible to optimize the content of school education and ensure that it was of the same standard in all general secondary educational establishments.

Recasting and enriching teaching materials

The increase in the volume of information assimilated in secondary schools calls for a new approach to the preparation of textbooks, visual aids and training facilities, so that they are effective in helping pupils to assimilate instructional material more accurately and rapidly.

In present conditions, textbooks should pay far greater attention than before to emphasizing the essentials in the content of educational material. In addition to the traditional use of bold type to draw attention to certain definitions and formulas, notions and laws, it is most important to give special emphasis to conclusions and generalizations. It is necessary to find the means of bringing out the principal ideas put forward during the course of their presentation, to focus pupils' attention on them, not only by visual and graphic means, but also by logical emphasis. It is very useful to include short summaries at the end of chapters or sections. Additional material, which pupils are not obliged to learn, is now included in some textbooks, as well as reference material which does not have to be memorized. The use of algorithmic directions helps to stress the essentials. Such directions can be most widely used in setting out spelling rules in the mother tongue, in drawing up instructions for laboratory work in physics, chemistry and biology, and also in working out labour assignments for industry, agriculture, etc.

Now that the wave of enthusiasm for programmed teaching aids has subsided, it may be noted that it does not follow that programming elements should no longer be introduced into the content of some chapters of textbooks or in sections dealing with control over the assimilation of given topics. The reasonable use of programmed control will help to bring out the most essential elements of the information being absorbed.

To strengthen individual sections of teaching material and generalize educational information, there has been a trend to reduce the number of paragraphs in textbooks. This makes it possible to set out certain notions and laws in a more integral text, including the type of additional information which is usually introduced in a separate paragraph.

Another means of improving the presentation of educational information and intensifying cognitive activity in absorbing it at the same time is by the simultaneous presentation of opposite notions, properties and operations in textbooks. For instance, Professor Pyurvya Erdiniev has written mathematics textbooks in which addition and subtraction, multiplication and division, integration and differentiation, etc. are presented together.

The increase in the relative importance of the deductive study of educational material, when skilfully combined with inductive study, contributes to the more thorough and more generalized presentation of educational information.

The introduction of new sections into the curriculum contributes to the remodelling of Soviet textbooks in this direction. The first such section emphasizes the main notions of each topic and the practical skills formed in the course of studying it. This section of the curriculum is called 'What should the pupil know and be able to do?' The second section is called 'Inter-subject links'. It makes concrete recommendations on the inter-subject links which should be revealed in studying the topic.

In this way, fairly substantial changes are introduced into textbooks in conditions in which the amount of educational information is increasing rapidly with a view to achieving more thorough assimilation of the key points of the subject.

The system of visual aids and training facilities is also being restructured. At present, efforts are made in preparing visual aids, posters, illustrations, diapositive film strips and overhead projector slides not only to reflect facts but to bring out comparisons between various facts, phenomena and processes, to compare and classify properties, signs, types, instruments, equipment, etc. Posters bringing out generalizations and algorithmic directions in the mother tongue and also foreign languages are being prepared even more widely. Posters and slides have been produced showing the causal connections between various phenomena under study, and other aids contain graphs.

Educational films also are being improved with the same aims in mind. They are increasingly acquiring a research and problem-oriented, rather than a merely visual and illustrative nature, although the latter retains its own importance.

The use of video techniques in the teaching process contributes to the consistent concentration of information and to emphasizing its essentials. For example, an educational excursion registered on video-tape, after being reviewed by the teacher, may be presented in a more concentrated form at a lesson summing up the material studied.

Over the past decade, the preparation of encyclopaedias for pupils (both universal encyclopaedias and encyclopaedias dealing with specific topics) has been intensified in many countries. In the USSR, for example, large encyclopaedias—*The Young Physicist*, *The Young Astronomer*, *The Young Farmer*, etc.—have been published. Large numbers of reference books on physics, engineering, chemistry and other subjects are produced for pupils. The considerable increase in the publication of reference material for pupils makes it possible to reduce the presentation of references in textbooks and to change the approach in testing pupils' knowledge and skills. In any event, pupils are no longer obliged to memorize a large amount of reference material but are now allowed to use reference material in answering questions.

A natural reaction to the growth of scientific information is the desire to elaborate various training methods to speed up the reading and writing processes. In many countries devices are being invented to make it possible to master more rapidly the technique of diagonal reading, to read much longer texts, and not to resort to letter-by-letter or syllable-by-syllable reading.

The improvement of the quality of education today was contributed to by the preparation in the USSR of study sets for all subjects for teachers and pupils which are called 'teaching sets'. They comprise a set of textbooks on the subject, instruction booklets for teachers, visual aids, teaching material for distribution to pupils, printed texts of assignments and laboratory work, and cards of different degrees of difficulty for the individual testing of pupils. The use of these sets saves the teachers' time, and differentiates the teaching process, helping all pupils to acquire new knowledge and skills more rapidly.

In the conditions created by the information explosion, particular hopes are naturally pinned on training facilities that speed up the learning process. Film excerpts, diagrams and epidiascope slides highlight the essentials in instructional material, focus pupils' attention on them, systematize, classify and generalize educational information and do not simply add innumerable new facts to it. The use of language laboratories in studying the mother tongue and foreign languages makes it possible to absorb more information in a shorter time. From the point of view of time-saving, overhead projectors have proved to be very useful. They enable teachers to place one transparency over another, showing how a complicated image is built up, and to use colour illustrations to stimulate the perception of information.

At the same time, educational experience has shown that to use training facilities without first determining the best method of using them can lead to an excessive loss of time and slow down the teaching process. To eliminate these drawbacks in the use of training facilities, the USSR Academy of Pedagogical Sciences has worked out special methodological cards to assist in selecting the most rational ways of using training facilities in the teaching process. At present more attention is being given to making short educational films and film excerpts which become an organic part of the content of lessons. Recently microcomputers have been used more extensively in the educational process, especially for calculations during practical work in physics, chemistry, technical drawing, training for work and other subjects. The use of this training facility and the development of pupils' basic calculating skills and know-how are optimally combined in mathematics classes.

Automated control classes have proved to be useful in saving teachers' time and in speeding up the assessment of pupils' knowledge. Most such classes take place at schools in Leningrad.

The mass transition over the last decade to the use of special subject classrooms is a great achievement of Soviet schools. This accelerates the process of using didactic teaching sets during lessons, spares teachers from spending extra time and effort on moving equipment from one classroom to another, and allows the use of more sophisticated instruments and installations.

Developing teaching methods

It can therefore be concluded that teachers have been equipped with new educational literature based on quite new principles over the past few decades, and also with modernized training facilities that enable scientific information to be absorbed more rapidly and its most important features highlighted. This new technical and methodological basis calls for the broader development of pupils' skills and abilities in the rational processing of scientific information.

Although the above-mentioned criteria for selecting the essential content of education ensure that it is accessible to pupils, it should be borne in mind that the flow of scientific and practical social information is constantly being renewed, expanded and replenished, and that at the same time it is, to some extent, being outdated. This means that teaching methods should not only ensure the successful assimilation of the material contained in the curriculum, but should also prepare pupils to acquire and understand new information. For this reason, special attention should be paid to the development of pupils' general skills and abilities. The most important of these in ensuring a pupil's progress are the planning of studies, the highlighting of essentials, an appropriate pace of work and self-checking of studies.

Teachers' experience shows, for instance, that systematically requiring pupils to prepare answers to the next questions they will have to answer during given lessons as part of their homework and to use these answers at school is an important means of training them to plan their studies.

Building up planning skills is closely linked with developing the ability to pick out the essentials in a text. For this purpose, teachers explain assignments and ways of studying given topics, drawing attention to the main issues, notions, facts and conclusions. Teachers make short notes and drawings on the blackboard and advise pupils to take similar notes in their notebooks and clearly stress the main points involved in describing them.

When pupils are working on their own during lessons, teachers systematically give them special assignments: to find the main ideas of the text they are studying, to choose a title for the various parts of the textbook's instructional material, to express the main idea of the text in a single sentence, to give a generalized summary of some of the facts considered during the lesson and to draw appropriate conclusions, to give a brief description of the main ideas in the text studied to draw up specimen questions on the text, etc.

At the same time, pupils' abilities to use textbooks and reference material are built up by teaching them to find the texts they need by using tables of contents, to use tables, diagrams, drawings and graphs, to draw up summaries and brief outlines of the material they have read, to find the books they need with the help of library catalogues, to compile bibliographies for the literature referred to during the preparation of reports, etc.

Teachers talk to pupils about acquiring their own libraries and about the most interesting radio and television programmes so that they can develop the ability to add to their knowledge on their own.

Pupils at modern secondary schools are taught how to use diapositive films, slides, microfilms, films, sound and video recordings and the simplest teaching and consultation machines.

But it is not enough to teach schoolchildren to work with books and training facilities. They must absorb information far more rapidly today. They must read, write and count at the optimal speed for their age envisaged by the curriculum. For instance, in the fourth and fifth forms pupils should read at the rate of 120–150 words a minute. The development of their reading speed is important not only for accelerating the assimilation of educational information, but also for identifying the main ideas in the text. The fact is that a slow reader is unable to compare the significance of the individual elements of a text rapidly. Of course, rapid reading and writing have a negative aspect as well. In certain conditions, it can decrease pupils' attention and their understanding of what they are reading. For this reason great attention is also paid in Soviet schools to developing reading habits that ensure pupils understand what they are reading.

Various methods aimed at developing the pace of learning are used in many Soviet schools—for example, in the city of Kharkov under the management of Professor Ivan Fedorenko. Certain amounts of compulsory reading are set each week and the pupils' work is checked on a selective basis. At the same time, exercises in reading a text within a specified time are held. To accelerate the speed of writing, the importance of writing quickly is explained by Kharkov teachers. The ability to write quickly helps pupils to follow ideas and grasp the main points. Kharkov teachers give exercises that help to develop the habit of writing quickly. Plasticine modelling lessons are given in primary classes to develop the finger muscles. During physical training lessons, exercises are given to develop the hands. As part of their homework, pupils are required to copy given texts within a specified time. At the end of every term writing speed is measured and entered in a special table, and pupils of primary classes and their parents are informed of this. These are the main methods and activities used to develop pupils' abilities to absorb scientific information rapidly.

In studying physics, wider use is now made of a single approach to the study of variations in different physical properties, the deductive study of gas laws, of electrical phenomena on the basis of the electron theory, etc. Such methods make it possible to take in a larger amount of educational information within a shorter period.

A long experiment in the phased building up of knowledge, skills and abilities, and in the use of programmed instruction in elementary schools has been conducted under the guidance of Professors Pyotr Galperin and Nina Talyzina. In the experimenters' opinion, active control over the process of assimilating new material and the gradual transition from practical work with objects to 'inner monologues' and active thinking accelerates the learning process and makes it more effective.

The elements of problem-oriented education are widely used in the Soviet Union. They enable pupils to tackle certain problems, describe the causes of certain phenomena and prove their point, thus making progress in assimilating new educational material. In recent times, specialists in the field of problem-oriented teaching (Professor Mirza Makhmutov and others) have been striving to discover the limits to the effective use of problem-oriented teaching, to determine the conditions of its optimum use in various age-groups studying material of different degrees of complexity, etc.

As the content of education becomes more and more complicated, slow learners can experience particular difficulties. For example, our surveys on reading, writing and counting speeds among pupils of the fourth, fifth and sixth forms in the 1960s showed that on average slow learners took more than six minutes to copy a fifty-word text whereas pupils making good progress took only four minutes to do so. The reading and counting speeds of the former were almost 50 per cent lower than those of the latter. In addition, slow learners made almost three times as many mistakes in copying and almost twice as many in reading and counting. This led Soviet educational psychologists, under the direction of Professor Natalya Menchinskaya, to study psychological factors involved with a view to avoiding poor pupil progress. These studies make it possible to differentiate the teaching process better and thus to ensure the satisfactory assimilation of educational information by all pupils.

Soviet teachers and psychologists are seeking ways of rationalizing assessment methods in the teaching process. An experiment in teaching pupils at primary schools without giving marks has been carried out for several years in the Georgian SSR under the guidance of Professor Shalva Amonashvili. The experiments proceed from the assumption that it is very important to create positive stimuli to learning at primary schools, to reduce the negative effects of the stress experienced by pupils when marks are given. In the course of the experiment, emphasis is laid on analysing the quality of pupils' work, on finding typical mistakes and difficulties and on indicating ways of avoiding them.

Optimizing instruction

Now that it is necessary to solve more complicated educational problems within the same period of schooling, the elaboration of the general theory and methods of optimizing the teaching process assumes particular importance. In other words, education should be organized in such a way that greater educational results will be attained within a shorter time than usual, or at least without exceeding the time allotted for the teaching process by the current curriculum. In this connection, considerable efforts to elaborate the theoretical foundations of optimizing instruction have been made in the USSR during the past decade. The main criterion for the optimization of instruction is the attainment by every pupil of his maximum capacity to absorb educational information at any given time, bearing in mind the health standards for homework established for pupils of every age-group.

To optimize instruction, the use of a scientifically based system of methods for optimum planning and use of all the basic elements of education—its tasks, content, forms, methods and means, as well as an analysis of the results of education—is recommended.

For us, the method of optimizing education consists in ensuring combined efforts by teachers and pupils aimed at obtaining the maximum possible efficacity of education in given conditions while respecting established standards concerning the time required for given activities, that is to say, without overburdening teachers and pupils. Optimization methods thus differ from the methods of intensifying, modernizing and improving instruction, which naturally are oriented solely towards obtaining better results and not towards saving teachers' and pupils' time and efforts. Optimization, however, logically combines these two activities.

The optimization of instruction calls for the use of all methods of making the best choice of each main element in the instruction process (its tasks, content, methods, etc.). Beside the term 'system of methods', the term 'system of the elements of the optimization of instruction' may therefore also be used, since each method is also an element of the integral optimization of the instructional process.

The teacher starts planning the instructional process by thinking over its tasks. The teacher should be guided in this by a principle stemming from the laws governing education, the principle of ensuring the unity of the instruction, education, and development of pupils. To indicate the tasks of instruction in the most rational way in each case, two principal methods of optimizing the tasks of instruction should be used. In the first place, comprehensive planning of the tasks involved in the instruction, education and general development of pupils is required and, secondly, these tasks should be more precisely defined, taking into account pupils' real possibilities, using various methods of studying them for this purpose.

Comprehensive planning also makes it possible to cover a wider range of activities, thus optimizing the work of the teacher who no longer needs to spend extra time on fulfilling educational tasks at special lessons. With skill, the teacher can fulfil these tasks simultaneously with instructional tasks.

Clearly defining the tasks of instruction makes it possible to take fully into account the specific learning behaviour of the pupils of a given class as well as their attitude towards learning, to reveal the weakest points in their knowledge and skills and to take the appropriate corrective action. This means that the teacher can single out the main feature of the work of a given class and adjust assignments accordingly. Instruction thus coincides with the real capacities and wishes of the pupils, encourages them to make greater efforts to widen their knowledge, and makes it possible to obtain adequate results more rapidly.

The next method of optimizing education, which mainly concerns the content and structure of education, is that of laying emphasis on essentials, ensuring co-ordination of teaching material between subjects, choosing the optimum level of difficulty and a rational structure of education. In accordance with this method, emphasis has been laid on essentials in the new Soviet curricula, questions that are too complicated or of minor importance have been eliminated from them, the basic requirements with regard to knowledge and skills have been indicated, instructions on inter-subject links introduced, concentration on individual subjects reduced and the role of deduction in the study of a large number of topics strengthened. But a great deal will still depend on the efforts of the teacher himself. At every lesson the teacher should focus pupils' attention on the most important points and make use of the appropriate problem-solving methods in an effort to achieve better results with fewer exercises.

A necessary means of optimizing education is that of stimulating motivation in pupils. In the past, pedagogics stressed the importance of interest in learning, but only as a kind of additional psychological condition for effective learning. At present, special methods have been elaborated to encourage pupils to adopt positive attitudes to learning: learning games, discussions during lessons, the creation of new learning situations or of situations arousing emotional experience, etc. At the same time, a more thorough study has been made of the motivating influence of all other methods of education, including methods of organizing educational activities and methods of assessment and self-assessment.

An important means of optimizing education is that of selecting which combination of teaching methods will enable the problems arising within a prescribed period to be solved most successfully. Such a choice may be made through the comparative evaluation of the effective completion of different assignments by different teaching methods appropriate to the group. Taking into account the specific content of material and the capacities and individual aptitudes of pupils, the teacher will have to choose, for example, a problem-solving or a repetitive teaching method, to select a combination of verbal, visual and practical methods. To ensure the unity of teaching and learning, the teacher should pay particular attention to developing the pupils' independent working methods.

At the same time, the best educational instruments are chosen—training facilities, visual, illustrative and demonstrative aids, laboratory equipment etc. It is, of course, more difficult to select teaching methods and means taking into consideration all factors relating to the content of education, pupils' capacities and prevailing conditions, than simply to adopt one of the teaching methods in fashion, whether problem-oriented, programmed or based on technical teaching means. But the use of such a method of optimizing education will justify itself and will save teachers and pupils time and effort wasted on repeated study of the same topics.

The choice of a combination of organizational forms that enables assignments to be fulfilled most successfully within the prescribed time is also a method of optimizing education. In accordance with this method, the teacher relies on the rules and principles calling for a combination of various forms of organizing education. More specifically, this method of optimization presupposes the need for a differentiated and individual approach towards slow learners, the most advanced learners and all other pupils. Incidentally, it should be noted that during the first years spent on the elaboration of the optimization theory, the individual approach was regarded by some authors as the only possible method of optimization. A more rational place has been found for it today in the overall set of methods for optimizing education.

In differentiating education, attention should be paid not

so much to simplifying assignments for slow learners as to adjusting the amount of help given them in fulfilling assignments given to the whole class. This will assist in avoiding gaps in knowledge, skills and abilities.

The final optimization method is the analysis of educational results on the basis of the criteria set for optimizing education. This involves establishing that the results achieved are fully in line with the tasks set and that the time pupils and teachers spend in reaching those results does not lay undue strain on them in the light of prevailing health standards for schools.

It should be stressed that all the above-mentioned educational optimization methods, while primarily intended for teachers, also call for corresponding efforts to be made by pupils, since their aim is to enhance classroom performance. In this way, when the teacher makes a comprehensive set of assignments and gives them to his pupils, he teaches the pupils how to tackle the assignments and to set themselves further related tasks. By defining assignments, the teacher shows how they should be approached in the light of the pupils' capacities. By emphasizing essentials, he builds up pupils' abilities. By choosing the best methods of education, the teacher builds up pupils' abilities and teaches them to organize and check their work themselves and to encourage themselves to make further efforts. By rationally combining various forms of education and adjusting them to individual cases, the teacher builds up pupils' abilities to develop their strongest points and to strengthen their weak points. By choosing the best teaching speed, he develops pupils' ability to work as fast as possible and to use their time to the best effect. By including pupils in the general effort to improve the basis of education, teachers develop in them the valuable ability to create the best conditions for learning. By analysing the educational process from the point of view of its results and of the time spent in achieving them, the teacher trains pupils to judge what their highest performance should be. The above-mentioned optimization methods as a whole thus concern both teachers and pupils. It should also be pointed out that each optimization method also enables improved educational results to be obtained in a shorter time and without overburdening pupils or teachers.

Since 'optimum' means the best that can be obtained in given conditions, the optimization criteria and methods will vary with changing requirements and conditions in schools. The set of methods for optimizing education is therefore subject to more variations than any set of regulations would be. It can also be more easily updated as educational experience advances and as typical strong and weak points of the educational process are revealed. The optimization system provides teachers with means of using new information on the pedagogical and psychological aspects of education by establishing the optimum measure of their use in combination with other teaching elements.

The elaboration of the theory of optimization makes it possible today to formulate an integral set of requirements for building up the educational process at every stage of development of the school.

New demands will be made with regard to the content and tasks of education as science, production, culture and society progress, and also as a result of scientific studies of typical weak points in pupils' progress, in the quality of curricula, textbooks and methodological aids. As educational methods and means improve, fresh demands will be made to improve the methodology of school education. The preparation of new teaching materials designed to differentiate the assistance provided to pupils will lead to more specific demands for an individual approach to education, judiciously combined with general classroom work. Rational means of saving the time and efforts of teachers and pupils will be discovered. New criteria for analysing results will be put forward. With the increase in study possibilities for pupils, demands will be made for the assessment of the effectiveness of lessons in educating pupils and developing their talents.

Such a system of measures will enable the school successfully to prepare school-leavers to continue their education and continuously add to their knowledge at a time when scientific information is increasing at a tremendous pace.

Theoretical issues and practical possibilities*

Len Masterman

The following discussion presents a fairly simple model of media education, and indicates some of the theoretical questions which it raises. Initially, however, I would like to say a word or two about some major theoretical and practical difficulties which have bedevilled media education in the past. It is important that we all recognize that the origins of media education lay in a profound distrust of the media themselves. From the very first the media were seen as baleful influences, seducers of the innocent, and as creeping diseases, the cure for which was 'inoculative' doses of education. What has always alarmed educators and large sections of responsible middle-class opinion, has been the overwhelming popularity of what seemed to them the tawdry, the trivial and the third-rate in the media. Indeed it seemed to many people that the worse a particular media product was, the more popular it was likely to become, and the concept of discrimination was called into action from the outset as a weapon to protect the young from experiences which they actually found quite attractive, and, indeed, to protect civilized and civilizing cultural values from what F. R. Leavis and Denys Thompson called 'the competing

* This article is taken from a Keynote Lecture given to the Australian National Media Education Conference, held in Adelaide, Australia, August–September 1982—Ed.

exploitation of the cheapest emotional responses' and 'satisfaction offered at the lowest level' by the mass media.¹

Ambiguity of thought on the media

The origins of media education then were middle-class and deeply paternalistic. Media education was based on the murky perceptions of those who peered down with a kind of squeamish horror at the curious tastes and tawdry habits of those beneath them on the social scale and who disapproved of what they saw.

This tradition is, of course, still alive and well in the concept of discrimination, a concept which has survived as a cornerstone of media education from Leavis onwards in spite of its changing formulations and the different functions it has been called upon to serve. The word itself indicates a curiously split function. On the one hand, there is a positive sense of 'exercising fine judgement'. On the other, the sense of 'unfair exclusion' which we find in such terms as sexual or racial discrimination. There is no doubt historically that hidden behind the positive connotations of the world (of which few of us would disapprove) that element of exclusion—in this case of the tastes and preferences of large numbers of pupils—was working strongly in practice. And this is almost certainly the most potent reason why media education, in spite of reports, recommendations, and conferences urging its implementation over the past twenty-five years, has made somewhat halting progress in the classroom.

Discrimination, as I suggested, was originally called in in order to be exercised against the media. The concept remained intact though its function changed dramatically in the 1960s, when what we might call the 'popular arts' movement advocated discrimination betweeen media products. In the words of Hall and Whannel:

In terms of actual quality the struggle between what is good and worthwhile, and what is shoddy and debased is not a struggle *against* the modern forms of communication but a conflict *within* these media.[2]

The mass media were, in the 1960s, sifted for newer art forms, forms which could nevertheless be evaluated by quite traditional aesthetic criteria. In classroom practice 'discrimination' in this new formulation could be quite simply equated with a preference for Continental European cinema over popular cinema (and incidentally with film as a medium over television), with serious newspapers over tabloids, with portentious current-affairs programmes and documentaries on television over game shows and cartoons. Discrimination could be equated, that is, with a preference for the rather highbrow 'serious' media tastes of teachers over the popular media offerings most avidly consumed by their pupils. The target for change—the media tastes of most pupils—remained the same, as it has done through the ever-more refined notions of discrimination that continue to this day.

Discrimination does not seem to be simply an unworthy and undesirable aim to pursue, an aim which works in fairly straightforward élitist ways. It is also an impossible aim. It does after all assume that clear criteria for evaluating media products do exist. This is far from being so. In a field where snap judgements and easy generalizations are common enough, the few serious attempts that have been made to erect and defend generally agreed criteria of judgement have been singularly, often spectacularly, unsuccessful.[3]

Indeed a tendency often observable here—to apply to the media evaluative criteria derived from other fields, particularly literary criticism—is turning back upon itself. For an enormous question mark now hangs over the concept of literary value itself, a doubt largely fostered by critical debates within cultural studies and media studies.[4]

If the prospect of a media education based upon the improvement of pupils' tastes is unsatisfactory, what more constructive and honourable position can be adopted?

Let us accept a fairly uncomplicated position. The media are massively 'there'; they are pervasive and self-evidently significant elements in our society. Over the next decade they will undoubtedly attain a newer and greater significance. They influence our perceptions of the world in fundamental ways which we all need to think about and understand, and for that reason they are worthy of the closest investigation. Let us be quite clear: media education should aim to increase students' understanding of how the media work, how they produce meaning, how they are organized, how they go about the business of constructing reality, and of how that 'reality' is understood by those who receive it. And that word 'understanding', with its emphasis upon the development of a critical intelligence in relation to media, will need to be given a centrality previously accorded to discrimination and to related concepts such as 'appreciation', with its implication of passivity before accredited works of value. The value question will not, however, simply lie down. Questions of value will inevitably be raised in relation to the media, as they are in relation to the arts, though I want to suggest that it might be more profitable to raise the issue in a rather different form than its historically dominant one. What is strategically necessary at the moment in media education is to move value questions away from centre stage, and to give up any Platonic or transcendental motion of value in relation to the mass media. It is not helpful to talk of 'good' or 'bad' television programmes. Rather we need to recognize, as the literary critic Terry Eagleton has suggested, that value terms are always transitive terms, and that if a text is valuable at all, it can only be so for particular people working within particular criteria of thought and feeling in particular societies, and for particular reasons. And as Eagleton has stressed, value questions are always, finally, strategic questions. The reading of any text is the use of that text for particular purposes, and the valuation of that text will be dependent on what those purposes are. A television documentary that we consider to be valuable or important may not be so to those who are using it for quite different purposes:

to those who have different political perspectives, who are from different subcultures, who live in other societies or in different historical periods.[4]

Theoretical issues

A simple theoretical model of media education can be built up through a definite kind of logic. For to argue for the study of media is to imply—correctly in my view—that they are non-transparent. A 'window on the world' view of television or newspapers would make their study as pointless as studying a pane of glass. One would not be examining television, but other things—sport, current affairs or drama, for example. The case for media education must rest upon the idea that the media are actively involved in constructing 'reality' rather than neutrally transmitting it; that is, they deal in representations, and the ideological power of the media is roughly proportional to the apparent naturalness of these representations. The ideological potency of a medium arises precisely from the power of those who control and work in it to pass off as 'real' or 'true' or universal an inevitably partial and selective (and, in the United Kingdom, almost always a white, male, middle-class, middle-aged and heterosexual) view of the world.

Now if media products are constructs then four areas, at least, immediately and with some degree of logic present themselves for further investigation:

Who is responsible for these constructions (ownership and control of the media; the sociology of the communicating professions)?

How precisely is the ideological effect noted above achieved (i.e. what are the dominant techniques and codings currently employed for conveying meaning)?

What values are implicit in the world so constructed?

How are these constructions read by the audience?

In teaching about the media it is not necessarily desirable to treat these four areas discretely, for they are often inter-

Theoretical issues and practical possibilities

penetrating and mutually illuminating. For the sake of clarity, however, some of the problems and issues relating to each area will be considered separately.

WHO CONSTRUCTS MEDIA REPRESENTATIONS?

It may be considered axiomatic that the control of the media by very few hands, the lack of much in the way of democratic accountability in the media and the resulting unwillingness of the media to provide access and production facilities for the expression of the rich diversity of views and opinions that exist in society should all be regarded as key, overarching areas of knowledge and concern within media education. It would be difficult to envisage a conceptually coherent media pedagogy that did not take into account the large number of studies of media institutions, and of the routine working practices of media workers that have been undertaken during the last decade.[5] Media professionals themselves can play an important part in media studies courses. They can offer teachers and students alike important insights from their own day-to-day involvement in, and knowledge of, the industry; certainly in my own courses some of the liveliest sessions have been those in which film-makers, journalists, comedy scriptwriters, television playwrights and producers have talked about their work. It is important to stress, however, that this talk should not be simply a general 'chat' or—even worse—be formally prepared. It should, rather, revolve round the analyses of particular texts and the economic and industrial constraints within which they are produced. Of crucial importance, of course, is that the group itself should retain a critical perspective (which may or may not be shared by the professional) upon the dominant practices of the industry.

The question of who owns and controls the mass media may be one of the few areas of media education where some 'telling' may be necessary, where the teacher may feel that he should provide students with a certain amount of factual information. I remain convinced, however, that if this kind of pedagogy is to be effective at all it should take place within an overall context of negotiated involvement by pupils in group analyses, practical activities, simulations and other participatory modes of learning.

I do not support the suggestion of a number of writers—none of them, incidentally, practising school-teachers—that media education must begin from a concrete analysis of economic relations and the ways in which they structure cultural processes and products.[6] A text cannot be directly analysed from its economic determinants, and due weight should be given to its specificity, to the interest students may have in it, and to the pleasure they may get from it. What is at stake here is not any simple opposition between cultural and economic analyses, but the relative weight to be given to each. For as long as it can be argued that the relationship between media product and economic base is complex, mediated and indirect, then space certainly exists for the kind of close textual analysis in which literature teachers are experienced. This kind of analysis has to recognize its own limitations, however. The media are not ersatz forms of literature, and textual analysis will need to be informed at every point by the sociological and economic data available.

HOW DO THE MEDIA CONSTRUCT THEIR REPRESENTATIONS?

A critical understanding of the media will involve a reversal of the process through which a medium selects and edits material into a polished, continuous and seamless flow. It will involve, that is, the 'deconstruction' of texts by breaking through their surface to reveal the techniques through which meanings are produced. The project is analogous to that undertaken by Brecht in his attack upon the 'illusionism' of bourgeois theatre, a theatre in which the audience identifies with, and accepts as real, the play's representations, rather than being encouraged to reflect critically upon them. But if Brecht was concerned about the illusionism of theatre how much more should teachers be concerned about the illusionism of the media?

For however much we may be sucked into the realism of a particular play, we are always finally aware that we are watching representations—performances which have been scripted, rehearsed and acted—and not reality. This is far from the case with television and newspapers however, where even the most alert critic constantly needs to be on his guard against the apparent authenticity of what is seen or read. The necessity for deconstruction in television and newspaper analysis, then, is even more imperative than it is in the theatre or the cinema.

How does one begin this process of deconstructing complex media texts? A simple start can be made by deconstructing photographs. Much useful work can be done with family photographs which pupils bring from home. Are photographs more likely to be taken on some occasions rather than others? What functions do our photographs serve for us as individuals, or as members of a family? How faithful a representation of the event depicted (a holiday or a wedding for example) is the photograph? Is the event 'frozen in action', or has it been specifically set up for the camera? What is the effect of the camera's presence upon the event? How would the pupils themselves begin to change their appearances if they knew they were going to be photographed? Attention needs to be drawn to the presence of the unseen member of the group—the photographer himself. What were the intentions and purposes of the photographer who had selected that moment, that angle and distance, and may even have arranged or suggested that particular composition? What alternatives were available to the photographer and why were they rejected? And who was the photographer? Very often the precise identity of the photographer can be deduced—but why should it be that person taking the photograph and not someone else? These kinds of questions need to be discussed as methodically as possible. They will be taken up again later in the analysis of television images and programmes.

A second, and very important, step in analysing photographs is to show the ways in which a photographic print, which will for most pupils represent the finished product, is, commercially, merely the subject for further mediations—those of editing, selecting and cropping. A great deal of well-produced photographic material is now fairly easily available that gives pupils practice in constructing their own media products, and allows scope for creative cropping and layout exercises.

A third and crucially important step is the relationship between the photograph and any accompanying text—a caption, headline or article. Most people are familiar with this kind of work.[7] The polysemic nature of visual evidence, and the function of the written text in anchoring a preferred meaning within it, needs to be stressed here.

Having cut their teeth on this much simpler photographic material, pupils ought then to be able to look critically at the relationship between televised sounds and images. Acquiring the ability to 'shred' the visual image from its accompanying commentary is an important step towards tele-literacy, and the problematic nature of visual evidence can be demonstrated by showing television news and documentaries without commentary, so that a range of possible interpretations and anchorages may be explored before the commentary is revealed.

These exercises take the filmed material as 'given', but following a parallel process to that taken with photographic exercises one can begin to examine the processes through which filmed 'reality' is manufactured, and begin to lay bare some of the mechanisms of film-making. Every television image is of course a selected one. The camera, the lights, the microphone are pointing in that direction, from that angle, at that time rather than another. And what of the effect of a camera crew of between, say, six and thirteen people, upon the event represented? Television continually purports to present what can never be shown—the event that would have taken place if cameras had not been present. And then there are the constraints implicit in producing images and sounds of 'acceptable' quality and the necessity of 'setting up' situations specifically for the camera. 'Television is the only profession', in the words of a former television producer, 'in which the word cheat is an inseparable part of the vocabulary'.[8] The existence of this kind of rigging ought to be part of every secondary-school pupil's common stock of knowledge about visual communication. The teacher also needs to draw attention to the inevitable fictionalizing involved in the editing process, particularly the creation of fictitious meaning in supposedly factual programmes through the smooth juxtaposing of originally fragmented and unrelated images and events. To do this, however, involves more than the analysis of the images on the screen. This kind of analysis should be complemented, wherever possible, by practical video work, though I should emphasize that I do not consider any kind of video work will do. The common rationale of much practical work with television cameras—that it will of itself produce more critically aware viewers—is simply bogus unless that connection is positively worked for and actively made by the teacher and his students. It cannot simply be assumed. In this particular case, the student's own manufacturing of particular effects through editing needs to be carried on alongside the analysis of edited effects upon the screen.

The media do not simply construct events, however. They attach significance to them, give them meaning. How is this achieved? First of all it is obvious that the act of selection itself marks some events, issues or people as being more important or significant than others. The media tell us what is important by what they take note of and what they ignore, by what is amplified and what is muted. This is the media's agenda-setting function. But the media also define the way in which these events should be discussed, and the interpretative frameworks which should be brought to bear upon them. The teacher can introduce this issue through the simple notion of the 'angle' from which any newspaper or television story is approached. Pupils need to see how most stories are pretty well set before the reporter has even left the office. All too often the reporter's task is not to seek the truth of a situation but to seek evidence which supports the chosen angle.

It is also important for teachers and pupils to consider the more complex issue of why some interpretative frameworks and angles rather than others should become familiar and well established. This leads to a consideration of such crucial ideological questions as the ownership and control of the media by the wealthy and powerful, the essentially conservative and hierarchical nature of media institutions, their susceptibility to overt and indirect political and financial pressures, the middle-class bias of their personnel, the philosophic commitment within broadcasting towards 'balance' and consensual explanatory models, the extent to which journalists are reliant upon established institutions (the police, the army, the law courts, big business, football clubs, etc.) as news sources, the ability of such sources to manage news and set events within their own interpretative contexts, and the over-accessibility of the media to those in powerful and privileged positions in society. This in turn should lead to a consideration of those voices that are not heard in the media, and to those that are heard, but which form part of a 'secondary' discourse which it is the privilege and function of the medium's dominant discourse to place and evaluate for us. It should lead us on, that is, to problems of representation, and to a consideration of the images presented of those subordinate groups who have little or no control of the media and for whom, indeed, the media constitute a major problem.

How are these images realized? How do the media go about the business of shaping the events and images they portray? In television one important factor is the control exercised by a programme's anchor person. He tells us through the programme's dominant discourse—linking, framing, commenting upon and placing each item—how the programme's other discourses (the subjects it treats) should be read. In television programmes of all kinds—even given the inevitable slanting and selectivity inherent in every image—we are still very rarely allowed to judge such images, people and events on their own merits. As the audience, we are habitually nudged in the direction of this or that preferred meaning. This is an example of what Barthes called the 'imperative, button-holding character' of Myth,[9] its insistent imposition of meaning through pushing the viewer into simple and unproblematic 'positions' from which the events depicted may be viewed and evaluated. So it is important, for example, in analysing interviews, not simply to look at the interview itself, but to the way it is contextualized for the viewer, and framed by the anchor person. It is a framework that will itself occupy a position, and this position, inevitably, will be developed by the interviewer who will continually sign-post to us, by his or her tone, reactions, interruptions and gestures, how the words of the subject are to be interpreted.

The control exercised by on-screen representatives of the television companies is reinforced by the visual codings of the medium, which confirm the status of the presenters as guarantors of truth. And here it should be said that the whole area of visual coding deserves specific attention in any consideration of how the medium constructs its meanings. This would cover the hierarchy implicit in different eye-contact-to-camera patterns, but also take in the way in which the image is framed, the appearance, dress and gestures of participants, what is communicated by the sets, and the codes of geography within a studio which tell us who is important and who less so.

Finally, mention must be made of one of television's dominant techniques for shaping the events it handles: the use of narrative. Television tells stories. News, current-affairs programmes, documentaries, sports programmes all create little dramas with their own heroes, villains, conflicts, reversals, rewards and resolutions—and they can easily be analysed in these terms. Dramatic shaping is endemic to most forms of editing for television, and it is probably most sensible to regard even the most factual documentaries, for example, as primarily fictional in form. But the dominant fiction which underpins the media's penchant for narrative is that there does indeed exist an unproblematic and disinterested 'position' from which the story may be told. In the deathless words of a former president of CBS News, 'Our reporters do not cover stories from their point of view. They are presenting them from nobody's point of view.'[10]

Hence the strength of Christopher Williams' assertion that 'narrative militates against knowledge... because it attempts to conceal itself, to imply that this is how the world is'.[11] But as we have seen 'how the world is' contains the positions fed to the viewer by editing, framing, commentary, visual codings, etc. This militates against knowledge not because of 'bias' or the suppression or demotion of alternative viewpoints, but because what is concealed is the notion of the text as a site for the construction of meanings which should be considered and analysed in relation to the position, interests and intentions of their producers.

IMPLICIT VALUES

I have tried to show in *Teaching about Television*[12] how the world constructed by the media may be elaborated at denotative, connotative and ideological levels. The following simply suggests how even quite young pupils might begin to grapple with the concept of idology. This concept is necessary to us as media teachers because it is necessary to explain precisely why and how it comes about that the ideas of a ruling group in any society are the dominant ideas for the whole society.

Althusser has argued that there are apparatuses of the state, particularly the communications and educational apparatuses, that have the specialized function of continually reproducing dominant ideas, that is of reproducing those conditions through which the powerful will remain powerful.[13] It needed Barthes, however, with his notion of myth, to show precisely how it was that bourgeois culture could be transformed into a universal nature. Myth is a mode of signification which involves 'the miraculous evaporation of history', and, as history evaporates out of the signification process, nature floods in. Myth is simply 'depoliticized speech', and Barthes' *Mythologies* was written out of his resentment at 'seeing Nature and History confused at every turn' and from an imperative to track down the ideological abuse hidden in 'the decorative display of *what-goes-without-saying*'.[14] That decorative display of what-goes-without-saying is precisely the stock-in-trade of the mass media, and our children will begin to get a glimmer of ideological operations the moment they challenge 'what-goes-without-saying'; the moment they begin to see alternatives to dominant explanations; the moment they can put the history and the struggle and the politics back into the process of signification. That sounds like a big agenda, but what I tried to show in *Teaching about Television* is how at the very basic level of non-verbal communication, quite unsophisticated pupils could begin to question the apparent 'innocence', spontaneity and naturalness of gestures, hairstyles, modes of dress, and the function and design of objects, and begin to grasp how closely woven into these things questions of value are. Now it is that crucial relationship between values and objects, between ideas and non-ideas, to which the concept of ideology draws attention and which we need our pupils to cling on to in watching television. What needs to be stressed is the general idea that powerful and contentious ideas lie behind the world depicted by television, that those ideas have emerged out of concrete historical situations and struggles, that those ideas have important functions, that they have work to do, and that they produce, as a result, powerful material consequences. If our pupils can grasp those kind of relationships between ideas and material situations in studying television's different content-areas, then they will possess a very powerful conceptual tool for understanding the world in which they live, and one of the most important functions of the mass media within it.

READING MEDIA CONSTRUCTIONS

It is indicative of an important recent change of emphasis in media criticism that two of the most significant books written about television in the United Kingdom in recent years have been concerned with questions relating to the kind of sense that audiences make of particular programmes. The two books are David Morley's study of *The Nationwide Audience*[15] and perhaps most significantly, Dorothy Hobson's study of one of the most reviled, yet most watched programmes in the United Kingdom, the soap opera, *Crossroads*.[16]

By common consent *Crossroads* is one of the poorest shows on British television. It is thought to be badly written, badly acted and badly produced, and the *Crossroads* team turn out three episodes each week on a remorseless conveyor-belt system with post-production editing facilities denied them because the company which produces the show considers them too expensive to be wasted on this programme.

The problem is, of course, that *Crossroads* enjoys huge audiences. After *Coronation Street*, it is the most popular programme regularly scheduled on British television. It is this phenomenon, the vast popular appeal of a media product deemed to have little intrinsic merit (a phenomenon which has always caused difficulties for media educators), which Dorothy Hobson's study investigates.

The heart of the study is an account of one of the most cataclysmic events in the history of British television — the decision in 1981 by a single television executive that Meg Mortimer, the central and best-loved character in the soap opera, would have to be disposed of. The outcry was enormous. The company was inundated with mail; its switchboards were jammed for days. Noële Gordon (the actress who played the part of Meg) sold her story for a lucrative sum to a Sunday newspaper, and the whole story remained in the headlines for weeks. Overwhelmingly those who telephoned and wrote letters were those whose views do not count for very much with television companies and advertisers: middle-aged to elderly women, and an enormous number of old-age pensioners. What Dorothy Hobson did was to read all their letters, and then seek out some of those who had written in, and watch the show with them in their own homes. What she writes about what those people — mainly women and principally elderly women — got out of the programme is very moving and affirmative. It is a rare glimpse of the human reality of how people, and particularly the elderly, relate to the media, and it gives the lie to the kind of condescending generalization generally made by cultural critics whenever they think of audiences as undiscriminating 'masses'. What Dorothy Hobson writes is worth quoting:

Perhaps the single most surprising aspect of researching and writing this book has been the awareness which it has brought to me about old people and their lives. Quite incidentally, while they wrote letters in support of the actress, they gave information about their own lives and the importance to them of some television programmes. For the letters were often not simply about television but about the way that old people experience their lives and how they feel about their role in society.[17]

There was a sense of the writers expressing two contradictory feelings—a sense of wanting to say that they had reached a certain age and that their opinions should be taken into account, but also an expression of the feeling that they knew that their opinions would not be considered, precisely because they were now old.

I want to end by stressing that teaching about the media is something which could be done simply and effectively by many thousands of teachers. Indeed, it is important that they should begin to do so as quickly as possible if the profession is not to contribute further to what is already a dangerously wide gap between the priorities and concerns of most schools and the life-problems, situations and issues which confront students and adults in the real world. Yet at the beginning of the 1980s we are standing on the threshold of the most enormous and unprecedented expansion of television and video. Those teachers who continue to ignore or deplore these developments will be opting for the role of educational dinosaurs. On the other hand if we, as media educators, keep ourselves informed about these developments and work alongside our students in helping them to make sense of them, then we will have an important and honourable role to play in the future of our education services.

Notes

1. F. R. Leavis and D. Thompson, *Culture and Environment*, p. 3, London, Chatto & Windus, 1948.
2. S. Hall and P. Whannel, *The Popular Arts*, p. 15, London, Hutchinson, 1964.
3. See for example P. Abrams, 'Radio and Television' in D. Thompson (ed.), *Discrimination and Popular Culture*, pp. 50–73, Harmondsworth, Penguin, 1964.
4. I am grateful for many of the ideas raised in this paragraph to discussions held with Dr Terry Eagleton in his seminar on Marxism and Structuralism held at Nottingham University in June 1982.
5. See, for example, *Granada: The First 25 Years*, London, British Film Institute, 1981 (BFI Dossier No. 9); T. Burns, *The BBC: Public Institution and Private World*, London, Macmillan, 1977; P. Schlesinger, *Putting 'Reality' Together*, London, Constable, 1978; Glasgow University Media Group, *Bad News*, London, Routledge & Kegan Paul, 1976; *More Bad News*, London, Routledge & Kegan Paul, 1980; *Really Bad News*, London, Readers and Writers Press, 1982; S. Cohen and S. Young, *The Manufacture of News*, London, Constable, 1973; M. Alvarado and E. Buscombe, *Hazell: The Making of a TV Series*, London, BF1/Latimer, 1978; S. Chibnall, *Law and Order News*, London, Tavistock, 1977.
6. G. Murdock and P. Golding, 'Capitalism, Communication and Class Relations' in J. Curran, M. Gurevitch and J. Woollacott (eds), *Mass Communication and Society*, London, Arnold, 1977.
7. L. Masterman, *Teaching About Television*, p. 152, London, Macmillan, 1980.
8. Philip Whitehead quoted in J. Bakewell and N. Garnham, *The New Priesthood*, p. 173, London, Allen Lane, 1970.
9. R. Barthes, *Mythologies*, p. 124, St Albans, Paladin, 1973.
10. D. L. Altheide, *Creating Reality: How TV News Distorts Events*, p. 17, Beverly Hills, Sage Publications Inc., 1976.
11. G. Williams (ed.), *Realism and the Cinema*, p. 152, London, Routledge/British Film Institute, 1980.
12. Masterman, op. cit., Chapters 3 and 4.
13. L. Althusser, 'Ideology and Ideological State Apparatuses', in *Lenin and Philosophy and Other Essays*, London, New Left Books, 1971.

14. Barthes, op. cit., pp. 11–12.
15. D. Morley, *The 'Nationwide' Audience*, London, British Film Institute, 1980 (Television Monograph, No. 11).
16. D. Hobson, *Crossroads: The Drama of a Soap Opera*, London, Methuen, 1982.
17. Ibid., pp. 147–9.

New tasks for teacher training

Ferenc Genzwein

These last few years, with the ever faster changes in the needs of society, studies on teaching and learning and on schools and their duties have been many and varied. All point to the same conclusions, namely that, compared with the results already produced by socio-economic development, the intellectual vision shows an increasing time-lag. The experts also agree that continuous, autonomous learning and the ability to change are vital requirements. Schools cannot avoid imparting new scientific knowledge, which demands more and more abstract thought, whether or not this is consonant with former notions of what is proper for different age-groups. At the same time, the quantity of knowledge to be acquired is constantly increasing while, clearly, the duration of schooling generally cannot be prolonged, or only insignificantly. This process is irreversible and can only become more marked in the future. Consequently, the only solution available lies in the intensive development of education. The changing and constantly increasing needs of society demand continuous development in schoolwork, while, at the same time, scientific and technological progress make this possible and provide the necessary conditions for it.

Thus, in the last few decades the question of how to teach has become just as important as those of what to teach and how much. Schools cannot ignore this fact. It entails not only educational research but also some urgent action with respect to school practice.

As social conditions change, educational curricula, methods and means must be changed accordingly. This is also urgent because, whereas for centuries schools were almost the only established source of knowledge in society, nowadays—and in the future this will be increasingly so—more and more other factors interfere indirectly, and even more pervasively, in the process of teaching and education. The mass media, especially radio and television, have entered homes and schools alike, and there has been a parallel development in other audio-visual media that can make the process of teaching and education in school more efficient. The mass media have been educational 'tools' for a long time now, and their existence shows that the era of the omnipotent teacher with his *ex-cathedra* pronouncements has come to an end.

Given this awareness, plus the availability of other new services designed to facilitate the running of schools and the changes that have occurred in the whole infrastructure of schools, it makes us realize that the universal backwardness of educational research and school practice is really paradoxical.

Making schools relevant to life

The main criticism levelled against schools nowadays is that conditions inside are not in harmony with conditions outside. To improve this situation, attention must be paid to three important requirements: (a) adaptation for pedagogical purposes of the ways in which abstract knowledge is acquired; (b) development of up-to-date principles and methods of illustration; and (c) much better practical use than hitherto of the possibilities implicit in audio-visual techniques.

According to Marcel Hicter,* schools are divorced from

* Marcel Hicter, 'Education for a Changing World', *Prospects*, Vol. II, No. 3, 1972, pp. 298–312.

real life, from young people's daily problems. This state of affairs is intolerable. Hicter sees recurrent education as the solution to the present situation. In the future, schools will increasingly have to become places for the processing of information obtained outside. Their task will be to promote the acquisition of knowledge offered by the mass media. I wish neither to refute nor to confirm Hicter's categorical opinion. I only refer to it, as it may lend support to the idea that the existence of the mass media entails some urgent tasks for schools. To show their growing influence, allow me to quote a few facts:

According to an international pedagogical conference held at Trogen (Switzerland), children under 14 are spending more and more time in front of their television screens. For example: in Austria the figure is 58 minutes per day; Switzerland, 70 minutes; Federal Republic of Germany, 79 minutes; France, 101 minutes; and Italy, 117 minutes per day.

These figures show how popular television is. Directly and indirectly it has a tremendous impact on the quality of schoolwork and already exerts a determining influence on the knowledge acquired by children and young people outside school and, consequently, on the development of their whole personalities.

This points to the obvious conclusion that where the training and further training of teachers are concerned, or attitudes to teaching and learning, or education as applied in schools, or the relations between school and home, our principles and practice must be placed on a new basis.

If we believe that the aim of schools is to 'open doors' and educate people to gain the maximum self-fulfilment and a versatile command of knowledge, this cannot be achieved really well without the help of the mass media. The mass media are the school's partners, not its rivals.

Partnership with the mass media

Thus, since the existence and development of the mass-media network undoubtedly influences school practice, the following have become key questions for our times:

How far does the relationship between learning inside and learning outside school change under the influence of the mass media, and particularly of television?

Are the special educational programmes of the mass media properly planned and co-ordinated with school syllabuses?

Do we know what effect, good or bad, the mass media have on pupils' personal development?

Are teachers equipped with the special knowhow in educational methodology necessary to utilize the mass media?

Are pupils competent to select and understand mainly audio-visual mass-media programmes?

Within the narrow limits of this article there is no room to expand on these questions, but I should like to emphasize a few basic points.

INFLUENCE ON LEARNING

When answering the first question, it must be borne in mind that, in all probability, the greater part of pupils' information already comes from 'life', of which the 'secondary' information abundantly flowing through mass-media channels is part. Schools used to consider that their task, apart from providing information on a large scale, was to systematize, structure and complement the experience acquired by pupils from other sources, but they never succeeded really well. That task is now increasingly important and, at the same time, increasingly difficult. In addition to supplying information directly, schools must devote much more attention to structuring the knowledge pupils already have and to teaching them how, or rather rendering them able, to collect and process information on their own. The relationship between learning inside and learning outside school will change accordingly, which means that in school pupils have to absorb not somewhat less but something different in a different way. This 'something different' is, on one hand, clearly a methodology for processing information on their own, and, on the other, an understanding of structures in the real world outside school that they cannot fully comprehend without guidance. Schools must, of course, possibly under the usual syllabus of compulsory subjects, also supply what cannot be acquired from the secondary information channels.

CO-ORDINATING THE EDUCATIONAL SERVICES OF THE MEDIA

Our second question is connected with the relationship between schools and television and radio for schools. In this field, practically every country has its own theory and practice. In Hungary and in the East European socialist countries generally, the functions of television and radio for schools are not identical with those of schools, hence they are not interchangeable but complementary systems. Programmes for schoolchildren, which are devised taking into consideration the standardized state curriculum, are called 'curriculum service programmes', and their fundamental function follows therefrom. That they should be worked on in schools is, accordingly, not compulsory, but it is desirable and appropriate. Since in our particular case this model has stood the test of experience, I should like to mention two of its advantages, which may help in the development of suitable relations between the mass media and schools.

One of them is that radio and television for schools allow pupils consciously to build up an audio-visual culture and in so doing are true to their nature. Thus, not only do they contribute directly to pupils' grasp of the school curriculum, in the first place precisely in those fields that go beyond the possibilities of classroom teaching, but the information supplied by the mass media can also be developed in practice, under guidance. It is no accident that in the sphere of aesthetic education and visual culture, for example, school television broadcasts numerous programmes not only for pupils but also for teachers.

The other conclusion to be drawn from the work of Hungary's television and radio for schools is that the multimedia system, useful and often indispensable for the grasping of particular areas of the school curriculum, can also be established on a nationwide scale, since co-ordination between the programme designers is guaranteed by their common approach, in our case as a result of the common curriculum. This is essential, because it is now well established that multimedia are much more efficient than single-medium teaching systems, because more allowance can be made for each pupils' individuality, and consequently the information supplied can actually be differentiated.

EFFECTS OF THE MEDIA ON PERSONALITY DEVELOPMENT

As to the third question, a comparatively short answer can be given. Since our knowledge in this area, owing precisely to the exceptionally rapid development of the mass media, is necessarily inadequate, the research and pedagogical and socio-psychological tests already begun must be continued and completed and the results made accessible, especially to teachers, not only during their training but also later on, during their further training. Wide-ranging studies such as those carried out by researchers in connection with the American *Sesame Street* television programme focus not only on the question of the effect school television programmes produce on teaching and personality formation but also generally on that of the special pedagogically valuable characteristics of the mass media. Since in this respect schools and teachers are usually at a disadvantage, it is up to the research and development institutes to speed up these investigations and to see that the results are translated not only into school practice but also into teacher-training and further-training programmes, as well, of course, as being made known to the media programme designers.

A MEDIA-FOCUSED PEDAGOGY

The fourth question is connected with the previous one: the question is whether, over and above the traditional teaching methods and strategies, teachers are expressly equipped with an educational methodology specifically designed for the mass media. This question is increasingly pertinent in so far as hitherto the main emphasis in schools has been on the instructional aspect. Where education is concerned, the process is always basically ideological and ethical. If it is true, as maintained by Enrico Fulchignoni, that the development of the mass media has brought about a 'parallel' school, and if what has been said about the 'latent' curriculum, 'school' curriculum and 'home' curriculum, suggesting the existence of several parallel schools, is true, then there is a greater need than ever for teachers and parents to have some knowledge of education, in the original sense of the word, and expertise in teaching. I must now return to the first question: the position of schools has changed, and so has their function and what is expected of teachers. As the development of 'parallel schools', though not inevitable, is likely, one of the teachers' main tasks is to ensure that they acquire the aforementioned capacities, and indeed in most countries they are legally responsible for doing so.

What has happened is that pupils, as consumers of audio-visual culture, have gained an undoubted 'advantage' over earlier generations. It is a paradox that schoolchildren brought up on the mass media should have to be trained to use them intelligently primarily by schools, which are becoming acquainted with them only slowly and often use them only haphazardly.

A global approach to integrating knowledge

The science of mass-media-based education must therefore be developed and taught to teachers, for otherwise they will continue to work empirically in that area as, unfortunately, in so many other areas of teaching. Although empirical teaching is not ineffective and far from useless, it is not efficient enough nowadays.

Thus the main problem is how to achieve a better and increasingly satisfactory marriage between school curricula and knowledge acquired through the mass media, and to instil a sense of 'wholeness' and 'comprehensiveness' into the process of gathering and absorbing knowledge.

The purpose of this article is not to explain possible solutions in concrete detail but to call attention to what needs to be done in that direction. However, let us not avoid answers completely.

To reduce the proportion of empiricism in teaching, research, above all, has an important part to play, given the novelty of the task. This is a specific new field for research. The main consideration is to find out how to combine the knowledge acquired inside with that acquired outside school, or more exactly how to weld into a whole items of knowledge acquired through the mass media and the school curriculum for pupils of a given age. As the content to be acquired is specified, the task can be tested experimentally. The aim is optimum learning, and not only do psychologists already have more to say about how to reach this aim than teachers are prepared to use, but it may be assumed that they could undertake further research and even deeper analysis on the subject.

The training of teachers should include integrated material providing an education in mass information ranging from the pre-school to the university and even to the adult-education age. During these courses, trainee teachers should acquire such knowledge and capacities as will enable them to teach their pupils or at least familiarize them with the process of evaluating the knowledge obtained through the mass media critically, systematizing it and integrating it with the knowledge obtained at school, while realizing that the mass media can never be responsible for ordinary teaching but only for the 'different sort of teaching' that can assist ordinary teaching.

Developing concentration

Apart from a few people in exceptional situations, we all spend more time listening to other people than reading or writing. This is even more so today with the rapid spread of television, radio, film and tape-recorders, and the increasing number and length of meetings and conferences. One of our great worries is that few people are able to concentrate on what they are listening to. We therefore find it difficult to understand properly what we are told. Schools have always been concerned about this and are and will be increasingly so, since a failure in communication or misinterpretation of information becomes a source of trouble, especially at a time when people obtain a considerable proportion of their information from listening to others. It is not only that people should be able to listen attentively to what they are told. Several other factors are also important. On the one hand, they should be able to understand and appraise what they are listening to, that is to say that the occurrence and number of misunderstandings should be reduced; on the other, they should be able not only to register but also to understand the content of the information they hear, to decide how to use it and come to conclusions.

One may wonder why people are not as attentive as might be desired. The reasons are complex. Here I shall mention just one, perhaps the most important, factor: that the power of concentration is not an inborn but an acquired faculty. It follows that schools must train pupils to develop it.

This problem has been insufficiently explored; teachers are not, or only minimally, prepared for the task in the training institutes, and attending to, understanding and digesting the spoken word requires greater concentration than reading. It is more difficult because the pace of reading can be determined by the reader, and, since what he reads is printed or written, if his attention strays he can turn back the pages or take up the text again and re-read it. The spoken word, however, 'flies away'. We cannot usually listen to it again if we have not understood it. It might be added that the modern way of life does not help people to learn how to concentrate. Constant rushing about is bad for concentration.

New tasks for teachers

The teachers' position is made even more difficult by the fact that scientific logic is not the same as learning logic, and when explaining scientific facts the mass media generally pay scant attention to learning logic. Teachers are thus called upon to teach and accustom their pupils constantly to go over what they have already learnt. There are still many questions pending in this area. It also means that those who prepare programmes for the mass media have a prime duty to become increasingly familiar with the sciences of teaching, psychology and communication.

Attention should also be drawn to another danger. It will no doubt be apparent from what has been said above that schools are inevitably increasingly involved in the process of exploring avenues, but in addition to realizing this and reacting accordingly we must also bear in mind that human beings cannot stand quick, unexpected, frequent changes without damage. Changes to increase the efficiency of educational work are inevitable but often counter-productive. A frequent change in aims may be good, in principle, but in practice these aims mostly become distorted, especially if teachers are not made to understand and accept the reason for, and essence of, the change, and if they are not properly trained to carry out their new duties correctly.

Today, for example, lecturing in class is rejected as being, generally, inefficient. The use *inter alia* of television, radio and audio-visual media generally is recommended, in order to improve teaching efficiency, but this becomes the source of a new danger in practice. We can attest to the fact that the use of the audio-visual media for the delivery of conventional lectures is common because teachers do not know how to use these media.

Teaching practice must also take into account the harmful effects of the mass media on young people. In this connection some mention must be made of the common responsibilities and duties of schools and families, for these problems can be solved only by co-operation between them. It is not only the schools' duties but also those of the parents that have changed and are changing. They have become more complicated. Potentially there are more opportunities to exert a favourable influence, but there are more temptations and opportunities to do harm too.

Modern parents' knowledge of good educational principles and methods has not increased in proportion as their duties have become more difficult. If this problem is to be solved, that is to say if parents are to become increasingly competent to carry out their more onerous educational duties, more and more help will be required from the schools and, consequently, teacher-training courses must also prepare trainee teachers for this task. The importance of this has not yet been fully realized by educational policy experts, teachers or parents.

No scientific investigation has yet been carried out on the effect of this mutual relationship. The subject has never really been explored from the angle of teaching, psychology or sociology. As a result, families and schools have not developed the mutual understanding and interdependence that is generally necessary for efficient education and that, in particular, is essential for integrated use of the mass media in education.

My aim here has been to put forward and describe a few thoughts and concerns relating to our subject and also to draw attention to a few new tasks for research and teacher training. I could not undertake a detailed analysis of all the problems identified, and even less suggest concrete solutions, within the limits of this paper. To get down to the root of these problems and find a perfect solution will require thorough research, a change in teacher-training and further-training courses and also wide-ranging societal collaboration. Society must establish an increasingly satisfactory partnership between the familiar traditional schools and the radio, cinema and press, so that traditional schools and schools developing along parallel lines should not work independently of each other but should have a complementary influence. To achieve this, teachers need not become mass-media experts; they only need to be able to appreciate the influence of these media on traditional schools, to acquire an increasing understanding of the educational capacity of the mass media and to use that understanding in their practical teaching.

Integrated approaches

Norway: critical consciousness and effective communication

Asle Gire Dahl

Media growth over the past few years has been formidable. All forms of media have increased their fare, and the turnover of transistor radios, video-recorders, micro-computers, cassettes and magazines is constantly reaching new heights. Some say that this is only the beginning of the second media revolution. The prognoses suggest that within the turn of the millennium there will be forty television satellites in Europe alone. This expansion of the culture industry will in the long run broaden the media's capacity for influence, and lead to a greater internationalizing of its content. The pressure from the media-conveyed culture has led to a greater consumption among most age-groups, and to other changes in media habits.

The need for media upbringing seems to be more important than ever. Progress has destroyed monopolies, threatened ideologies, shaken patterns of authority, turned both young and old into involuntary media consumers, and created a magnetic field in the socializing process which was unknown to previous generations. Yet, if the individual citizen is still to be able to digest impressions from the messages of the media, he needs a basis for evaluation. This basis must come from upbringing. Such a pedagogic challenge must be taken up by cultural institutions as well as the authorities, but the major responsibility lies in the home. The latter is the consumer arena where the criteria for right and wrong in our relationship to the media are formed. The adult generation perhaps lacks the requirements necessary for establishing criteria. It does not have any more of a conscious relationship to the media than does the younger generation. Many parents have fallen behind in current events and often see television and comics as the lesser of many evils to which children are exposed. Media politics at home give children a specific attitude towards the mass media. Already, the conflicts of authority seem obvious. What sort of magazines should be left lying about? Who decides whether or not the television should be turned off, or changed to another channel? How loud should the radio or stereo be when other family members wish to talk? Such questions sound trivial. But if parents do not have the authority to answer them, how can they bring up their children?

Schools' contribution to media education

Schools were for a long time passive in their relationship to the mass media. That is why they were at a disadvantage in terms of experience and authority in counselling parents about practical or pedagogical media questions. They still have a supplementary role to play, first in bringing up the topic at parent-teacher meetings and in other local forums, and, second, in consciousness-raising efforts with camera clubs, libraries, women's clubs, etc.

Both the school and the home can offer children clearing-up sessions; in other words, time for follow-up work in conjunction with media consumption. Children often retain a great deal of undigested impressions from television, radio or comics, and it is therefore necessary to clear things up in which frightening or violent scenes are brought into the light; the inexplicable is explained, and one tries to draw moral conclusions. Such an exercise can only be accomplished by giving children information about the ideas behind the programme, explanation of foreign words and information about the special effects such as lighting and camera angles. It is also favourable to create discussion situations concerning those experiences each individual receives from the programme and its message. Here, the teacher and student, parent and child can meet on common ground by talking about their own experiences so that the distance between the individual and the media is established, a distance which gives everyone the opportunity to make independent decisions in relationship to them.

The schools' most important contribution to media education is nevertheless to offer pupils a systematic introduction to the world of the media. Up to the last few years, this possibility has only been partially implemented. Now one can see that more and more schools are attacking their educational assignments with vigour. They wish to give their pupils a set of facts, attitudes and abilities which are the prerequisites for facing and understanding products from the cultural industry. An adult audience that demands more from, and discerns more concerning, the mass media can progress only by use of such means.

Aims for media education

It is often emphasized in didactics that you must have clear goals in order to know not only where you are headed, but also the path you will follow. What is the point of studying mass communications? What should the aim of such work in school be? These questions must be answered based on the national scholastic tradition, the age-group involved and the school's overall goals. It is always required that new subject areas help the school in realizing its general intentions. The study of curricula from many countries shows, nevertheless, that in spite of varying points of departure, there is a rather broad agreement on two aspects.[1]

THE CRITICAL IDEAL

The cultivation of a critical attitude towards the mass media is a goal that is formulated in many ways. The curriculum plan for Norwegian primary schools views such teaching as a necessity in order that the pupils can 'develop their ability to form remonstrative attitudes towards suggestive influences, whether these are from their nearest circle or from the mass media'.[2] The idea here then is to lead pupils to a definable attitude of protection where they can question both media coverage and their own media habits. People of the 1980s are going to be overwhelmed by information and entertainment many hours a day. This current inevitably involves a false sense of proportion, hidden conflicts, and norms which do not fit very well with those that the school and the home try to espouse. Perhaps the most serious problem for many is that the media replace personal experiences and activities with second-hand consumer goods. The critical student reflects on roles, values and arguments in the media as a force of habit. Such a student has put a psychological distance between himself and the media, knowing that they are only surrogates. But this does not prevent identification with the leading character in a film, or participation in detective-inspired games. Living like superman, or thinking like the rock-music idol, however, provides no temptation. They can be enjoyed for what they are. In a sea of impressions, the critical student manages to resist the pressure to conform and remains able to form independent opinions on the material at hand.

THE COMMUNICATIVE IDEAL

The strengthening of pupils' ability to express themselves through different media is also an important educational goal. This ideal represents a fundamental role change for pupils: working with the mass media puts them in the broadcaster's booth. They can see for themselves what challenges the production process offers. The course of putting together a radio programme, for example, can say a lot about just what coincidences can mean for the finished product, and what team-work is all about. In addition, they will notice that their friends do not always interpret the programme's message as it was planned.

The argument for this goal is both social and political. Allowing pupils to develop their own message serves a general pedagogic purpose by having them practise presenting themselves to other people both in and out of their own milieu, something which is not deemed so very important in the traditional classroom situation. It also stimulates non-verbal communication. Cine cameras, tape-recorders, video and offset machines are fast becoming common fare in many schools. This machine menagerie is tempting, so long as pupils are exposed to the composition of pictures and sound, drama and mime. This goal is also a reaction to the mass media's élitist one-way character. It is rather odd that in a democracy only a tiny percentage of the population write books or produce newspapers and magazines, and even fewer get a chance to work in television or radio. If the desire is for discussion on a broad basis throughout society, possibilities for others than the purely professional to have a say must be found. Instruction in the use of media equipment will be an important step in the direction of saving local and national culture from disintegration.

What chance do the schools have for fostering critical and communicative pupils? Even though the realization of these goals lies in the future, schools can provide important requisites for achieving them. They can give a factual foundation, skill-training and stimulation of a conscious relationship and attitude to the media. Concrete objectives must be deduced from these points at the individual school, which can give the pupil a wide understanding of the process of mass communication, its goals and effects. Without such demands, mass-media teaching will be merely scraping the surface, providing a non-binding orientation about day-to-day happenings.

Variation in media education

The concept of media education functions today as an umbrella covering various educational forms, with different emphases on individual media and different problems. Experiments are being carried out concerning content and methods, and many points of attack have been tried in the hope of reaching the goals that have been set. The proposals are based on fact, traditions, demands and intentions which change from country to country. It is therefore difficult to give a general description of just what is practised within the subject. I have instead elected to discuss the situation in Norway, which has a number of similarities with other European countries, but where special patterns have also been developed.

Teaching about the media is found at practically all levels of the Norwegian school system. For the sake of clarity, I will concentrate on 12- to 18-year-olds, for whom the most has been done in the past few years. These pupils are offered two types of education on the subject, the integrated obligatory type, and later, special elective courses.

INTEGRATED EDUCATION

Traditional media education usually takes place as a part of social studies, art or mother-tongue education. Integration spanning all subjects is a principle which is meant to provide a meaningful and holistic exposure to the material. Such units can be termed, 'communication and the mass media', 'from handwriting to communication in our time' or 'media influence'. Such teaching does not present a holistic view of the subject. The term 'mass media' is used, but a great deal of time goes to presenting the film industry, radio, television and the press separately. New presentations and advertising are examined. Information concerning the national media structure is also presented, and the media's role in society especially is brought forward. The wider context can nevertheless be perceived in so far as the media make up greater wholes, for example the history of printing or great inventions.

The theoretical basis for education is first and foremost the teacher's general knowledge. Textbooks offer a certain support with chapters on the press, broadcasting and the cinema, and additional theory on the subject. This makes evaluation possible, but it will be an evaluation on the premises of the traditional subject.

Integrated education is offered on the whole in primary school (third to sixth grade). Exposure is most often gradual along with current-event orientations in which the material at hand is connected to the individual information about it. The problem with this form of organization is that there is no way of calculating the time spent on the subject. The entire subject is constantly under pressure from other subjects. When a teacher works out what ought to be covered, mass media are likely to end up at the bottom of the list. Hence the instruction becomes fragmentary. There is good reason to fear that the pupils' perception of the characteristics of the mass media becomes the exception and not the rule. Therefore, integrated education can not be said to satisfy the demands for fundamental media teaching for all pupils.

SPECIAL COURSES

Pupils can choose individual courses dealing with the media from fourth grade all the way up to college. The usual course is two hours a week (on the average, sixty hours per year). During the school year 1979/80, 46 per cent of all secondary schools offered such courses, mostly for eighth and ninth grades. The most common form consisted of individual media courses, with most having official course descriptions.

The oldest and most widespread of these is photography. Here pupils work mostly with camera technique, subject-matter, composition, and the developing and enlarging of photographs. The work is time-consuming and demands precision. The main emphasis is on the technical side of photography, and a holistic view is found only in the process cycle: taking the picture, developing the film, enlarging and cropping the prints, and mounting them for exhibition. The course seems to lack a theoretical foundation in terms of the mass media, but there are vast stores of handbook knowledge about photography. The pupils are quite active during these classes, but they do not get much training in saying something with their pictures. Visual mass communication is also left in the background.

Behind the course title, 'Newspaper', one seldom finds a study of the press as such, but rather the school newspaper. The pupils join in with one or more of the teachers in producing the school newspaper, as an extension of a short or long local tradition. The emphasis in this work is on the collection of material and the writing of articles, but lay-out and printing are also important parts of the activity. The finished product is inspired by the local newspaper, the office of which the class has probably visited in the course of their studies. But the school paper is only distributed to a few, and has more the character of a humoristic rather than a news-oriented endeavour. The editorial responsibility is set down in the rules depending on the type of school. The remaining theoretical basis can vary greatly, and there is much trial and error. Together with the usual uncertainty about the data of issue, these aspects can give the work a feeling of 'printed matter' production rather than of mass communication in the school environment.

The study of film is less widespread. It is based on film analysis, and/or the production of super-8 mm films. In both cases, knowledge of the elements of film and a little film history are included. The courses have a holistic view of the media, as forms of communication and as forms of art. Filming and the evaluation of amateur as well as professional products provide the pupils with some of the picture. None the less the somewhat one-sided concentration on the technical side of filming can often obscure the mass-media context.

Television courses are just beginning and are seldom offered. Evaluation of programmes is attempted. Also some classes use portable video equipment for making their own short segments in the same way as with film.

These special courses have concrete goals which guide them in their work with a specific medium. The idea is to be able to handle equipment and particular working processes. Quality evaluation is seldom undertaken. They must be seen as forming a group nevertheless, because they all use media techniques in order to make something concrete. They can to an extent be compared to arts-and-crafts courses, and fit into a hobby perspective. They give pupils the ability to continue with similar products in the future, and can to a degree be seen as bringing out the pupils' creative impulses.

MEDIA INFORMATION

The subject is covered in a new type of course which received its official course description in 1974. It has the same resource framework as the other courses, but is unmistakably different as far as content is concerned. Courses are commonly begun with a little communications theory, in which vital terms such as transmitter, channel, message and influence are introduced. Next, work is done systematically with many different media. The teacher provides an overview of the media structure in Norway and much time is given to discussion of television programmes, advertising and pop culture. These classes become forums for discussing local radio and cable television, which are new phenomena in Norway. A mass-communication model can be said to make up the theoretical basis of the courses. Here, important characteristics which the different media have in common can be seen: the idea behind the message, the heavy-handed editing and influencing mechanisms that are used. In this way, students get a better picture of what the mass media really are and how they function. In the practical work, a certain emphasis is given to visual media and the press.

Media information consists of many components which are part of a more or less stable, integrated education. It is not aimed at any particular hobby, and therefore pupil participation is often more cognitive than manual. Pupils receive a broad view of the media world within a critically holistic perspective. They are encouraged to relate their own media experiences, and receive training in evaluating media content. Along with a study of the media institutions, the special course takes on the aspect of social studies. This course stands today as the best means for achieving those goals established for media upbringing, and great effort will be made in its further development.

Necessary teacher training

It has taken a long time for schools to begin teaching about the media. Little interest in the subject and a lack of equipment can explain a good deal; but the most serious hindrance to the expansion of media teaching appears to be teacher training. It does not help much that the course description gives official status to media information so long as the would-be teachers do not receive the didactical and methodological background necessary to do their job well. In many countries, the connection between poor media education and insufficient teacher training is clear.

Because there was no tradition for such training at the teachers' colleges in Norway, it was necessary to experiment. For the last ten years we have had a one-year programme in media pedagogy, mostly in order to satisfy the need for school librarians and assistants in the use of audio-visual equipment. The mass media have been a part of this programme, but greater emphasis has been put on integrating such media in the normal curriculum, rather than giving the students work in teaching about the media. Over the same period, there has existed a six-month programme in film in which films and personal productions are seen from an artistic perspective. At the university level, there is a one-year course in mass communications, basically of a sociological character, and there are also possibilities for taking an MA degree in pictorial pedagogy in the areas of drama, film and theatre.

What these studies have in common is that they are higher-education programes with minimal enrolment capacity. It has therefore been necessary to develop a type of media education on a more elementary and general level with room for more students.

The most radical pilot project up to now is called Media Acknowledgement. It is run by night-school organizations in conjunction with a correspondence school and a regional college. It is designed for teachers, public-relations people, those in business and industry, and organization chairmen; in short, adults who are to inform others about the media, or who are involved with the media in a a professional capacity.

The course is initially designed to give a general view of forms of communication and media, so the participants can form a holistic impression of the media's limitations and possibilities as a means of information and contact between people.

The programme combines correspondence-school work and upper-level work in the classroom. It is made up of two half-year courses which can be terminated by an examination giving some sort of certification. Altogether it will take two years to complete the study. It has been said that most of the students want to go on further in their training, though they have to work under pressure because most of the training takes place during the evening, and most of the students teach in their own schools during the day. On the other hand, they can use what they learn in the evening in their daily work.

The programme also provides the opportunity during the second year to specialize in one of the main subjects if the student reads about 1,000 pages of literature by himself. Each half-year course consists of 150 school lectures, one practice teaching assignment and answering of correspondence, thirty letters in all. To date, there have been primary courses in between sixteen and twenty different locations with groups ranging from twelve to forty. Both the training and the examination take place at the course centre, saving money which can then be used for the practical media work.

The results have been positive and it appears that most of the students wished to take the second-year course. This level was therefore tried for the first time in 1982. It consists mainly of students from the primary courses, although anyone else with the same background could take part.

This pilot project aims at offering a flexible model that can stimulate individual study where media consumption is at its highest: in private homes. Teachers can try out their qualifications on members of their family and in discussions with their colleagues and pupils. They have to discuss many of the letters with the local teachers at work before answering them. In the production assignment, the course stimulates debate between colleagues and participation in local mass communication, which can get the individual out of the traditional role of consumer.

Innovation problems in a new field

Even though we in Norway have got over the early phases in the field, it would be expecting too much to think that the field of information has already reached its goals and is totally problem-free. The lack of tradition and experience often leads to uncertainty, and a number of schools have started eagerly on the projects only to abolish the entire programme a year later. Continued progress is therefore dependent on work with course-planning theory and subject didactics that can improve the quality of media information. I would like to point out three things of a general character in this context, which all planners must solve if they are to succeed in introducing mass-media education on a broad basis.

SELECTION OF SUBJECT-MATTER

Schools base their curriculum on more or less clearly defined aspects of the common culture. Mass communication is a meaningful cultural phenomenon in many countries. Additionally, it is often an industry with increasing impact on society. Therefore the authorities expect schools to make it a part of their curriculum. But questions arise as to what is to be studied, what we want to know about the subject, and what reflection of culture is expected to be provided by the schools.

We must remember that the school day is quite short. Only a fraction of those questions can be covered. What shall then be selected? The answer to the question of content involves taking into consideration: (a) knowledge of the media and profession; (b) goals to be achieved; (c) pupils' needs and interests; and (d) local resources. I am not about to set up a curriculum which demands pattern applicability. Others have already made valid efforts.[3] I am simply pointing out certain aspects which ought to be considered when forming a syllabus, whether it be prepared for local or national level.

A number of school subjects have a basis of collected knowledge and capabilities in the environment where the subject is reviewed. In our case, this review occurs within research and the media industry. In particular, there are three elements of this foundation which influence course content. The most obvious of them is the terminology. Terms such as 'transistor radio', 'editor' and 'advertising' have become part of people's everyday language. To teach without using the names of equipment, processes and professions within the field is impossible in the long run. If the words are first chosen, they must of course be explained; something which draws the subject and examples along and in that way fills the period with content. The media's subject categories often decide the division of material for teaching. Films have genres such as westerns and horror pictures. Newspapers have set space for the leader and advertisements. Radio programmes broadcast news and television offers entertainment extravaganzas. These categories must to a certain extent be followed in the course structure so that it remains clear. Planners take points of view from research, which is reflected somewhat in the textbooks and which says what the experts feel is important when studying the media. What do we do with the mass media? What does it do with us? These are questions that can provide many interesting hours of work in the classroom.

THE GOALS

Aims for the course describe a conceived, desirable situation. As intimated earlier, they are so broad and general that it is necessary to expand their meaning and reformulate them into specifically local goals. If this effort is not made, the goals' influence on the teaching will be minimal.

THE PUPILS' NEEDS

To ignore the interests of the pupils in planning is the same as losing a motivating power, and thereby risking that little or nothing is learned. But such wishes and needs change rapidly and diverge in many directions. What should be the deciding factor? Age-determined characteristics in terms of media habits and subject preference ought here to be the decisive factors. They make a rough, beforehand judgement possible. Among the youngest, comic strips and television are preferred. Young children like fiction, while they do not care much for the news. During adolescence, teenagers listen to a lot more pop music than they used to and television is used more selectively; interest in films grows. This sort of information can tell the teacher a good deal about what media material would be most appropriate for use in class. Other more concrete desires will turn up in the course of the year and the programme can be appropriately adjusted.

RESOURCES

An important consideration which is seldom mentioned is the local supply of school time, classrooms, equipment, material and teachers. These are factors that can limit the choice of course content, something which again forces the programme to be narrowed down, superficial or largely theoretical. Lack of equipment has usually been the largest problem, but such courses do not need advanced technology. It appears that what is more important is whether or not the teacher has the know-how and whether or not there is enough time available.

Curriculum planning for mass-media teaching is often characterized by chance, something that accounts for plentiful variation in course content. If we are to hope to be able to put together information about the media in a way that both meets professional standards and at the same time is comprehensible to the pupils, these major considerations must be taken more fully into account. The teachers responsible ought to do so on their own; they cannot rely on textbooks alone.

MEDIA-SPECIFIC METHODS

To be selective and analytic, to be able to compose and deliver a message are all skills that are difficult to teach in the traditional way. They must be learned by the individual pupil. The pupil must display a critical attitude and formulate a concrete message. The school is placed in a new position, where one cannot expect to transfer the old ways of working. What is necessary are media-specific methods, which are not to be found without experimenting. Belief in method neutrality has meant that the point is neglected. But traditional assignments, themes and drawing problems ought to be exchanged for methods that are compatible with controversial material: content analysis, manuscript writing, collages and wall newspapers.

One senses strongly in this area the influence of professional ideals. Media research spent a long time using the Laswell formula for analysis (which asks What, to whom, on which channel, with what intent and what effect?). Masterman bases his work on the idea that the media are active formulators of opinion,[4] but he is nevertheless sceptical about studies of power and control for the very young. Even though many teachers seem to be very concerned about just these things, pupils have a difficult time following them. Here, the teacher can ask questions that guide interest: What sort of feelings did the film stimulate? What message was made by the story? How realistic was the film? Are there connections between it and your own life? Why are so many emphatic words and exclamation points used in this article?

The study of norm transmission is also a form of content analysis. Comic strips are an excellent practice material. We can study 'heroes' and 'bad-guys' and make collages of their images. What sort of values does the hero stand for? Which moralistic conclusions can be drawn from the story? If pupils can answer such questions, they will be on the way to becoming more conscious of the influences to which they are subjected.

During the formulation of the message, it is easy to imitate professionals and use their quality criteria for evaluation of the results. Such an exercise is not recommended for school work with the media; creative processes and personal experiences are at least as important. Journalistic techniques of reduction and exaggeration have received much critical attention in the last few years, and it is an open question whether or not this sort of media twisting ought to be held up as the norm for work in the classroom. It is probably more appropriate to let the pupils try out the channels of communication on their own premises. This activity ought not be too closely tied to language gymnastics or advanced techniques.

A tape-recorder is a simple aid which is appropriate for as important a media form as the interview; people with special knowledge can be interviewed. An interview can paint a portrait by means of the calm atmosphere of the discussion. In both instances, the pupils must divide the assignments among themselves and put together a recording manuscript. There it is decided who is to be interviewed, where the interview is to take place, necessary noise-reduction and, especially, the formulation of short, concise questions. Later work will include editing, addition of music and choosing an appropriate title.

As a result of the usual school work, many pupils are tired of concentrating on others' knowledge and abilities. They would rather collect and evaluate their own encounters with the media. The workbook satisfies their need for individual study, while it can also stimulate class discussions. It provides an opportunity for ascertaining and systematizing the flood of information about and in the media. It compensates to a degree for the lack of a textbook. The workbook, preferably a loose-leaf notebook, becomes a personal documentation of the course which the pupil can use for many years. Film and television reviews and personal comments on the same theme can be put together in the workbook. New issues of the school newspaper can also be put in it.

The work in the classroom must have the atmosphere of pedagogically planned media-play that corresponds to the pupils' visual world and their cognitive development. The goal must be to bring them away from the accustomed role of viewer/receiver and lead them towards an analytic and active relationship to the media. There is a lot of trial and error yet to come before the goal is reached.

The general problems mentioned here are tied to concrete education, which must be considered to be in the preliminary phases. Enthusiasm for the subject is undeniable, but unless mass-media education assimilates a well-founded subject matter and an appropriate methodology in the course of a few years, there is a danger that schools will be saddled with a new subject with fragmentary material and traditional control-mechanisms which neither increase understanding of communication nor stimulate further expansion of the subject.

Organization

When things are well under way, difficulties as to structure and continuity begin to appear. Many children arrive for their first day of school as experienced media consumers with many thousands of hours of television watching, film going, and comic reading under their belts. Therefore the subject of the media ought to be taken up as soon as possible. Starting with an informal presentation, the teacher can progress into more systematic teaching in the course of primary school, gradually replacing the elementary material with material of deeper character during secondary education. Media information cannot be totally dealt within the course of a school year. If pupils have had special courses over a few years, and wish to continue with media studies at a higher level, the question of subject-matter arises. In order to avoid boring repetition, the material must be spread out over the different grades, with a progression that fits the increasing difficulty in other school subjects. Planning by the central school authorities is required. They must see to it that media information is given a coherent structure through the formulation of yearly guidelines. There can be a different theme each year in which the title draws attention to the main points of the course. The amount of work must be evaluated in relationship to pupils' abilities and the time available for the subject; for example, an average of two hours a week. Such plans can never be detailed: the local control of content and assignment selection must not disappear.

Complete knowledge about the media cannot be easily taught in any logical order. To provide a structure and secure continuity will be a question of discretion and co-ordination with the official course descriptions in the other subjects. The result might be the following list of subjects from third grade all the way up to the college level: (a) identification of the field; (b) presentation of the major media; (c) the eye of the journalist: observation and presentation; (d) systematic review of the media institutions; (e) how the media have made the world smaller; (f) what is meant by communication; (g) the media's means of action; (h) entertaining the masses: the language of the media; (i) the media in local society; and (j) the processing of information.

This sort of overview will provide for a more systematic way of working and will ease test-courses enormously. It can also be a guideline for publishers of educational aids and for broadcasting companies wishing to produce their own material on the subject. It also makes it possible for planners to decide which terms are to be introduced and in what order. One thereby provides continuity in the pupils' comprehension while building up an understanding of important aspects of the subject material corresponding to their own level of maturity.

Teaching about the media is no fad, though fads are often found in teaching. It is a constructive answer to technological and cultural challenges in the world today. Although this sort of work is only beginning in most countries, and many problems remain to be solved, the education that is presented here is fundamentally important. It is the beginning of a continual formulation process that makes it possible to keep in step with development within the field of the media.

Notes

1. A. Gire Dahl, *Mediakunnskap-laereplanteori for et nytt fag,* Oslo, 1982.
2. *Mønsterplan for grunnskolen*, pp. 13–14, Oslo, KUD.
3. S. Minkkinen, *A General Curricular Model for Mass Media Education,* Paris, Unesco, 1978.
4. Len Masterman, *Teaching About Television,* London, Macmillan, 1980.

The canton of Fribourg: media education from primary through secondary school

Gérald Berger

Switzerland is a confederation of twenty-six states known as cantons, which are sovereign in the domain of public education. This particular situation affects the problem discussed here in two important ways. In the first place, the government of each canton develops its own educational policy in accordance with its specific cultural, linguistic and even religious traditions. Integrated experiments in education, sometimes of considerable originality, may thus be found within a single Swiss canton, as in the case of media education in the canton of Fribourg. Secondly, the school-age population in each canton, large or small, is relatively limited. In Fribourg, for example, there are 29,000 pupils. It is, then, a relatively simple matter to introduce new courses with some flexibility, to monitor successive stages very closely and change direction if necessary. In view of the fact that in the canton of Fribourg there are in all 600 primary-school and 800 secondary-school teachers, it is quite feasible for the canton's Chief Education Officer to maintain direct personal contact with the teachers concerned. These particular factors have played a not inconsiderable role in the introduction of integrated media education courses in the canton of Fribourg.

Origins

Early in the 1960s a group of Fribourg teachers got together in order to work in the area of film education. They were aware of the psychological impact of the cinema on their pupils, and they wished to take advantage of the cultural and educational potential of the seventh art. Accordingly, they organized film presentation programmes in schools. Each year they would choose a number of feature films and show them to the various classes. After each showing there was a discussion under the guidance of the teacher. The group approached a number of Catholic academics in France (notably Henri Agel) and Belgium, and asked them for help in developing the programme. The outcome was that courses in film education were introduced in several schools. These courses, while unofficial, were accepted by the school authorities. From its grass-roots origins, the movement soon spread. On the strength of their success, the originators decided to ask the canton's Department of Public Education to give the experiment official status. In 1965 a committee was established for the purpose of setting up the necessary official educational structures. By 1967 Fribourg had become the first Swiss canton to establish a film education programme designed not only for primary schools but also for lower and upper secondary schools. This programme provided for weekly sessions throughout the entire duration of the compulsory school-attendance period. Before long, however, the programme organizers began to encounter difficulties which ultimately led to the suspension of the experiment. The partial failure of this initial attempt at integration may be attributed to several causes. In the first place, the organizers were not in a position to provide teachers with training while, secondly, the programmes were too general and really amounted to little more than lists of vague recommendations, and lastly, and perhaps most important of all, the grammar of film which was the basis of these programmes disappointed both teachers and pupils.

Strategy in lower secondary education

In 1975 the entire problem was considered afresh. The Department of Public Education established the Centre d'Initiation aux Mass-Média (CIMM) and gave it the task of re-examining the issue. The centre spent its first two years considering and drawing lessons from the successful and unsuccessful aspects of the previous experiment. In the end, the following strategy was framed. Instead of imposing a ready-made programme and ready-made structures, use was made first of all of the potential of the teachers, who formed the basic resource. A number of teachers were showing interest in this educational endeavour, so they were invited to join in the work of the centre and, together, a number of basic methodological approaches were worked out. For a year the teachers tried out these approaches, with the approval of their school principals, and student response to this type of work was highly positive. Encouraged by this promising start, the centre continued to develop its work, with the result that two years later a coherent methodology had been produced. This was perfected and tried out in schools in both rural and urban areas, and in both the long-course programme (for students intending to go on to university) and the terminal-course programme (for students intending to take vocational training).

During this experimental phase, encouraging comments from students aroused the curiosity of teachers who had initially regarded the work of the Centre with suspicion. They asked, during the experiment, whether they too might join the group. The initiative, like its predecessor, was making a progressively wider impact. In due course several school principals visited classrooms and were surprised at the quality of the work being done.

It was at this crucial moment that the Centre decided that the time was ripe to approach the senior education officers. In the course of several meetings, at which discussions sometimes proved delicate, it was agreed that the method would be tried out for one year in all schools at the lower-secondary level (*cycle d'orientation*, ages 12–15). A decision would be reached subsequently.

The earlier experiment had shown that it was necessary to adopt a grass-roots approach, starting at the source and creating the necessary conditions to enable what amounted to a process of spontaneous generation to take place in widely different educational environments. In 1979, the official introduction of this course was approved.

Training of secondary-school teachers

An essential phase in the establishment of any educational process is the training of the teachers. In a period when in-service training courses abound, the difficulty tends to be as much psychological in nature as it is educational or financial. Here also it was important to work out a suitable strategy. The centre decided to rely entirely on a voluntary approach. The first trainees and those who came after them were all trained during their vacation periods by means of one week of intensive work. The holding of this one-week in-service training course every year since 1976, has enabled a relatively large number of teachers to be trained over the seven-year period. These courses are organized by the person responsible for the administration of the centre. Accordingly, the same person undertook to negotiate with the official bodies and senior education officers concerned to secure the acceptance and subsequently the integration of the experiment.

The decision to adopt a voluntary approach was of critical importance. Given the method used, a teacher who, whether he or she liked it or not, was obliged to give media education courses would certainly risk failure, for the student-teacher relationship might well prove difficult. In addition, the gradual spreading effect would not have occurred with a large-scale training scheme, so that the psychological advantages of that effect would have been lost. A voluntary approach also made it essential for those in charge of the experiment to tread very carefully in seeking to have the courses accepted in the schools.

The process of integration proceeded in concentric circles, with the result that at every stage it was possible to make adjustments to fit particular situations.

The fact that the same person was in charge of both training and relations with the authorities was important as well. As he was personally acquainted with all the prospective teachers and also constantly in touch with the actual classroom situation, he was well placed to detect potential conflicts during the process of negotiating with the political and educational authorities the details of the structural, financial and administrative integration of the media education experiment.

It was decided not to include any systematically presented theoretical or technical information about the media in the training programme. During their thirty-five hours of training, the teachers are placed in practical situations. The practical work and exercises that the students are required to do are presented just as they are, and are gone over with the teachers. This is a highly effective method of preparing them to overcome the difficulties they will encounter in the classroom. The problems of group dynamics, leadership phenomena and the difficulty of accepting a variety of opinions arise in exactly the same fashion. After training is completed, the course director attends a few of each teacher's classes, with the consent of the teacher concerned. This allows the director to assess the effectiveness of the method under actual working conditions, and it provides the teacher with an opportunity to make comments or ask for advice, if he wishes.

After they have finished their training, the teachers may continue to keep in touch with the Centre d'Initiation aux Mass-Média through additional sessions in various fields which the latter organizes each year. Every teacher is free to attend these sessions or not, as he or she may see fit.

General objectives

An effort was made to ensure that training was based on objectives and a method that were acceptable, without excessive conflict, to both students and teachers. It had been necessary to recognize that the students (and the Centre) had rejected the grammar of film. In addition, the audio-visual media explosion of the early 1970s had given a boundless horizon to the field of investigation. Lastly, the work of Roland Barthes in the area of semiology and that of Jean Piaget in phenomenology called for reconsideration of the entire issue. This task was carried out jointly with the original group of initiators, consisting almost entirely of people trained in the grammar of film. Before objectives and methods were established, experiments under way at the time were, of course, reviewed, and a great deal is owed to the work of the Institut de la Communication Audio-Visuelle (ICAV) in Bordeaux, and the Ligue Française de l'Enseignement et de l'Éducation Permanente in Paris.

Teachers have long thought of the media in terms of rivalry. They have seen in them a form of parallel schooling, largely beyond their control and tending to promote a mosaic image of culture at the expense of the analytical reasoning and logical process so dear to the hearts of traditional educationists. However, attitudes have gradually changed, and the audio-visual media, as teaching aids, have become omnipresent in the school environment. These media, with their stress on image and sound, are of the greatest interest to the world of education. They are characterized by the special faculty of faithfully reproducing whatever they record. Hence the child viewer establishes a relationship with them more sensual than intellectual, seeking in the image a source of pleasure. The use of the audio-visual media in the school environment has resulted in some degree of educational ambiguity, an effect which has been intensified by the proliferation and expansion of educational bodies that produce audio-visual aids and programmes. When it uses images and sounds for the purposes of instruction, the school unfortunately tends to eliminate the pleasurable aspect, either by selecting images that are unsatisfactory from an aesthetic standpoint or by arbitrarily placing stress on one meaning at the expense of the others.

Even when they are made part of the school environment, images and sounds should continue to be a source of pleasure and arouse a subjective response. Consequently, audio-visual messages that are rich in meaning cannot be confined within a system of methods that would inhibit, by an arsenal of procedures, the free reading of the message.

The mass media create forms of language that are clearly distinguishable from those resulting from the culture of the written word. In addition, they sometimes assume a greater place than real-life relationships and practical activities. The changes brought about by modern communication media have a sociological and linguistic impact first and foremost. And, as we know, the learning of social behaviour in conjunction with language activities is one of the basic functions of education.

In the light of this analysis, a series of general objectives have been worked out which may be summed up in two words: understanding and action:

Media education should make pupils something more than passive receivers of messages. They should understand that they are experiencing a communication process in which they too can play an active part.

Pupils should understand how multiple meanings result from the nature of the audio-visual message. In this way they will become aware of the formulae governing the devising of certain messages, while at the same time they will experience the density of expression that allows the meaning to emerge in other messages.

By encouraging the production of audio-visual messages by the pupils themselves, media education will enable them to become actors within the audio-visual communication process.

Specific teaching approaches

One dubious distinction of conventional education is that old teaching methods are sometimes applied to new educational objectives. Having regard to the objectives that had been decided upon, media education courses could not simply be added to the traditional curriculum. It was thus necessary to propose specific types of approaches for the benefit of teachers:

- A child is an individual whose view of the world is not identical with an adult's, especially in the case of visual images. The teacher should therefore accept the polysemous nature of such images.
- When teacher and pupil are discussing an audio-visual message, they find themselves on the same footing in that both of them are unavoidably compelled to proceed by way of the document in order to express themselves. The teacher should respect this equal relationship. Such unmediated contact between the pupil and the audio-visual document represents a break with the traditional approach whereby the teacher precedes the pupil in interpreting the message or else stands between pupil and message. In due course the pupil will spontaneously ask the teacher to provide further explanation.
- It is very frequent to find that pupils have difficulty at first in spontaneously expressing their feelings about an audio-visual document. Because of the leadership phenomenon, only two or three interpretations will be provided in class, almost invariably from the same individuals. In order to enable the shyer pupils to participate, the teacher should begin by asking the class to give their views in writing. Each pupil writes down his or her interpretation, briefly, and the various replies are then gone through. At this stage, each pupil supports his or her position by referring to elements in the audio-visual document itself, which everyone in the class has seen and heard. Accordingly, no pupil's response will be dismissed out of hand as ridiculous or obviously wrong. All the pupils are doing here is making natural use of the polysemous nature of the document, or unconsciously criticizing its inadequacy of expressiveness.
- The impromptu reading of an audio-visual document, that is, with no prior preparation, will enable pupils to discover

possibilities of expression that would be prevented by a more organized presentation in which they are told what to watch for. After extracting as much meaning from the document as possible, a child will naturally feel the need to systematize and rank-order the interpretations he has discovered.

As the course also endeavours to teach pupils to seek something more than experience at second hand, direct experience should be encouraged through the use of documents brought in by the children themselves and through individual or group production of audio-visual documents.

Methods

Several strategies were tried out before a decision was reached. The initial idea was to have one hour of media education inserted into the timetable on a completely independent basis. This experiment was tried out and then dropped, as it would have encouraged the proliferation of new teaching posts for specialists in media education, and a specialist would probably teach 'media' to several different classes on the basis of one hour per week. This would mean that contact with his classes would not be sufficiently regular and continuous, and hence would be more difficult to establish. In addition, the teacher would know his pupils only through that single course, and this would mean that media education would not be firmly rooted in the day-to-day experience of the class. In any case, specialists tend to speak a language characterized by esoteric jargon.

Ideally, media education should be taught as a component of every subject in the curriculum. For the time being, at any rate, this strategy is quite unrealistic. It would require every teacher in the school to undergo retraining, and it would make it necessary to work out methodological adjustments in already overloaded curricula designed along quite different lines. Experience showed that the result was a process of dispersion, with the pupils failing to learn how to handle the critical tools placed at their disposal. The various constraints affecting the preparation of curricula and timetables at present, especially at the secondary level, make it difficult to achieve large-scale interdisciplinarity.

The final choice was a compromise solution that included the desirable features of both the above methods. If media education is to produce worthwhile results within the context of the present school system, it must be organized on the basis of two complementary phases.

INTRODUCTORY PHASE

Initially (that is, during the first year), the media education course enables pupils to acquire a certain quantity of factual data, which are presented through the specific types of teaching approaches referred to above. In order to make sure that media education will be firmly rooted in the day-to-day experience of the class, it is coupled with one of the subjects of the regular curriculum. In view of the socio-linguistic objectives of media education, it was felt that the subject which would be most appropriate for this procedure was French (the children's mother tongue). Once a week, always during the same class period, expressly set aside for the purpose, the French teacher takes the media education class. The fact that the French textbooks used refer on occasion to the media helps to reinforce the lession during the rest of the week. Teachers and pupils are provided with a special kit of reference cards, slides, video recordings, etc., for the purpose of this activity.

CRYSTALLIZATION PHASE

During the following two years of the *cycle d'orientation* (lower secondary level, ages 13–15), media education should move out of its introductory phase. Students should learn how to look with a critical eye at the various audio-visual messages associated with particular subjects. At this stage there is no need to set aside a class period exclusively for media education: it may be brought in as the need arises, depending on the subject and the teacher. A number of means are currently emerging that will ensure that this crystallization phase remains real and meaningful. In the first place, contact between students and teachers who have been through the introductory phase necessarily continues during subsequent school years, depending on the timetable, and the habits that have been acquired at an earlier stage are deep-rooted. In the second place, the same students naturally apply the critical skills they have acquired when studying history, civics, etc., in subsequent years. In many instances, they initiate a discussion with the teacher on the real meaning of a document. Lastly, there are plans to organize teacher-training courses in the very near future for subjects not included in the introductory phase (that is, all subjects except French). Here again, a voluntary approach will be used. The aim will be to show teachers how to adopt a critical approach with their classes in response to a supporting audio-visual document, without, however, losing sight of the specific purpose of the course (for example, the study of history). It is expected that in the course of time a considerable number of teachers will be able to receive in-service training in this way. The crystallization phase will then come fully into effect, and media education will take its place as a normal part of school activities.

Programme

A clearly structured programme was developed only for the introductory phase. As for its content, there was a brief moment of hesitation. Should a number of possible approaches simply be suggested (complete with accompanying documents) or should a detailed programme be worked out? The former solution had the advantage of giving full scope to the class and teacher in organizing the introduction to media education in accordance with their own particular criteria, whereas the latter involved the potential danger of an excessively academic approach. Despite the inherent risks, the choice fell, with no regrets, on the detailed programme. In the first place, by clearly explaining to the teachers during their training what types of specific teaching methods were called for, we were able to reduce the potential danger of an excessively academic approach. In the second place, there was obviously no question of adopting any marking system for the subject. Difficulties were encountered here for this was a precedent that frightened some educational administrators. The decision to develop a structured programme was taken in response to the very reasonable preference expressed by the teachers themselves. Virtually all of them were afraid that they might be unequal to the task of teaching such an unusual subject. Their already fairly heavy workloads (twenty-six teaching hours a week) meant that they could not devote a vast amount of care and attention to the preparation of every media education lesson. The programme comprised three essential segments: (a) the media; (b) how to read an image; and (c) connotation processes.

Within each of these segments, there are a number of sequences that may be tackled either together or separately. The students have sixty unnumbered exercise cards that can be organized in any way the teacher wishes. There are three different but complementary approaches for use with each sequence:

The intuitive approach, which enables some property of the media to be discovered through play activity.

The practical approach, which enables pupils to create a message relating to the sequence.

The theoretical approach, which defines the sequence. No memory work is required. This approach is essential in order to mark out the ground that has been covered, and in addition it is useful for revision purposes when a class returns to a concept after being away from it for a week.

For each sequence, supplementary activities are suggested, and these are usually creative in nature. One of them should be particularly intensive. To deal with the programme as a whole, the teacher needs two terms (out of three). Thus he can set aside the equivalent of the class hours of the third term for the purposes of the intensive activity.

The overall objective of the segment on the media is to define the media and study their effects. Most of the sequences are linked with an approach to the printed message (the press). In the case of television, the course relies on educational television. (For example, every week the Swiss French-language television authority broadcasts media education programmes coproduced by the Departments of Education of the French-speaking cantons.) In the segment on how to read an image, pupils devote most of their efforts to reading advertising messages. They are also introduced to the concepts of denotation, connotation and connotation processes. The final segment reviews the various connotation processes (nine in all) through a large number of sequences which may be taken separately or in groups. In this segment the scope of the media education course is extended to artistic documents, as it was observed that the pupils quickly tire of advertising images. Artistic productions, in contrast, give them an opportunity to savour the richness of multiple meanings to the full, and enable them to discover images that differ from those that constitute their daily fare. Strip cartoons form the thread running through the study of connotation processes. Theoretical aspects and a number of practical exercises have been compiled and are presented in a book entitled *La Marque Jaune* (Jacobs), a copy of which is given to each student. Teachers will find some dozens of copies of other books of cartoons available at the centre for their use.

This segment also makes provision for learning how to view films. The centre has prepared a short film on the subject, with an accompanying montage sequence which has been distributed to all schools.

In addition to these two phases (introduction and crystallization), the students are given other forms of media education during their three years in the lower secondary school. The circulating film programme, that pioneering venture referred to at the beginning of this article, has been retained. Each year, the classes view three feature films within the context of their curriculum. The centre sends the prints round to the various schools. The task of selection is entrusted to a group of teachers, who organize a series of 'screening days'. Before and after the film is shown, the class is told something about it, and the students may discuss the film with their teacher.

The future outlook

Media education in the lower secondary school thus involves several complementary educational processes, of which the introductory phase is the most crucial. In 1982, this period was regarded as completed. A decision was taken at the outset against the adoption of any form of large-scale scientific evaluation, for it was realized from experience how seriously premature evaluation can inhibit a process, prevent an experiment from achieving its full development, and even block the thinking of initiators and teachers. The preferred method has consisted of informal evaluation carried out by means of visits to classrooms and interviews with senior education officials, teachers and students. In this way it has been possible to make any necessary adjustments unobtrusively and in all cases through personal contact. A more explicitly scientific form of evaluation is currently being prepared, with the idea of entrusting this to students preparing for a university degree in education.

If media education is to be a success in future, its objectives and methods must continuously be reviewed. This situation, of course, is related to the continuing development of the media, their forms of penetration and language, and changes in the perception of the receivers, who in this instance are the teachers and students. For this reason it is essential that responsibility for media education be entrusted to a specialized body. The Centre is now considering a project for the remodelling, in the very near future, of the course and the materials that it makes available to the schools as teaching aids. In brief, one experimental phase is about to be terminated in order to make way for another!

Primary level

Concurrently with the action taken at the lower secondary level, a form of media education has also been introduced in primary education (ages 7–12). At this level the fundamental situation is rather different: in the first place, each class has only one teacher (a generalist), and in the second place, the Centre is in constant contact with future primary-school teachers throughout their professional training.

TRAINING

From a psychological standpoint, it was essential for the Centre to be located in the heart of the institution where prospective primary-school teachers received their training, and this requirement was accordingly made clear at a very early stage. As a result, contact is established with students from the very beginning of their training. In addition, the Department of Education has entrusted the Centre with the task of providing them with training in the media, which extends over a period of two years. The student teachers are first given a general introduction to the media with a substantial degree of theoretical content (sociological aspects of the media, the semiology of images, etc.). Next, they become accustomed to the methodological implications of media education. No distinction is drawn between studying an image or newspaper article in a media education context and studying it as a teaching aid in some other subject. The object is to teach the student teacher to adopt, wherever possible, a critical attitude towards documents that he takes from the media and from educational documentation centres. He must respect the polysemous nature of the document, where this exists, and allow his future pupils to give expression to their sensitivity and their personal points of view wherever possible.

PROGRAMME

No provision is made for a structured programme during the first four years of primary school. A booklet is currently being prepared for distribution to all student teachers during training. It will contain a number of individual or group exercises which will give the pupils an opportunity to use various forms of communication, while also discussing the processes that give rise to them. It will be readily feasible to use these exercises in oral or written expression classes or in creative activities.

In 1981 a structured programme was introduced in the last two years of primary school (fifth and sixth years). This programme is more modest than its counterpart, at the lower secondary level, containing as it does only twenty-four teaching units in all, and it fits smoothly into the existing subjects (environment, arts education, language, etc.).

The initial group of exercises deals with the reading of images. The pupils are taught to understand the concepts of objectivity and subjectivity through pictures. They are then set to comparing the pictures they encounter in their environment (postcards in particular) with the reality of that environment. In a second group of exercises, the pupils learn at first hand how the meaning of a reporter's message may be altered by the sender, the transmitter and the receiver. The programmes of the French-language educational television service may be used as a source of supporting material in classrooms that are equipped with a video tape-recorder.

Upper secondary level

At the other end of the school system (preparation for the secondary-school leaving certificate) a number of specific activities have been undertaken which vary from one school to another. As a rule, issues related to semiology are handled by the French teacher as part of his task of developing his students' response to the world of language. At this educational level, efforts have been concentrated on the seventh art: each year, the students view several feature films dealing with a particular theme or set of themes. Each showing is an occasion for a lesson in film-reading. Here again, there are several possible types of supplementary activities: making Super-8 films, photo documentaries, video, etc. The question of whether a weekly media education course should be introduced is still under consideration. As the preparation of timetables at the upper secondary level falls within the jurisdiction of the federal authorities, it is relatively difficult to develop programmes at the level of a single canton. However, in view of the positions adopted by the federal commission on the media, as stated in the report reported by that body, the future can be faced with some degree of optimism.

Lifelong education

By the age of 16 students have finished the compulsory part of their education, and leave school in order to learn a trade or to go on to higher education. It is at this age that they are keenest on seeing films. Furthermore, viewers prefer to watch feature films shown on television. The appearance of cable television in Switzerland and the rise of video clubs are not likely to alter these preferences. It is clearer than ever that a cultural policy covering the field of film and designed for the public at large is required. Over five years ago, and using only the resources that were ready to hand, the centre introduced a cultural development programme designed for the general public and, with the co-operation of a cinema proprietor in the canton, CINEPLUS was launched. For a variety of reasons, many art and experimental films never reach Fribourg, and the aim was to motivate the potential audience for productions of that type. The centre assumed responsibility for this task, while the cinema proprietor contributed his technical and commercial facilities. The audience consisted, in the main, of very young people. Very soon the operation had to be decentralized. Today, CINEPLUS is pursuing its activities even in towns where there is no longer any commercial cinema. Every year nearly 100 films are shown, attracting in all some thousands of spectators. In addition to the traditional film-club formula, CINEPLUS sponsors, every year, various showings devoted to some particular film-maker or theme. It is hoped, within the very near future, to extend the scope of this activity to other contemporary media, including photography, video and comic-strips.

The centre's operations, which are carried out within the framework of lifelong education, are well designed to serve the objectives of media education in schools. They enable an entire segment of the population to have access to works that are in a different category from those commonly available on television or through the ordinary commercial cinema. Contact with film-makers and producers is frequently possible, and the audience is able to exchange opinions, with the result that a cultural initiative assumes a social dimension.

Towards general integration

After seven years of integration efforts, the picture is beginning to change to a more consistent mosaic. Media education is now perceived as a necessity in both political and educational circles. The main obstacles to its integration are, in general, psychological and institutional. The solution undoubtedly lies in a pragmatic approach to individuals and institutions. Instead of designing a pilot project that is jealously restricted to a single domain and aimed at a particular school-age population, it is salutary to adopt a differentiated approach. Wherever suitable ground is found, experimental programmes must be launched. It matters little how tenuous and fragmentary they may be, provided they are governed by the same objectives. As time goes by, the experiments build up, reinforcing and enriching each other. Regular reviews and reminders of the common purpose will help to avoid dispersion and will pave the way for the formation of an organized system. Such a system will appear by itself, once all the psychological and institutional obstacles have been overcome in the course of the individualized phase. As a result of the mutual influence effect, every organized system must contribute to the genesis of its predecessor and its successor. The lower secondary course, for example, called for the development of the primary-level course. Both of them were factors in the launching of the upper secondary course, while all three helped to shape the lifelong education programme known as CINEPLUS. Ideally, the integration of media education will not need to be supported by methods and programmes, it will undoubtedly be a perfectly natural adjunct to teaching for the children of the twenty-first century.

Finland: reducing informational and cultural inequality

Sirkka Minkkinen and Kaarle Nordenstreng

According to its uses mass media can be an enhancing factor in the individual's life, and means of national identity and development, international understanding and peace, by giving more real and adequate information on each other's lives. It can, however, turn out to be a new opium for the masses or it may deteriorate the norms and become a means of cultural supremacy.

This extract from *Proposals for an International Programme of Communication Research,* formulated by Unesco with the assistance of an international panel of experts in 1971,[1] provides a typical perspective into the question of mass communication in the contemporary world. Throughout the 1970s, this perspective has been more and more widely recognized at the national as well as international level, as demonstrated by the debate about a 'new international information order'.[2] Well-known landmarks in this development are the Declaration on Fundamental Principles concerning the Contribution of the Mass Media to Strengthening Peace and International Understanding, to the Promotion of Human Rights and Combating Racialism, Apartheid and Incitement to War (adopted by the General Conference of Unesco at its twentieth session in 1978), as well as the final report of the MacBride Commission.[3]

Part and parcel of this overall perspective is a recognition of a problem created by the mass media with regards to school education. The problem was first posed in an international expert meeting converted by Unesco in Montreal in 1969:

The flow of information which young people now receive from the media outside their formal schooling calls into question the whole content of school programmes. On the other hand, the meeting was of the opinion that schools should help students develop critical attitudes towards the media so that they will demand and receive better media content.[4]

At the same time, in 1969, the same ideas were independently written into the first curriculum of the newly established Finnish comprehensive school system. The curriculum was published in 1970 as a State Committee report, with an appendix entitled 'Mass Media Education in the Comprehensive School'.[5] Thus a new subject known as 'mass media education' was included in the Finnish educational system in connection with a comprehensive school reform at a time when consideration of the matter was at its earliest stages elsewhere in the world.

The case for mass-media studies

In the Finnish view the bases for the reasonableness of mass-media studies in the school context are drawn from two main streams of thought. On the one hand, it is not a matter for indifference as to how children and the young use periodicals, books, radio, television, films and records, or how they view the information and values presented by these media. Children are, in fact, regular consumers of the mass media before reaching school age and for many young people who have finished their schooling they are the most important channels for acquiring information about the rest of the world. On the other hand, the activities of the mass media must be considered as one of the most important institutions of an industrialized society without which production, cultural life and social life would be unable to function. The mass media are an important and inseparable part of society, and at the same time a part of society within the reach of each schoolchild.

Such an overtly societal approach was further emphasized in the communication policy debate that went into motion in the early 1970s. In his contribution to this debate, the President of Finland, Dr Urho Kekkonen, made this relevant point:

> Wide sections of the population are lacking in the most basic social information, and do not have sufficient knowledge to form opinions about society and act as democracy would demand. People can of course learn from experience, and their opportunities to obtain information are growing all the time, but the knowledge they have does not form an organized entity. There is a shortage of information which would give them this cohesive whole and the possibility to connect matters with one another.
>
> But a democracy cannot function properly unless there is original, critical thinking among its citizens. The realization of democracy is not possible if only dominant patterns of behaviour and the pressure of public opinion offer content to people's view of the world. In such conditions one cannot speak of the will of the people, but of the people merely echoing the message put across by a small privileged group with control of both power and the channels of influence. When this is the case, a so-called free-market economy which claims to offer free choice is in no position to point an accusing finger at societies it considers totalitarian.
>
> The conscious channelling of future development towards democracy requires that the vast bulk of the population does not remain in the position of bystanders without initiative. By improving the lot of those in a weaker position, we equalize the opportunities for participation. By directing communication and education to the development of spontaneous thinking and the independent assumption of knowledge we make possible the search for consciousness so much desired for the future.[6]

The Finnish philosophy of mass-media education was heavily based on such reflections of social equality and inequality with regards to information.

Globally speaking, improved communication and an increasing amount of information have not been able to alleviate the informational inequality that prevails in the world. The number of illiterate people is constantly increasing, and even in the industrialized Western countries it is the best educated and informed people who gain the greatest benefits from the new improved channels of information. Inequality in information and knowledge is increasing rather than decreasing.

Studies which chart the levels of knowledge attained by people have indicated that a low level of knowledge can be related to a limited education, a routine job, few or merely physical and non-intellectual leisure-time activities and to a low level of income. At the same time it has been found that a low level of knowledge often indicates informational passivity. Even available information is not being utilized for one reason or another, and thus informational inequality only deepens. The mass media have aggravated informational inequality. Entertainment and factual information are often presented without discrimination or factual analysis. The term 'higher level of knowledge' should not be crudely equated with middle-class status or the difficult and unstable term 'intelligence'.

Informational inequality tends to be transmitted from one generation to another. Parents who have limited knowledge, do routine work, and lack intellectually stimulating activities, pass on their informational passivity to their children. They are not able to offer their children stimulation and guidance to the same extent as people with access to knowledge and the ability to discuss the meaning of that knowledge in political and cultural terms. Those with lower economic means are, of course, unable to offer their children the same toys, books, hobbies and recreation as can families in better financial circumstances. Their habits of cultural consumption are often limited, and through their example they lead their children into a use of light entertainment material. Furthermore, it appears that the lightest and most superficial area of juvenile culture— comic magazines, cheap picture books, advertisements— reaches just those children whose intellectual environment is already disadvantageous in other respects. In poorer homes both parents often go out to work and consequently children have to spend a lot of the time alone or with other children from early childhood.

The role of schools

The school, however, is particularly significant for those children whose home environment cannot offer them stimulation which is beneficial from an educational point of view. Thus mass-media education could, at least to some extent, alleviate the informational and cultural inequality in home backgrounds.

The quantity of information transmitted by the mass media is fairly large, but the quality of the contents has not increased correspondingly. Commercialization and concentration both at national and international levels are characteristics of information transmission in the capitalistic countries. Mass communication has become a flourishing business.

Concentration has led to an ideological bias in mass communication, and the opportunities for different ideologies to become known to the public have been narrowed down: for example, the proportion of political party newspapers has decreased, whereas the role of the commercial papers—which claim to be independent—has increased. Left-wing information transmission has experienced the heaviest loss in the competition. Thus, the bulk of mass communication, for example in Finland, supports, more or less openly the prevailing ideology, and critical opinions seldom reach the general public. Thus the ideological distribution of mass-media contents is far from identical with the distribution of the political opinions of the people.

Moreover concentration is seen in consumption, too. At the same time as we have more and more mass communication at our disposal, the marketing mechanism attempts to focus consumption on a few products, which are then consumed by millions of people all over the world. The question is not only of mass communication but of culture as a whole, of the creation of a commercial way of living. When a product 'gets through', it will be exploited in every possible way: popular products come out as different mass-media products (such as Jaws, Superman, Donald Duck, Saturday Night Fever, etc.). A Swedish research group studying children's culture writes that sometimes when we look back at the cultural policies of the 1970s, we see it as a time when commercialism intentionally and inevitably took over culture.[7]

This is why schools need systematic education in the use of mass media. Although the entire problem cannot be solved merely through education, it can lead to more systematic results. In short, the problem situations that could be facilitated by proper instruction at school are the following:

School could facilitate understanding the means of communication. As the role of mass communication as a mediator of new information and as a means for continuous education will probably increase—as will the possibilities for manipulation of the mass media—it will be necessary to teach children how to analyse the language of mass media as well as their semantic and aesthetic nuances.

School could help children to use mass media in a meaningful way. Investigations show that children develop undesirable habits early. If they have not learned to concentrate and if they do not know how to select information, they tend to accept what is easy to digest. Although much time is spent with mass media, the range of content often remains rather narrow, and habits learned in childhood tend to remain unchanged. One learns to avoid things that differ from the familiar and abstains from making efforts to understand them.

School could help children to benefit from information available in current mass media. Children could be interested in a variety of contents and obtain guidance for selecting relevant information and for accumulating knowledge and integrating it with what has already been learned.

School could also help children to avoid contents that are

not beneficial from the educational viewpoint and that are manipulative. They ought to learn to be critical. Children ought to learn to see the difference between messages that lack proper information and have a low aesthetic level from material that is valuable and beneficial.

School could also implant in children a desire to affect the mass media, to demand mass communications of a high aesthetic, informational and ethical level. The growth of mass entertainment is partly due to the fact that people do not know how to affect mass media, and also to a lack of conscious desire to influence them.

Objectives in Finland

Although an awareness of the need for mass-media education had been aroused and recognized, those who formulated the curriculum for Finland's comprehensive schools were faced with a quite difficult problem. It was necessary to start from scratch as there was no ready model available. The main background material for the comprehensive-school mass-media curriculum was drawn from mass-media studies, especially those concerning children and mass media, and only secondary consideration was given to the curriculum for audio-visual education and film education in other countries. Thus the curriculum was very much in the nature of a draft formulation of problems.

The objectives of mass-media education in the comprehensive school were expressed in the curriculum in three statements of purpose each of which can be characterized as sub-goals:

To train students in the examination and interpretation of messages emanating from the mass media. The attainment of this aim will require that students learn to utilize the mass media: (a) for both the acquisition of information and the enjoyment of leisure; (b) to form proper and sensible habits for reading, listening and viewing; and (c) to understand the expressions used by the different media—the nuances and aesthetic qualities of these expressions.

To train students in the critical reception of messages. The attainment of this aim will require students: (a) to learn to select mass-media messages with understanding and according to their needs; (b) to check and increase the information they receive from the mass media; (c) to analyse mass-media messages and their relationship to reality; (d) to understand the position of mass-media communications in society and the socio-political dependence of mass media; (e) to detect and distinguish the influence of the medium itself, the communicator of the message and its interpretation; and (f) to relate the information acquired from the mass media to their wider framework of knowledge and, with discrimination, to their view of the world.

To encourage students to develop their own independent opinions about messages transmitted via the mass media and other channels of information. The attainment of this aim will require students: (a) to learn to select the ingredients needed for the formation of their own views from among the mass-media messages they receive; (b) to distinguish between facts and the interpretations of facts which form the basis of messages; (c) to search for the most reliable and relevant facts to support their own opinions and learn to appreciate the role and significance of their own ethical thinking and their own view of the world in the formation of their opinions; and (d) to express their opinions confidently.

Curriculum content

The content of mass-media education is divided into several fields. The first area of study, the transmission of information in society, includes: (a) the early history of the transmission of information; (b) the era of mass communication; (c) the era of mass communication in Finland; and (d) the structure of world communication. A second area of study examines the structure of mass communication in Finland. It covers: (a) control of mass information; (b) channels of mass information; and (c) the financing of mass communication. The third group of topics includes the content and means of expression of mass communication ranged from fact-based messages to fictional messages, to the nature of fictional presentation, the share of opinion in fictional exposition, the main types of fictional exposition and means of expression, and to advertising. A fourth study area covers the reception and influence of mass information: the reception of the message, understanding the message, the influence (or effect) of the message, and the future of information policy.

Mass-media education is included in the curriculum of the comprehensive school as a so-called 'pervading subject'. This term means that mass-media education has no lessons of its own but is taught in points applicable with the teaching of Finnish, art, history, social studies and study of the environment. Mass-media education can be given throughout the school day or, alternatively, concentrated into shorter periods.

In the senior secondary school, mass-media education is also integrated into overall instruction but it is possible to arrange special courses of about thirty-eight to seventy-six lessons. The teaching is concentrated in the first two years. However, the teachers have relatively broad scope in arranging the teaching of mass-media education.

In vocational schools, no mass-media education is included in the curriculum. It can, however, be taught in connection with general culture and it is evident that when the educational plan of general culture is reformed, some parts of mass-media education will be included in teaching also in vocational schools.

Teaching the media curriculum

No nationwide study has been carried out concerning the implementation of the mass-media education curriculum in

Finland. A number of regional inquiries have revealed, however, that not all teachers in practice give instruction in mass-media education, and instruction generally covers only part of the curriculum. This result was indeed to be expected in that it was a question of implementing a new, pass/fail subject in which the teachers had not received training during their own period of studies.

The curriculum of the comprehensive school contains a number of other pass/fail subjects such as international studies and family education, which have also met with great difficulties. The establishment of the comprehensive school meant rather large changes in all subjects and for all teachers. Training during the transition period was a major task. The new pass/fail subjects were seen as an inconvenient addition, which required an unreasonable amount of effort from the teachers.

During the comprehensive school transition period instruction in mass-media education was only a few hours long. Many teachers' organizations have attempted to supplement teacher knowledge and skills through voluntary professional and academic courses. The position of mass-media education in the basic training of teachers has not yet become firmly established. It is still an elective subject, and only training for visual-arts teachers includes a mandatory course in mass-media education.

There are no special textbooks on mass-media education, rather instruction materials are divided among other subjects such as visual arts, history, language, etc. The disconnected and irregular nature of the teaching materials has been a problem. Writers are rarely experts in mass-media education but prepare material because it is required by the curriculum. Similarly, very little audio-visual teaching material related to mass-media education is available. Quite a lot of activity in producing teaching material has been undertaken by newspaper and periodical publishers, who have both organized courses for teachers and produced material for use in the schools. One problem in this material, however, has been a certain bias: the goal is just as much to cultivate new consumers as it is to promote education, even though it is not a matter of open marketing. Still, the issue is important in terms of school policy. Publishers hardly consider as their main objective the development of critical consumers and influencers.

The availability of such partisan material is in striking contrast to the distracted state of the scientific body of knowledge about the mass media. To be sure, mass-communication research as an academic study does exist (in Finland it has been at the professorial level since the 1940s), but it is still too young and underdeveloped to provide a solid theoretical basis for the mass-media education. Rather, it is a controversial field where several academic 'schools' compete in the very essence of human communication—some stress the technical means of transmitting messages, whereas others capitalize on the social significance of the contents of communication. In such a situation practically all interest groups, including private publishers, can refer to some 'facts' and academic authorities of their choosing. Consequently, teachers and school authorities are left in an awkward situation orienting themselves in a field which offers little uncontroversial theory, especially for those who are not thoroughly acquainted with the problems involved and few teachers are.

The dispute over theory has in part increased the lack of desire by teachers to give instruction in mass-media education. Teachers will willingly remain 'objective' and above disputes in society. The presentation of opposing methods of approach and the multiple interpretation of matters in teaching are felt to be difficult; which they undoubtedly are, especially if the teacher's own knowledge of the subject is weak. The teaching of mass-media education also includes questions of morality and taste about which the teacher and the pupil, or the pupils' parents, may disagree.

Mass-media education affects the daily life of pupils' families much more intimately than many other subjects. Parents may view the teacher's directions or attitudes as interference in private affairs. Mass-media education requires much closer co-operation between school and home than is the practice today. It does seem, however, that parents are gradually realizing the importance of and need for mass-media education as regards the home as well.

Children and young people today are major consumers of the mass media, and as such know the products of the mass media, at least in part, incomparably better than the teacher does. They very readily sense the teacher's well-intended moralizing attitudes regarding their favourite material. Instruction requires effort, discretion and a feeling for psychology on the part of the teacher—above all a rejection of authoritarianism.

Planning and co-operation in the teaching of mass-media education also cause problems of their own. Co-operation among teachers seems to be amazingly slight and rare in Finnish schools. However, in order to succeed, mass-media education demands co-operation among several teachers because lessons in any one subject are not sufficient to carry out the mass-media curriculum.

The introduction of mass-media education into the Finnish schools came during an interesting social period, the decade of the 1970s, when student movements began to spread from the universities into the schools. There were demands for school democracy, increased decision-making powers for pupils, closer ties between school and society. Politics also came into the schools, especially in school elections. Discipline was criticized and the authority of teachers even as sources of information was shaken when pupils got information about various matters from outside the school as well.

It seems almost a miracle that, despite the difficulties, many teachers did an enormous amount of work in developing mass-media education. The problem is that these teaching experiments have never been systematically brought together, analysed and published for use. Teachers have had to work alone unaware of the work of others. In connection with a Unesco mass-media education project (1974 and 1976) it was however possible to compile and publish the results of the work of several dozen teachers. Examples were also published in the curriculum written for Unesco.[8]

An encouraging innovation

The authorities, namely the National Board of General Education, have been involved only twice. In the mid-1970s the National Board of General Education arranged, in cooperation with the Finnish Newspaper Publishers' Association, a campaign in the schools. During one week the pupils received periodic teaching about newspapers and the mass media, according to the directives of the National Board. The National Board also prepared an 'information package' for teachers relating to the campaign, and some examples with exercises. No systematic assessment of the impact of the campaign has been made, but the directives of the National Board allowing the schools to subscribe to newspapers representing various political parties for teaching purposes for four months of the school year can be seen as one consequence of the campaign. Several studies relating to the use of newspapers in school teaching were made during the 1970s; these reveal that the use of newspapers has expanded and that a fairly large share of the teachers who use newspapers in their teaching also teach about mass media.

In the school years 1978/79 and 1979/80 the National Board of General Education arranged a so-called mass-media entertainment project both in the comprehensive schools and the upper secondary schools. The aim of the project was to deal with different forms of mass-media entertainment and to get pupils and teachers to discuss their use among children and youth. In connection with the project, teachers and pupils discussed television, films, entertainment, literature and music. The National Board prepared teaching and reading material for the teachers dealing with different sectors of entertainment, and many different sectors supplied schools with additional material relating to the subject. It included material aimed at developing the pupils' critical sense of judgement as well as some more commercially oriented material. Much other useful material was also produced during the project: for instance, the Association of Film Clubs published a catalogue of dramatic and documentary films and the Finnish Broadcasting Company a list of television films suitable for teaching. The education department produced television series including six parts on the methods of the cinema, the Films for Children and Young People Centre dedicated two issues of its magazine to the topics of the project.

The National Board of Education made a survey of the outcome of the first year of the project. The survey revealed that about 90 per cent of the schools had discussed mass-media entertainment during the lessons, but the average length of the time devoted to the topic was small, the upper secondary schools and the upper level of the comprehensive schools eight hours, and the lower comprehensive schools five hours. Some 40 per cent of the schools arranged programme evenings for the parents dealing with mass-media entertainment which were attended by more than 100,000 parents.

The mass-media entertainment project thus activated a large number of teachers and parents, but the results seem to have been very modest. The teachers were dissatisfied both with teacher training and the teaching material. What the teachers seemed to lack most were concrete teaching examples, material for exercises and detailed teaching plans. The National Board arranged two evaluation seminars related to the mass-media entertainment project where many researchers directed rather harsh criticism against the project. It was accused of having adopted too narrow an approach, and of not having carefully defined the basic concepts. Many have asked themselves if the project produced anything beyond the initial enthusiasm.

An effort to be followed

The preceding examination shows that Finnish mass-media education, twelve years after the appearance of the first curriculum, is still in its infancy. The need for it has been recognized. A great deal of work has been put into developing the curriculum and formulating teaching methods. Attitudes towards it have become increasingly positive, but many practical problems, including teacher training and the production of teaching materials, remain unsolved.

The mass media, especially television and other visual forms, have begun to be seen as competing with school just as strongly, or even more strongly, as a system affecting the child's entire personality. American media professor Neil Postman has compared the significance of the 'curricula' of school and television. In terms of time, television is ahead of school: an American child on average attends school for thirteen years, some 11,500 hours. At the same time in addition to school, he watches television for some 15,000 hours. Furthermore, he has begun television viewing as a small child and continues it after completing school. Additionally, television for a child is pleasant and voluntary. Its 'teaching' takes place in the kind of psychologically pleasurable atmosphere that school will perhaps never achieve. Postman emphasizes the significance of school especially as a teacher, its effects on the child's ability to concentrate, to observe and on language skills. He views television's short time-spans, the overly easy and fast solution to all problems, as a hidden danger.[9] Postman's compatriots Gerbner and Gross see the significance of television in its role as a medium for presenting surrounding culture and a picture of the world, directing our concept of reality.[10] In this situation it is even more important that we stop to analyse what is most essential in mass-media education. In our view the answer can be summarized with the general objectives of the mass-media education curriculum model prepared for Unesco mentioned above.[11]

Mass-media education aims at teaching children and young people the knowledge and skills to enable them to formulate a critical assessment of available mass communications and to use it as a source of stimuli for their own creative expressions. In addition, it enables them to express their own thoughts and feelings through these media, and as citizens and members of civil organizations, to influence available communications. This goal is demanding and requires a lot from the rest of teaching at schools. A narrower goal is not sufficient, to our mind, if we want to go into this problem more deeply and seriously.

Finland, like Unesco, began an early development of the curriculum for mass-media education. It now seems that many other countries have managed to edge ahead of Finland. Interesting development work on the mass-media education curriculum has been done *inter alia* in the United Kingdom at the BFI, in Norway, Australia and Sweden to name a few. Also, the mass-media education curriculum project begun by Unesco in 1974 has slowed down, become generalized and non-specific. It is indeed important to extend mass-media education to the adult population as well, but the emphasis should remain on the development of curricula for the schools. The earlier mass-media education can be started, the more probable it is that it will produce results. An even worse mistake would be to view mass-media education outside its social context, as the simple teaching of a 'new language', as a communication problem.

Notes

1. *Proposals for an International Programme of Communication Research*, p. 1, Paris, Unesco, 10 September 1971 (Document COM/MD/20).
2. For a review and analysis of this 'great media debate' of the 1970s, see, for example, Kaarle Nordenstreng, *The Mass Media Declaration of Unesco*, Norwood, N. H., Ablex Publishing Co., 1983.
3. Sean MacBride et al., *Many Voices, One World,* Paris/New York/London, Unesco/Unipub/Kogan Page, 1980.
4. *Mass Media in Society: The Need of Research*, p. 26, Paris, Unesco, 1974 (Reports and Papers on Mass Communication, No. 59).
5. *Peruskoulun opetussuunnitelmakomitean mietintö I-II*, Helsinki, Valtion Painatuskeskus, 1970 (Komiteanmietintö 1970: A4–5).
6. *Television Traffic—A One-way Street*, p. 45, Paris, Unesco, 1974 (Reports and Papers on Mass Communication, No. 70).

7. *Barnen och kulturen: En rapport från Barnkulturgruppen*, Helsingborg, Publica, 1978.
8. *A General Curricular Model for Mass Media Education*, Madrid, ESCO/Unesco, 1978.
9. Niel Postman, *Teaching as a Conserving Activity*, New York, Delacorte Press, 1979.
10. See, for example, 'Living with Television: The Violence Profile', *Journal of Communication*, Spring, 1976.
11. *A General Curricular Model...*, op. cit.

Austria: theory and practice of media education

Thomas A. Bauer

Why media education?

Many reasons can be adduced to argue the urgent need for media education in the individual and social educational process. Although problems are still encountered in Austria in establishing media education as a scientific discipline in universities and teachers' training colleges, we can nevertheless look back on a history of nearly twenty years of practical experience in schools, churches and adult education institutions. This means that media education has achieved a status of indispensability. In communications science circles in Austria, there has also been a growing awareness in recent years that the science of communications is a discipline that is concerned with the achievement of consensus in the practical everyday life of society and is therefore qualified to develop theories and methods to resolve the problems of social communication by educational means.

THE EDUCATIONAL ROLE OF THE SCHOOL

In an information-intensive world, the provision of educational information can no longer be adequately carried out by the school, either in regard to subject content or in the formal organizational sense. It is becoming increasingly clear that gaps exist between the knowledge supplied in the classroom and the daily demand for the factual knowledge, guidance and information necessary to solve problems arising in the course of social evolution, and that these gaps cannot be filled by the traditional school. But we also know that the knowledge gap between lower and higher social classes caused by social stratification cannot be completely bridged by the mass media; on the contrary, it can be made more acute.[1] It is readily acknowledged that the mass media fulfil an integrative function in society, but they can do so only if the users of the media are in a position to accept the media supply, or access to the media, in a democratically competent manner. It is in the psychological and social, political and cultural climate in which the individual develops his media behaviour that private and public knowledge meet and are rendered mutually useful.

THE SOCIALIZING ROLE OF THE MEDIA

From a technological point of view, mass media are first of all merely technical and organizational systems for the conveyance of information. Since, however, information, and its selection, supply and effect, are inseparably linked with the problem of power and influence, and power has the dimension of a social problem, the mass media, as areas of decision in the private and public socialization process, constitute a problem that is of relevance to education. The mass media provide experience of life without the interpersonal relations that obtain in other socialization contexts (such as family, friends, school). They construct realities, and offer evaluations and models for living that to some extent compete with those of other areas of socialization. To this must be added the experience, and the suspicion borne out by experience, of manipulation by the mass media. They are instruments of expression and impression in our society. They provide access to information, entertainment, knowledge and education, and help to enlarge our environment both in time and space. The mass media must now be numbered amongst the most decisive forces in every area of cultural, economic and social life.

What conclusions are to be drawn from these findings that could be useful in the establishment of media education?

School facts and media facts, school knowledge and media knowledge are both second-hand experiences, even though their respective contents and the quality of their transmission differ. If these two fields of socialization are to cease competing with each other, or are not to compete with each other still more, the question of educational methods must be brought in as an intermediary. If we bear in mind that political socialization processes operating through mass communications function in a much more subtle and telling way through media entertainment than through the actual political programmes[2] offered by the media, the political dimension of socially relevant educational approaches cannot be ignored. Interest in education and training is always accompanied, either openly or covertly, by an interest in the political evolution of a society, and vice versa. To be convincing, an interest in political development must be accompanied by an interest in education and training.

But in a highly-organized society, the more the balance between first-hand and second-hand experience becomes weighted, through the increasingly decisive role of the mass media, on the side of information that we no longer select from our immediate field of experience, the more important it becomes to ensure without delay a capacity for independent orientation. Since the inexperienced person assumes reality as constructed by the media to be a presentation of true reality (because he cannot perceive that it is an aggregate of items selected to serve specific interests) he receives an inaccurate picture of reality, on the basis of which he develops an incorrect relationship to his natural, social and political-cultural environment.

The preparation of programmes on industrial lines means that communication and experience undergo a qualitative change.[3] All media products are so planned that they can be multiplied and distributed at will. Their preparation is based on industrial planning, that is, they are produced by one party and consumed by another. Thus the socialization process goes beyond an exchange of experience: as labour is divided and roles are assigned, it takes place on a new basis and conforms to different standards.

The originally communicative, interactive, integrated relationship between social partners (parent-child, teacher-pupil, apprentice-master) loses some of its functions. It thus becomes clear that media education must be more than merely education in the meaningful use of the media. Because what is at issue is not primarily the media, but the structures of communication in our society. Media education is meaningful and credible in the context of education policy only as *education for communication*.

Communications education

It cannot be denied therefore that there are certain problems whose solution involves communications and the media. Since media problems are not really problems of the media alone but problems of communication in our social system in general, the formulation of objectives calls not, as hitherto, for a media-centred approach, but for an approach focusing on the problems of the system as a whole. If we consider the question in this light, it follows that the polarization of media influence and media education in an individualistic education cannot be a good thing. The problem of unwanted or undesirable media influences is a problem of society, and cannot be solved through moral rearmament to make it the responsibility of the individual. On the contrary, socially useful media education should help to resolve any contradiction between the socialization performed by the media and that of educational institutions by achieving a situation in which the latter use the mass media on a selective basis as teaching instruments, as well as for their content, in the teaching structures of kindergarten, school and adult education systems, while the mass media in turn interest themselves in the subjects dealt with by educational institutions.

It cannot be the aim of socially committed media education with a critical approach simply to leave the development of social communication to the media technocrats and to turn education, which itself uses the media and trains students in their use, into a sort of repair shop for unsuccessful or misguided attempts at socialization. What purpose does it serve, for instance, to observe presentations of social violence in the media and to learn to deplore them, if the various forms of structural, psychological and physical violence practised in society continue as before? Media education which concentrates in blinkered fashion on the effects of the media makes the media a scapegoat for a malaise affecting the individual that is in fact created by the basic ideological structure of our society. The aim of socially useful media education can be meaningfully formulated and organized only in a comprehensive way, that is, through comprehensive, diversified efforts to create and provide the structural, social and psychological conditions which will at an early stage foster the ability of the younger generation to form balanced judgements without the intervention of repression, prejudice or dogma. The key concept of such media education as education in communication is the communicative meaning of social judgements regarding the media.[4]

Media will always be necessary when time-space relationships become so complex that people can no longer conduct satisfactory exchanges of information in conditions of mutual perception. Again, media always become necessary when, through the growing complexity of the world in which they live and of exchanges of experience connected with it, people find themselves in a situation where they are obliged to concern themselves with problems and contexts with which they were previously unfamiliar or in which they were not interested. As interpersonal exchanges of experience became increasingly structured by technical organizing agents, the possibility of direct, spontaneous control of meaning was lost. New ways of controlling perceived meaning (that is, controls of subjective usefulness, applicability, assimilability, life orientation, etc.) must therefore be made part of the adolescent's repertoire of behavioural skills and an apparatus for sense perception developed that will make possible a well-founded social consensus.

Media education in the school

This attempt to describe the potential and fields of application of work on the media in Austrian schools is largely based on subjective experiences, judgements and analyses, because as yet no systematic analysis of media education as practised in Austrian schools is available[5] and it is therefore difficult to form an objective view. The professional organization of media and communications education is not yet fully developed, and it is a field in which private initiative flourishes. This means inevitably that charlatanism blossoms forth, detracting from the efforts of serious practitioners and affecting the credibility of the demand for media education in the context of social policy or associating it with private interests.

Initiatives in media education on the official educational level, as distinct from private initiatives, have been taken in Austria only since 1963–64. Initially, these consisted of providing instructional aids for media courses or for technical approaches to media education. It was only a decade later that the development of media education, which had meanwhile been approved in theory, was carried a step further in the public educational field with the promulgation of decrees concerning media education in general[6] and political education.[7]

On the practical level, the central problem in media education in Austrian schools is that of teacher training. Up to now, there has been no synchronization of training for media education with the normal professional training of teachers so that the problem has to be overcome by means of further training for teachers. However, it is virtually impossible to provide adequate further training in this way for all the teachers concerned. Since the decree of 1973, the inclusion of media education in the curricula of all Austrian schools has been obligatory. In the decree, in which media education is defined as an integral part of general education in communication 'covering the theory and practice of the emergence and use of the media', a structural distinction is drawn between 'media science' as a specialized subject and 'media education' as an 'educational principle'. The 'educational principle' is a feature of the Austrian school system.

This principle (by analogy with political education as an educational principle) assumes that educational action is an emancipatory process enabling pupils to acquire practical mastery of the communicational use of the media with a view to testing out and establishing by empirical means the conditions for social consensus amongst themselves and with other groups, and on the basis of this experience to ascertain to what extent the established mass media fulfil or fail to fulfil these conditions.

At first committed teachers who had been campaigning for the inclusion of media education in the Austrian schools' curriculum were disappointed. They considered the introduction of media science 'only' as an educational principle under the title 'media education', instead of as a subject in its own right like mathematics or geography, to be a half measure. But it encouraged all teachers to organize media- and communications-related instruction within their primary subject, and to treat the mass media in thematic fashion whenever this was relevant. It is now clear that this decision was a very farsighted, comprehensive and flexible way of dealing with the problem and that it corresponds very closely to the theoretical considerations outlined above. The aim is not to turn schoolchildren into pocket-size journalists, but to turn out men and women who, whatever their role in life, will be in a position to act in a politically responsible and democratic way and to make good use of the media in so doing. The aim corresponding to the concept of the 'principle of education' is not primarily the imparting of specialized knowledge of the media but the shaping of the pupil's personality. The pupil must become familiar with the various forms of social communication and practise them. He must acquire experience of the social problems of our socially organized communications system as a reality and find out how he can define his own role within it. However, the practical application of the 'educational principle' by the teachers is still left to the latters' discretion and to their sensitivity to problems of social communication.

Teachers who have learned to see their role in the context of a functionalistic concept of education see themselves as purveyors of specialized knowledge and will therefore hardly be in a position to carry out with sufficient sensitivity the teaching task associated with such a principle of education. In Austria we still have a functionalistic, specialist-orientated system of training teachers at universities and teacher-training colleges. In these circumstances it is not surprising that the dispute as to which school subjects should actually give a place to the principle of media education has not yet been settled. At the moment, a number of different subjects are involved, as shown in Figure 1. It is impossible to determine objectively how and to what extent the teachers of these subjects deal with mass communication problems as a theme. Moreover, the possibility that teachers of physics, chemistry or even mathematics might also deal with media themes is not to be ruled out.

The following is a list of participants by subject in further training courses organized for secondary-school teachers in Austria as a whole: first come teachers of German (often with history as second subject), secondly art teachers (with manual training as second subject), thirdly teachers of foreign languages. Thereafter, interest is shared amongst teachers of religion, philosophy, history, geography, vocational education (for example, in training establishments for kindergarten teachers) and, to a lesser extent, amongst teachers of physics, mathematics and other scientific subjects.

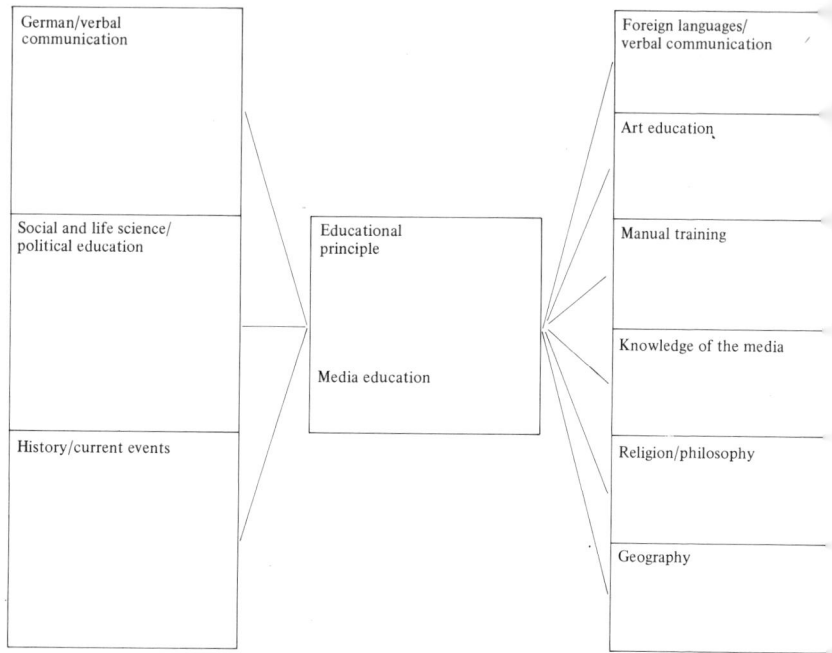

Fig. 1. Subjects involved in media education.

It may be helpful at this point to describe how further training courses in media education for teachers are organized in Austria.

Since 1977, the Federal Ministry for Education and the Arts (Organization), in collaboration with the Institute for Communications Science in Graz (Seminars Division) has been organizing further training seminars on a regular basis. The structure of these seminars is shown in Figure 2.

These further training seminars proceed as follows: first of all the teachers themselves are made aware of problems that may be caused by their own attitudes towards the media. Then, with the aid of the seminar directors and participants, they construct teaching models for schools and act them out.

Type of seminar	Content priorities		
Seminars in the basic elements	Problems of communications science in general, social structures, functions and effects of mass communications, general information about the media, communications pedagogy, the technology of education		
One week since 1977 once or twice a year			
Modular seminars	Media-oriented	Function-oriented	Theme-oriented
1978, 1979, 1983 ⟶	Television		
1979, 1980, 1983 ⟶	Press		
1980, 1981 ⟶	Radio ⟵	Cross-connections	⟶
1979 ⟶	Film		
1981 ⟶	Comics	Entertainment	
1982 ⟶		Information	
1983 ⟶		Opinion formation, propaganda	
Planned for the coming years ⟶			The world of work Violence Politics Image of youth

FIG. 2. Typology of seminars on media education.

The further training seminars follow an obligatory pattern of objectives, shown in Figure 3. As the figure indicates, special stress is laid on the seminars' workshop character, so that the specialized knowledge and teaching qualifications of the participants, as well as the problems and uncertainties raised by the teachers, are made part of the training process to the benefit of all concerned. The participative, action-orientated methods employed make it easy to do this. I consider the fact that the communicative role of the teacher in the school—and hence in society also—is increasingly dealt with as a theme in the course of these seminars to be particularly advantageous. Obviously there is little sense in seeking to master the subject of social communication if the structures of communication within the school are not also dealt with.

Thanks to this provision of further training, some 600 Austrian high-school teachers have now been familiarized with

	Behaviour	Knowledge
Personality	1. Critical experience and analysis of subjective attitudes to the media and communications	1. Cognitive mastering of intuitive attitudes to the media
Personality	2. Observation of the attitudes of others and their assessment in relation to one's own	2. To develop everyday knowledge of communications and the media into an intelligently orientated awareness
Personality	3. Practice of communication-conscious - attitudes to the media and - interactions in everyday life (e.g. in the school)	3. Theoretical and empirical basis for socially desirable communication via the media
Teacher's role	1. Communicational teaching on the media/mass communications 2. The communication-conscious role of the teacher 3. Pupil-centred model for media education	Basic knowledge concerning communications models (interpersonal communication, educational communication, mass communication) - sociological aspects - psychological aspects - politico-economic aspects - cultural or socio-cultural aspects of media production and media reception

FIG. 3. Objectives in teacher training for media education.

the subject of media education since 1977. This is still an infinitesimal percentage of the total number of teachers.

At the elementary school (Volkschule and Hauptschule) level, the organizational development of media education is left to regional working parties or regional youth training institutions. This explains why some provinces are more active in this field than others. For instance, in the Steiermark[8] and the Tyrol[9] the teachers have formed project groups for the purpose of elaborating teaching models for elementary schools. However, both the Styrian and the Tyrolean autonomous organization models have shown that the success of these projects depends upon the availability of a few particularly committed teachers and their willingness to make a personal effort. Support for these activities from official quarters (Provincial Cultural Departments, Provincial Youth Services or Teachers Further Training Institutes in the Provinces) has declined considerably in recent years and is confined increasingly to organizational assistance. The official funds that are necessary for further development are lacking. This leaves only individual ad hoc arrangements which, it must be admitted, are no more than a stop-gap. This regressive trend is certainly due, on the one hand, to the fact that resources have become scarcer but also, on the other, to the resigned attitude of those with political responsibility towards technological developments in the media. In the 1970s, there were still hopes that it would be possible to break the monopoly of the national radio service by setting up regional or local radio or television services (at that time cable television was the rallying point for those concerned with the development of media-policy), but since then new developments in media technology (such as satellite radio)[10] have made the possibility of developing local communications technology seem more remote.

The parallelism between changes in media technology, a media policy that remains resolutely unchanged, and diminishing official interest in education connected with the media lead one to suspect that the higher level of official interest in media education shown previously was inspired by ulterior motives of a technocratic nature. Otherwise it is difficult to understand, for instance, the haste with which an audio-visual centre was set up in Graz between 1977 and 1979, only to be dismantled in 1980.[11]

Media education, which was pioneered in Austria with film and radio education, has on the practical level been less successful in the context of educational and media policy development than might be considered necessary. It has nevertheless improved its educational and methodological standards and has clearly and unambiguously transformed itself from a media science that sets norms and moral standards into an emancipatory, socially and democratically committed system of theoretical and practical communication education. If efforts to establish its status within the university and teacher-training system in the next few years are successful, it can be expected that the theoretical problems of media education in Austria as well as those arising in the field of educational practice and school organization will before long be resolved.

Notes

1. See U. Saxer, 'Medienverhalten und Wissensstand', in Deutsche Lesegesellschaft (ed.), *Buch und Lesen,* Gütersloh, 1979.
2. See T. A. Bauer, *Medienpedagogik. Einführung und Grundlegung.* Vol. III: *Didaktische Modelle: Unterhaltung durch Massenmedien.* p. 68 et seq., Vienna/Cologne/Graz, Böhlau, 1980.
3. See T. W. Adorno, Résumé über Kulturindustrie', in D. Prokop, (ed.) *Kommunikationsforschung,* Vol. 1: *Produktion,* Frankfurt, Fischer, 1972.
4. T. A. Bauer, 'Medienpädagogik als Aufgabe und Beruf,' *Kommunikationsberufe in Österreich: Österreichisches Jahrbuch für Kommunikationswissenschaft,* Salzburg, Neugebauer, 1982.
5. See I. Geretschläger-Pixner, 'Medienpädagogik in Österreich,' Österreichisches Jahrbuch für Kommunikationswissenschaft, Salzburg, 1979.
6. Bundesministerium für Unterricht und Kunst, 26 June 1973.
7. Ibid., 11 May 1978.
8. See T. A. Bauer and G. Haas, *Information durch Massenmedien,* Graz, 1977; H. Weigl et al., *Comics-und was dahintersteckt,* Graz, Landerjugendreferat, 1982.
9. S. Winkler et al., *Unterrichtsmodelle zur Medienerziehung,* Vienna, Österr. Bundesverlag, 1981.
10. See G. Bacher, 'Die ganze Welt wird ein Dorf: Medienzukunft mit Satelliten,' *Die Furch,* No. 14, 8 April 1981; H. Lenhardt (ORF) *Satellitenrundfunk,* Vienna, Entwicklungstand und Kosten, 1981.
11. See Thomas A. Bauer, *Cultural Development through Video: Austrian Experiments,* Strasbourg, Council of Europe, 1977.

Focuses on impact and experiment

Journalism and pedagogy

Gaspare Barbiellini Amidei

The new information technologies are giving rise to a new millenarian fear, one which is already producing the first of its irrational fruits. Our era, like its predecessors, has created its own fears. The two that are peculiar to it are fear of nuclear power and fear of mass communications.

The first of these, however, does not seem to be of such immediate moment as the second, for it can be dispelled by the certainty that man's instinct for physical self-preservation will prevail. So we may say that mass communications are Public Enemy Number One to people of today, and undoubtedly the object of their greatest fear. In other words, people are not certain that the spirit of the preservation of freedom is as strong as the spirit of the preservation of physical life.

What they fear is that the ruling classes, having hitherto held down the masses by assiduously depriving them of information and culture, are now going to condition them, by reversing the process and swamping them with information. There is of course some truth behind this fear. But it is just as true that there are some who stand to gain from it: those whose aversion to information is at bottom a fundamental aversion to democracy itself.

The members of a healthy society, therefore, while seeing

the danger of the homogenization of information, are also wary of false prophets who warn them to keep away from it. So rejection of 'doctored' or trivial information goes hand in hand with concern to make sure of information in the future, a concern that increases as the more informed study of history makes people aware that the processes of freedom and democracy are all too reversible. They see that history does not move in a straight line whose end is the attainment of the fullest and the best kind of democracy. The history of those countries that have but recently gained their independence shows the truth of this view, and the increasing number of dictatorships throughout the world, coupled with the increasing number of 'formal' democracies, confirms it.

But if technologies are evolving in opposition to man, may it not be that man's mind too is evolving so that he will attain the capacity to use technologies, master them and bend them to his universal purposes? All this is the province of education, which operates pre-eminently in the school. But the school must not feed upon itself; it must engage in a richer dialogue with society. In my view, this is what makes it increasingly important for journalists to make their way into the schools even before newspapers do.

In point of fact, only in the school can the world's new fears be effectively dispelled in time. In the school we perceive those generation-linked changes that so often upset our assumptions about the lines along which society is going to develop, and prove them to be wrong.

Projection of these lines or their extension into the future often leads to false predictions. When this happens, people say that contestation has broken out unexpectedly, that the waves of the sea have sucked in some political element unexpectedly, and that the tide as it recedes has unexpectedly laid bare something personal on the shore.

In all probability, these unexpected discoveries would not have been so unexpected if observation of the younger generations had not been confined to questions of productivity and of their behaviour in school itself. Furthermore, such observation is possible only when they are in a 'class' by themselves: that is, in a school class.

Moreover, behaviour can be determined as well as discovered. The idea that the school can be impartial is as foolish as the idea of impartial information. The school has not yet solved the problem of whether freedom of teaching or freedom of learning comes first, just as it has not settled the question of how far freedom of teaching goes. This increased freedom which the teacher is assumed to possess, but which is only a manifestation of the widest freedom of thought, is really only legitimate when it is combined with the duty to train the child in the ways of the society in which he lives (and, very often, the way in which society expects to use him). His freedom then becomes both duty and right. Only in the school, therefore, and without doing violence to anyone (or at least any further violence) can the 'new fears' as we have called them, be stilled in time.

The journalist should not of course point out any particular facts in the classroom, nor should he lay down rules. A journalist's job has always been to give an account of facts and comment on them. He has never been expected to teach, and certainly not to teach teachers. But the fact is that we are all convinced that the fate of the press, and especially of the free press, will be settled in the school in the next few years. And this is not only due to the need to spread expenses and to balance costs and income, which has now become urgent, nor is it only because we wish to break the non-reading habit, which for the last twenty years has kept Italian newspapers down to a total circulation of 5 million.

This is a problem of great importance to the publishing world, but it is one that concerns the externals and not the heart of our society. To take newspapers into the schools, therefore, not occasionally or in a superficial way, as people have tried to do in Italy in recent years (leaving aside the question of results and the efficiency of the means employed) is to try to change the very fabric of Italian society so that it includes news of the life of the community.

Anyone who can really read a newspaper can defend his own rights in the world of work. He can choose the party he wants to vote for. He can give or withdraw his mandate. Above all, he can lead his public and private life without letting other people's ideas be pumped into his head. Semiologists tell us that to read a newspaper, when one has learnt how to read it, is to 'decodify' a message, to understand why a thing is said in a certain way and what interests lie behind the fact that it is put in a particular place rather than elsewhere, and to appreciate the reasons for the page presentation. I am convinced that if every young person learns to play this decodification game he will be able to get every particle of information out of newspapers, putting together and pulling apart the principles and the imperatives imposed on him in the course of the years by life, love, fears and his daily work.

Obviously, then, what we want to do is much more than train young people or make them engage in comparative and interdisciplinary studies. Our real object is to do away with the conglomerating element in mass society, using the self-same tools that this society employs. 'Operation school' is of increased importance to us as journalists. Our aim, which may indeed take time to achieve, is to bring up a generation of school pupils to be journalists who are readers, or, if you like, readers who are journalists. Seen in perspective, this means that if we succeed in making citizens able to read the newspapers critically and with full comprehension we shall destroy the mechanism (which could almost be called diabolical) that divides society into those who talk and those who listen, those who impart information and those who swallow it—or refuse to do so.

Gobetti thought that we needed a society that would be capable of reading and writing about itself and of writing up its own news. From the sort of school we hope for a new generation of journalists might arise, journalists who are not just sons, nephews and cousins of journalists, publishers, party leaders, heads of factions or friends of friends, as they sometimes are today.

There is a lot of discussion in Italy about the role of newspapers in the school. So far, it has certainly embraced two aspects: that of helping the pupil to understand newspapers themselves, which is the first stage in the criticism and defence of information; and that of assisting him in the study of ordinary school subjects.

A newspaper that wants to render the school service of an educational and didactic nature should avoid confusing these two aspects. It should seek ways of helping to attain both of these separate—but not unconnected—ends.

The first service that the publishers of a newspaper can render, if they want to improve the use of newspapers in the schools, might be to provide the schools with tools that will help them in their study of the various problems posed by the use of newspapers, such as the two-volume publication *Il Quotidiano in Classe*[1] or *I Giornali, Guida alla Lettura e all'Uso Didattico*,[2] as well as an excellent French book *Lire le Journal* by Yves Agnes and Jean Michel Croissandeau of *Le Monde*.[3]

Some newspapers have evolved their own methods of directly helping the schools which are their customers. They make it a practice to include suggestions and exercises on the educational use of newspapers. Some issue supplements intended for classes, individual pupils, or teachers. Others send parcels of specially prepared material which teachers ask for, such as stocks of back numbers in which all the previous references to a story or a problem can be found, such as the different stages of a conflict, a news item or a discussion.

Sometimes national or international publishers' associations undertake and finance such operations in order to cut costs and enable more newspapers to use the service. In the United States there are fully developed 'school service' organizations, which are used by whole newspaper chains.

In Italy, a scheme for sending out newspapers to schools at a reduced price was tried out in 1970 by the Italian Federation of Newspaper Publishers (FIEG) but it could not be called a great success. The truth is that, while the newspapers attracted attention, no proper method of using them to advantage in the classroom had been worked out.

In Denmark, monthly issues are put out for the upper classes of secondary schools. They are intended for use in sociological studies, and contain newspaper headlines and articles. The disadvantage of this sort of arrangement is that the topics are ready-made, and the newspaper cuttings supplied deal with subjects that are often out of date. The system is operated by a publishers' association, the Committee for the Distribution of Newspapers (Pressens Oplysningsudvalg).

In France there is a Committee for Press Information in Education (CIPE). In the Federal Republic of Germany, the *Hessische Allgemeine* undertook a study of the question in 1965, which was widely discussed and which led the way to making proper use of newspapers in schools; and the Huber di Monaco publishing house put out a guide to reading, with exercises, entitled *Im Spiegel der Presse* (In the Mirror of the Press). In the United Kingdom, the *Bolton Evening News* is a pioneer in developing relations between schools and the press. It has a project, signed by Robert Foulkes, which is designed to facilitate the regular use of newspapers in schools. In the United States, booklets are issued containing exercises in using the various parts of a newspaper. The NIC system (Newspaper in the Classroom) is organized by ANPA (American Newspaper Publishers Association). It supplies 70 million copies of newspapers a year to 18,000 schools, which work according to 350 set programmes. The *New York Times*, too, has its own schemes. It runs a schools department in collaboration with the New York Teachers College and School Service, and publishes the *New York Times School Weekly* (twenty-nine issues a year), which gives a selection of the week's events, together with background information, figures and teaching aids.

Almost all North American newspapers have such schemes. If a newspaper cannot afford to run its own service, it subscribes to that of specialized firms such as the VEC (Visual Educational Consultants) in Madison, Wisconsin; Copley

Newspapers in San Diego, California; or the CDNPA (Canadian Daily Newspapers Publishers Association). The VEC prepares individual programmes, using a certain amount of ready-made material. Over 250 North American daily newspapers use its services so that they can provide schools in their area with educational tools for making the best possible use of newspapers.

In Italy there has been a revival of interest in the use of newspapers for teaching and study in the classroom. Since the end of the 1970s many regions and provinces have given financial assistance to encourage it.

Not a few teachers (and not only teachers in Italy) have been ready to denounce outright the idea that newspapers should be read in schools. Some still do so. They think newspapers are unwholesome vectors of noxious ideas, not realizing that in this sense there are dangerous teachers, who are more to be feared than dangerous newspapers. There are teachers who do not see that education is a sacred task and who allow it be used for the ends of some obsessive, all-pervading political ideology. (Teachers of this kind are a risk, with or without newspapers.) The political protection afforded by the provisions of regional and provincial laws have accordingly been of great assistance to teachers of good faith.

Financial assistance, however, while beneficial in itself, has usually been accompanied by the introduction of mechanisms which have directly affected the choice of a newspaper, under the pretext of the need to keep costs down, or sometimes under no pretext at all.

This has been done by making rules regarding the purchase of newspapers; by forcing people to buy only national newspapers in one region, or local ones in another, by fixing purchase quotas which put major newspapers on the same footing as those with a very low circulation, often papers that hardly anyone has ever heard of; sometimes by preventing people from choosing party newspapers; by making newspapers comprehensible to certain sectors of the population only, and so on.

Such decisions, handed down from above by the financing body—in short, by politicians—have shown that the freedom the school guards with such jealousy is restricted, more or less overtly, more or less deliberately. This state of affairs has certainly transferred some of the school's competences to the administration.

This has been a mistake. Many teachers were full of good will at the outset and saw the use of newspapers in the school as their own free choice, on condition that they were free to choose them and to choose how to use them. Subsequently they have seen their choice restricted and their methods questioned, to such an extent that they have given up.

The opponents of the use of newspapers in schools have been only too happy to confuse the problem of the extent to which public intervention should go with the cultural and social problem of the introduction of newspapers into the school. They have done so intentionally.

This is why we are today in a period of declining interest in newspapers as an educational tool for teaching pupils how to learn from the mass-media and, in particular, the daily press.

But it is a traumatic stage, a stage where we are searching for new balances, one that will inevitably achieve a proper relationship in which the triangle formed by school, newspaper and public institution will have the school and not the public institution as its base. It will be a relationship in which the public institution will reconsider its prescriptive role, and become more neutral and less inclined to interfere.

Journalists, for their part, should renew their efforts to grasp what it is that the schools need. The schools would like journalists at least to express themselves more clearly. But this is a journalist's duty to all readers. It is an objective that is within reach. It will be reached as new generations of journalists replace the old. Newspapers can never be of service to the school, however, if by that we mean that they serve the school alone. The school cannot expect journalists to write a newspaper the way a bedside book is written. A newspaper is published to record what happens in a community. It is for the school to read it, and to read it with understanding. Otherwise we should have a false state of affairs. It could be compared to the effect in the study of entomology if all butterflies were killed so that they would be like those that are pinned down in glass cases. Its parallel in physics would be the result of reducing the exciting reality of the subatomic world to the simplicity of the multiplication table. It is not too much to say that the school should be part of the fabric of society in all its reality. Newspapers should not forsake that reality so as to be suitable for the age-old institution that we call school. Journalism will never become education, for if it did it would no longer be journalism. However, to deny that journalism can be education is not to deny that undoubted fact that it can be a most valuable and indeed indispensable educational tool.

Notes

1. Nicola d'Amico and Luciana della Seta, *Il quotidiano in classe*, Milan, Zanichelli/Gruppo Rizzoli-Corriere della Sera.
2. Omar Calabrese and Patrizia Violi, *I giornali, guida alla lettura e all'uso didattico*, Milan, Espresso.
3. Yves Agnes and J.-M. Croissandeau, *Lire le journal*, Paris, Lobies, 1979.

Brazil: the press in school

Dymas Joseph

At a given moment, somewhere in the world, a teacher had occasion to mention—and even brilliantly illustrate—the fact that planets revolve harmoniously around the sun, in a pattern of discipline and symmetry which has been repeated over millions of years. But suddenly a pupil (perhaps the least clever of the class) got to his feet and asked for explanations about something he had read in the newspaper: a superconjunction. This was something that was quite unintelligible to him—and here, in the classroom, he was even more perplexed, for what the teacher had said did not square exactly with what he had seen in the newspaper on that morning of 10 March 1982.

The teacher's reaction to the pupil's question was likewise a noteworthy, although less uncommon, phenomenon. Displaying great self-assurance and some irritation, he gave his answer after glancing at page 43 of the textbook, where there were to be found the very words in which he had just described the harmonious arrangement of the planets, together with a handsome illustration showing the sun surrounded by its orderly and obedient attendants. The book was reliable (after all, it was in its fourteenth edition!) and the teacher was not wrong to take it as a guide. But 10 March 1982 was a special day—that the textbook had not foreseen—on which the nine planets of the solar system were due to change their positions transversely and all appear on the same side of the sun. And they had even made an appointment for the event: 8.30 p.m. Brasilia time. 'The planets will not lie in a straight line,' said the *Jornal do Brasil*, 'but inside a heliocentric segment defined by an angle of slightly more than 60 degrees. Six will be visible to the naked eye, and three—Uranus, Neptune and Pluto—with the help of instruments.' Because of these words, there was a confrontation in a classroom, on that morning, between a teacher (who repeated what a book said was true), a book (which proclaimed that truth), a pupil (who wanted to know the truth) and life (which is the truth in the world outside).

The news given in the press (which reported the living truth), and reproduced on radio and television, momentarily modified, in respect of one exceptional event, the truth repeated by the book in its fourteenth edition. Unwarned (or perhaps misinformed), the teacher did not know that a new fact had occurred and had made it necessary to revise his methodical teaching plan, which had gone so smoothly the year before.

The pupil's question showed that he was alert to what was actually happening here and now, and was endowed with sufficient curiosity and scepticism to unsettle the dogmatism of a well-established, oft-repeated and all the more respected concept. An unusual situation was created: for a moment, consecrated knowledge was put aside in favour of learning about something new that had recently attracted attention! Suddenly, the school, that stronghold of unchallengeable statements and concepts (some of which are only pre-conceived ideas), was going to be obliged to behave likewise in an exceptional way. The old agora of Athens was reborn, only this time the questioners found their answers, not in the subtle arguments of a master like Socrates, but in things that 'were there in the world for all to see once they had learned to do so'—as goes a song by a young Brazilian composer.

Learning to see

'Learning to see' is the same as the *Learning to Be* of the report by the International Commission on the Development of Education established by Unesco under the chairmanship of Edgar Faure,[1] who admirably explains it in Chapter 4, 'Challenges'. There he proposes that educators take on 'a fascinating task: that of discovering how to attain harmonious balance between rational training and liberation of sensibility', in such a way as to be prepared for changes and to allow questioning without being alarmed by doubts.

Let us return to the classroom with the teacher, the book, and the pupil whose question about a topic of the day was answered by the teacher's facile repetition of what he himself had learned once and for all. What happens in the mind of a child, an adolescent, if an item of information (so vividly projected by the media) conflicts with what he is taught in the classroom? Does it mean that the school is discredited, that it will have to change, or that school is dead, as Everett Reimer predicted?

Although it cannot be said that this is happening in all the schools of Brazil, it is undoubtedly the case in most of them. But is this true only here, or is it a universal phenomenon?

The thinking of John Dewey (in the United States) and Anísio Teixeira (the great disseminator of his ideas in Brazil) may suggest a line of approach to the problem that the American educator put in a nutshell when he said that school should imitate life and strive to be life itself. The effort to put into practice this idea, which almost became a slogan, ushered in one of Brazilian education's most brilliant periods, during which various educators made decisive contributions towards the revision of teaching methods.

Nevertheless, the problem arises both here and in other parts of the world: it is no longer enough for school to be part of reality; it must become a 'receptive creation', capable of shaping (not so much with the teachers as with the pupils themselves) the contours of a still unknown life—which will be the pupils' life years later when they have left the classroom. The school must be the place where the future is invented, for it will be in the fragile yet strong hands of children and adolescents. The objective is not to perpetuate the contemporary way of living, for this will be quickly swept aside owing to the speed of communications, but to be equipped to make the most of life in the world of tomorrow, precisely because of the extraordinary alternation of balance–imbalance–balance of modernity which is a continual process of renewal and self-transformation.

Galileo urges us on in his forthright way when he says that

science is written in that immense book which is always opening before our eyes (I mean the universe); but we will never understand this book unless we first learn to understand the language and to recognize the characters with which it is written.... Otherwise [he concludes], it is humanly impossible to make out a single word. Without this knowledge we can only wander aimlessly through a dark labyrinth.[2]

The characters referred to by the irreverent scientist in the passage quoted above cannot be deciphered by the adult generation to which the teachers belong; they raise questions to which the teachers are unable to give answers likely to satisfy the young generation, which is busy building another universe—different habits, concepts, values—and is showing, with strong encouragement by the media, that it has its own peculiar (and disturbing) way of seeing and re-examining, judging and choosing, acting and reacting.

Education rarely prepares the individual to adapt to change. It is true, however, that the teaching-learning process is being constantly enriched by a very wide range of technological aids. It is also true that the school is tending to relinquish its claim to monopolize society's educational functions. It is in this context that the media, and particularly the press—which enables news to be used as a teaching tool—can serve as a pedagogical alternative.

The role of the *Jornal do Brasil*

With this perspective, one of the country's best-known newspapers published the following statement by its editor, J. A. de Nascimento Brito:

The importance of news, not only for the shaping of public opinion, but also as a living record of history in the making, has for a long time seemed to us at the *Jornal do Brasil* to imply that it has a valuable contribution to make to the theory and practice of education. Today, one nation is stronger than another not by reason of its military might, but because of the quantity of information at its disposal. In accordance with our vision of the perpetual renovation of the world, we have realized that our social function would not be properly performed unless we established a service to help the community of young people by introducing news into the classroom as a factor to be included in the teaching–learning process itself as this is progressively focused on what is new and original. Nothing could be more logical, therefore, than to create an education department to arouse the school's interest in news—living, dynamic, up-to-date information—and to enable it in this way to play its role more effectively as the agent of change and the basis of the country's development.

We emphasize, in conclusion, that we are conscious of our responsibility towards the Brazil of the year 2000, which will be governed by the children and young people whom we are helping to train today.

Towards an education department

The question before us comprised a simple idea: news is indispensable for shaping an evolutive vision of the things of this world and also for enabling individuals to participate as actors in the evolutionary process, and not just as objects.

In order to set up an education department in an enterprise engaged in journalism and the dissemination of news—the *Jornal do Brasil*—it was necessary to work out strategies for pursuing its various objectives. There were many experiments, personal contacts, disappointments and frustrations, until finally the main theoretical principles on the basis of which it was to operate began to emerge. A series of meetings between journalists, cultural promotion workers, pupils between the ages of 13 and 18 and a model-maker resulted in the idea of creating a 'flying' editorial office which would take up quarters in a school for a given length of time.

According to this concept, the pupils would acquire some basic knowledge and skills in the fields of communication, editorial methods, creativity and team-work, and would practise observing, researching into and collecting documentation on the conditions prevailing in their community. They would also have to define the concepts of culture, community and the common good.

The experiment began in March 1972 with forty-eight sixth-form pupils, all belonging to the same stream, selected out of a school population of 850 pupils. The work was to be carried out on experimental lines with this stream only and without altering the curricula or the school timetable. However, we were allowed to use the classroom and ancillary school buildings out of school hours and to enlist the co-operation of the teachers.

During the first two weeks, we explained, in the most informal and practical way possible, how a newspaper is made, describing the respective roles of the editor, the reporters, the photographers, the illustrators and the page-setters, and giving some basic instruction in the preparation of texts, headlines and captions. We also organized exercises to develop the pupils' powers of observation and their ability to select and condense information, as well as games designed to teach them to pick out newsworthy items. At the same time, in order to make the conceptualizing work done at this stage more dynamic, we introduced (with the help of the teacher of composition, communication and self-expression) a wall newspaper for the use of the pupils in our group, with no restrictions as to content.

At the end of each meeting, we also used (with the unhesitating support of the science teacher) the technique of the 'spoken newspaper', which consisted in inviting any pupils who so desired (and in fact they were all willing!) to deliver an oral progress report, lasting one or two minutes, on the work done up to that point. This gave us an opportunity to correct or improve their oral expression by showing them how to present their ideas more clearly and making them appreciate the virtues of concision, without, however, inhibiting their creative capacity. During this stage, we concentrated on techniques of television and radio news reporting.

The spoken newspaper, as an exciting instrument for the self-evaluation process, was soon enriched by announcements of birthdays and parties and by bulletins that vividly revealed the children's interests as regards leisure activities, sports, culture and other, more unexpected matters. For example, we were occasionally faced with surprising demands, some of which were deep-rooted, but they were always voiced in a relaxed and cheerful atmosphere. We also observed a great improvement in interaction within the group.

As for the wall newspaper, it was made of a panel of soft-surfaced material measuring 2×2.5 metres, on which the pupils could fix slips of paper (or whatever else they chose) containing news. This noticeboard was hung on one of the classroom walls, not next to the entrance door (so that it would not be thought of as something to be only glanced at in passing) but on the opposite wall, which is the natural focus of attention. A rule was laid down at the outset; the wall newspaper was to be renewed every day so that no item of news would stay up longer than twenty-four hours (the purpose being to induce the pupils to read it every day). Later on we came to the conclusion that some information had to stay up longer, such as examination schedules, announcements of festivities, and so on. For this type of news item we therefore reserved a space (on the right-hand side of the panel) which was headed 'Coming Events'. But our guiding principle was that the wall newspaper should look different every day. To that effect, the news items in the 'Coming Events' space were arranged in chronological order, with the events closest at hand shown in red, the middle-term ones standing out against a yellow background and the rest shown in green. Every day, this column displayed a fresh illustration with a caption alluding to the next imminent event.

So as to ensure that the rule of 'looking different every day' was consistently observed by the wall newspaper, including the 'Coming Events' column, we found it necessary to use expressions such as 'tomorrow', 'today', 'two days left', and so on, in the form of subheads, thereby allowing the news to stay up but renewing its appeal from day to day and creating the impression that 'if you don't look at it today it won't be there tomorrow and you'll have missed something that practically everyone else knows about'. We agreed among ourselves that, as the newspaper would be stale after twenty-four hours, something new would have to be assimilated every day. The accumulated material was given to a group of pupils entrusted with the running of a research and documentation section, which classified the items displayed by the wall newspaper and other documents supplied by their classmates, thus making up files for reference purposes. This part of the experiment was later repeated by the Education Department of the *Jornal do Brasil* in other schools (involving pupils and teachers) in order to show how to organize and use files composed of cuttings from newspapers and periodicals. The library then made room on its shelves, beside its books, for these files, which covered such questions as the Transamazonian highway, petrol, energy (this subject being broken down according to the different forms of energy) and other matters arising out of work projects suggested by the teachers. Files soon began to be made up as fresh news appeared in the press. Among the subjects covered in this way were the space race, the death of Sadat and, more recently, the solar system (including the phenomenon of the superconjunction of the planets). We regularly contribute documentation material that the *Jornal do Brasil* has received but has not used, and we also run a column in the *Teacher's Newspaper* (one of the publications of the Education Department), giving more detailed information on recent events of major importance, which is also collected in these files.

Some school libraries have collaborated in the execution of this project by making up files of illustrations which the pupils can use for their academic work. Here too, the *Jornal do Brasil* enriches these collections with photographs stored in its own archives, but which happened never to be used in the newspaper; it donates one copy and keeps the negative.

To return to the wall newspaper itself, another rule was established: the material was to be harmoniously set out on the panel. To that end, a group was formed to be responsible for what the pupils had learned about page-setting, and every day it designed and made a model layout for the wall newspaper. It was the same group that introduced a modification in the work project in order to make the wall newspaper more attractive: instead of simply pinning slips of paper torn out of an exercise book on to the panel, the group had the idea of mounting the slips of paper on coloured cardboard, giving the effect of a frame, so that the news items were displayed in a more striking way. They then decided that one colour should be assigned to each day of the week, so that a change in the predominant colour of the panel would immediately tell the pupils that a new edition had come out.

What did the wall newspaper display? All kinds of things. Some critical comments on a television programme; an invitation to trade a book or some sports equipment; the football shirt a classmate was wearing when he scored the winning goal in the last match; a poem; a made-up anecdote; an invitation to take part in a research project on the life of an anthill. We could produce a long and fascinating list, but we shall stop there so as to leave the pleasure of discovery to anyone who carries out an experiment of the same kind.

One important activity deserves to be recorded here: the group that read the day's newspapers clipped out the most important news stories and pinned them up with a blank sheet of paper next to them, for their classmates to jot down their comments. At the beginning, the group cut out the whole article, but after a while the pupils in the group saw that no one read an article all the way through because it was too long and the letters too small, given the distance at which the reader stood from the wall newspaper. So some variations were introduced; they started by pasting up only the title or the subhead; then they saw that they should add on the lead and sublead, or the summary that always appears on the front page (which was, in fact, the name given to this part of the wall newspaper). Sometimes they only put up a photo or an illustration with its caption.

Nearby they placed a folder containing the rest of the press article which had been cut out and which was thus made available for a more thorough study of the question; the rule of providing a blank sheet of paper next to the news item (for comments and interpretations) continued to be observed.

Making a newspaper

By the end of the first month the pupils were enthusiastic. They were even asking to be given tasks in which they could make use of the instrument they were beginning to master. We then went on to the next stage of the project: the students wanted a publication that reflected their own experience. Where should we begin? Our suggestion was to make just the front page of a newspaper (like the *Jornal do Brasil*'s, for example). First of all, we distributed the roles of chief editor, editor, reporter, photographer, illustrator and page-setter. We divided the class into groups (about six or seven in each one), each one to be responsible for one of these jobs, and we studied the way in which the *Jornal do Brasil* had gone about setting up its front page. We described the task assigned to the *peuteiro* (the person in charge of suggesting how the content of the materials to be published should be presented), explained the rules applying to titles and captions, and identified the basic elements that go to make up a news item (who, what, when, how, where and why).

We then distributed page-setting sheets (models on which page-setters and illustrators work). The result was spectacular:

six front pages with 'photographs', different 'titles' and 'texts' hand-written by the pupils themselves. Each of these pages bore the newspaper's name and a rough logotype. The experiment was repeated twice, once using a collage of photos, texts and titles from newspaper and periodicals. The last production was a front page containing news of the school community, for which a 'press agency' (operating like a telex service) received information supplied by other classes.

A newspaper had been born and was faced with all the usual problems of layout, editorial policy, distribution and circulation. It was a home-made production of a kind which was close to Célestin Freinet's ideal means of fostering such things as: the team spirit; an experimental approach to problems; the organization and systematization of logical thought; participation in real work; the evaluation of one's work within one's own community; a critical mind; an aptitude for team-work; the improvement of skills of communication and self-expression; group dynamics (aimed at the socialization of all the pupils); participation in community life (at the levels of the school, the immediate neighbourhood, the district, the city and the world); curiosity and the active search for information; the habit of reading, researching and collecting documentation; and the free development of each individual's own idiom and modes of expression. In short, a project integrating art, education and communication, in which the school has become an open space and now thinks of its mission not as being expressly restricted to the transmission of knowledge, but as including the discovery of the vocation, talents and potentialities of each individual.

We carried on with our experimental project, which reached its peak after almost three months of work done in the school, in the editorial office of the *Jornal do Brasil*, and even in the homes of pupils or teachers, apart from the special meetings held for the 'editorial groups'. (Some of these were attended by professional journalists or cultural promotion workers recommended by us.) We had launched a venture and now pupils and teachers were ready to continue on their own, although they still needed some form of supervision, control and evaluation. The next stage in view was the publishing of a printed newspaper, for which we had to determine the extent of our participation, as well as trying to define what the Education Department of the *Jornal do Brasil* would be like and how it would operate.

At last, a programme

The experiment we had conducted with the forty-eight pupils could clearly not become their main activity. What we needed was a programme, rather than a project, whose scope would be wide enough, in accordance with our original aim, to activate the entire school community of a large area of the State of Rio, which comprised over 2,000 schools.

Nevertheless, we consider the work we did to be of the utmost importance, since it helped us to develop a philosophy based on the idea that news can be used to galvanize efforts to integrate communication into the art and education process. In the context of that experiment, some of our present forms of action took shape: preparing teachers and pupils for carrying out projects like those of the wall newspaper, the spoken newspaper and the printed (or hand-written) newspaper; encouraging school libraries to establish a research and documentation service to be responsible for keeping files of cuttings from newspapers and periodicals; launching the 'Young Newsman' project, which duplicates (with a few modifications) the experiment conducted with the forty-eight pupils, except that it is no longer concentrated in a single school, but is carried out by the pupils of several schools who come together for that purpose at the *Jornal do Brasil*; converting the 'editorial group' (which selected and displayed the news for the wall newspaper) into a newspaper-reading club.

We reconvened the group that had planned the pilot project and reorganized the Education Department on the basis of a programme reflecting the interests of fifth- and sixth-form pupils (between 15 and 18 years old) and providing for printed publications, projects, activities, the performance of services and campaigns (or promotion action). Two publications were planned: one for pupils and teachers, and the other for teachers only. The projects were designed to develop, within the school community, proposals related to subjects of public interest, most of which would be those dealt with in the *Jornal do Brasil*, for example, 'science clubs' and 'science fairs' (science and technology), an agricultural club, known as 'A Kitchen Garden in Every School' (health, food, agriculture), 'Ecological Reporter' (environment, ecology), 'Young City' (political education of young people) and many others. The activities were in fact less ambitious projects, like, for example, the one we called 'The Teacher Goes to the Theatre', in which the Education Department provides (for the use of teachers only) a free ticket for a significant play to be discussed afterwards with specialists. Another activity, called 'News School', consisted in publishing in the *Jornal do Brasil* material based on a news item enlarged upon by schoolchildren, for example, a new country's independence; in the case of an event of this kind, various aspects (geographical, economic, historical, etc.) can be dealt with in depth and prepared for publication in the press with maps, statistical data and other annexes illustrating them for didactic purposes. Other examples were the 'Occupational News Fair' and the 'Little Book Fair': during Book Week, some schools organize book exhibitions, talks with story-tellers and authors, who donate or sell their autographed books, exchanges of second-hand books, and so on. Yet another type of activity is the commemoration of events such as Health Day, Pan-American Day, or the anniversary of the birth or death of a public figure who has made an important contribution to the development of education in civics and cultural subjects.

As regards the performance of services, we have set up a Section for Assisting Educational Researchers. It keeps more than a hundred files containing news clipped from newspapers and periodicals and texts written by the Education Department itself, as well as books and collections that the pupils can consult in a room set aside for them, where they can study and select the material they need. If a pupil wants to obtain a copy of a document, we are able to supply it. Before a pupil begins his research, he is assisted by a professional who gives him advice as to the right way of approaching his subject.

We also keep a collection of all issues of the *Jornal do Brasil* that have come out during the last twelve months, so as to enable the pupils to refer to the material already published. The recent establishment within our enterprise of our own documentation centre has enabled us to offer a wide range of services, since this centre is equipped with microfilm readers, a cross-referenced index of published news, a valuable collection of documents dealing with the history of journalism, and a photographic library. Furthermore, pupils and even teachers can telephone the centre to obtain information.

Lastly, the campaigns are related to the major issues brought to the fore by the *Jornal do Brasil* or the community itself. Examples are the campaign called 'Plant a Tree', and another concerning child welfare which was conducted recently in response to Unesco's proposal.

Now that we have set up this flexible framework, which is renewed from year to year, we are sure of having a philosophy of action and a programme of projects that are well worth following.

A closer look at the Education Department of the *Jornal do Brasil*

In order to describe the functions of the Education Department of the *Jornal do Brasil* we must start by explaining the basic ideas underlying the *Wall Newspaper of Brazil*, the *Teacher's Newspaper* and the Section for Assisting Educational Researchers.

The *Wall Newspaper of Brazil* is the kingpin of our efforts. Unlike the previous experiment, this wall newspaper is produced by us and printed on the same presses as the *Jornal do Brasil*. It consists of an unfolded double page, the two sides of which are treated as two distinct parts. For the content of one part, we choose (with different groups of pupils) a subject related to the curriculum; the other part displays typical press material dealing with the most important news of the moment, provided that it has something to contribute to the pupils' school work. As in the case of the previous experiment, there is also a calendar on one side, showing the fortnight's most important dates and events. The *Wall Newspaper of Brazil* is published fortnightly and distributed free of charge, by mail, to all the schools and other educational institutions of the city of Rio de Janeiro. Its texts are short, printed in large type (as they are intended to be read at a distance of 2 or 3 metres) and well illustrated.

The idea of the *Teacher's Newspaper* arose from the need to give teachers a deeper insight into the subjects touched on by the news items presented in the *Wall Newspaper*, in order to enable them to deal with them adequately with their pupils. It is produced in the form of a quarter tabloid, is also published fortnightly and comprises sixteen pages that are mainly designed to facilitate the introduction of news into the classroom. It also features a brief review of major events that have occurred in the field of education, bibliographical notes, summaries of pedagogical theories and teaching techniques, personality profiles of leading educators and press reports on miscellaneous subjects.

The Section for Assisting Educational Researchers has already been referred to. It remains for us to describe the system which links together the three elements considered above and which (along with the activities, campaigns and projects) has made the Education Department of the *Jornal do Brasil* what it is. It operates as follows.

Every process begins with a news item. This item, which is taken from the *Jornal do Brasil*—for example, the super-conjunction of the planets—is presented in the appropriate language and typography in the *Wall Newspaper of Brazil*. This is hung up in the classroom and arouses the pupil's curiosity, inducing him to question the teacher about its content. Meanwhile, the teacher has been enabled by his *Teacher's Newspaper* to answer the pupil's questions and, using the suggestions made in that publication, to propose a line of research for the pupil to pursue. But where can information be found about the present superconjunction of the planets of the solar system, since it is too early for the information to be given in the textbook? Answering that inquiry is the function of the Section for Assisting Educational Researchers, which will, if necessary, direct pupils to external services to help them find better documentation and may even tell them who is the right person to see ('Go to the National Observatory and ask for so and so at such and such a time, or telephone him at such and such a number').

In this way a cycle is formed and the process is continually supplied with fresh material, since it begins by taking news from the *Jornal do Brasil* and ends by bringing it back to the Education Department, which is engaged, at the same time, in promoting activities (such as a visit to the Planetarium), writing up material of the 'News School' type for the *Jornal do Brasil*, and encouraging young scientists to study the matter for the next annual science fair, besides providing school libraries with reference material. In the same way, certain projects, such as the 'Young Newsman' project and its production of school newspapers featuring this kind of event, can benefit from the action taken to focus attention on news items. More and more examples can be quoted as the list of subjects lengthens. We do not have space here to enumerate all the forms in which this programme is being carried out.

On the strength of the results obtained by the Education Department of the *Jornal do Brasil*, we feel sure that its various sections are contributing, through their interaction, to a receptive endeavour, ideologically oriented towards the development of a critical awareness of the world and the things around us. In these twelve years of work, each of these sections has made its own impact and acquired its own credibility, although they are all integrated into a process in which news is both the point of departure and the ultimate goal.

Notes

1. Edgar Faure, *Learning to Be*, Paris/London, Unesco/Harrap, 1972.
2. Galileo Galilei, 'Poetry and Philosophy: The Book of the Universe', in *The Experimenter*.

Cuba: an introduction to radio broadcasting

Renaldo Infante Urivazo

The environment

On 25 April 1971, Fidel Castro inaugurated the Basic Secondary School in the Countryside in the Victoria de Girón Citrus Cultivation Plan area. The Citrus Cultivation Plan area is located in the Matanzas province, adjoining Jagüey Grande, a flourishing southern town that played a prominent part in the historical events of the 1960s.

The inaugural ceremony initiated what was to be the Victoria de Girón Plan, which now covers fifty-six schools and includes in addition to basic secondary schools, a large number of pre-university and technical and vocational establishments. More than 40,000 students are enrolled in this impressive network of educational institutions.

Demographically, the area consists of an extensive region that was divided up in the past into a patchwork of small-holdings. Woodland vegetation was interspersed with pastureland, and agricultural yields were high. The major obstacle to rapid development was the large quantity of stone per metre of land. The most valuable natural asset was an ample supply of groundwater, well suited for the application of irrigation systems.

It was discovered in certain small plots or former small-holdings that orange and lemon trees could be cultivated with considerable success, producing high average yields.

State management of the project ensured speed and rigorous organization; the long and valuable experience of the population of the region in the cultivation of citrus fruit was an important contribution to it. Despite the shortage of qualified technical staff, the plantation system was successfully introduced.

It was a risky venture in view of the lack of properly qualified personnel, but it also promised to promote economic development in the southern part of Matanzas province and to break the pattern of one-crop production by introducing a new and important type of cultivation that diversified agriculture and gave access to a lucrative export market.

The second complex was inaugurated in the same year. It was called 'Décimo Festival' commemorating the Tenth World Festival of Youth and Students. The rate of construction was to increase in subsequent years, and the present total now stands at fifty-six establishments.

The implementation of the Citrus Cultivation Plan and the presence of the schools in Jagüey Grande brought about a radical change in an extensive region that had previously been one of the most neglected in the country. The construction of dozens of new schools was accompanied by the growth of a new population centre with large housing projects to accommodate the workers and farmers. Miles of new roads form a constantly expanding network; electric power systems have been established for agricultural, educational and social uses, and telephone facilities have been installed.

Students attending secondary, pre-university and technical schools play a vital role in looking after the gigantic nurseries of millions of plants, in grafting, irrigating the plantations, pruning the trees, harvesting the fruit and performing many other tasks suited to the young. Seventy per cent of the harvesting is done by the students of the schools in the countryside.

Background

An appreciable number of students who had just left primary school moved to the area from other provinces. There was a really urgent need for secondary teachers and a titanic effort was required to reach a solution. This phenomenon, typical of growth periods at the various stages of development, had assumed alarming proportions in the early years of the revolutionary regime, necessitating emergency measures and meticulous planning for the future. On that occasion, many expedients were resorted to, including the use of radio and television in support of the national system of education.

The possibility of offering teaching posts to students who had completed secondary school was considered, despite their total lack of experience. Implementation of this idea led to the creation of what was to be the first contingent of the Manuel Ascunce Domenech Teaching Detachment.[1] Through its work in various courses in the schools, this reservoir of future leaders helped to educate thousands of young people at secondary level.

The young student-teachers made an effort to take part in all the activities of the school, joining with their pupils in the work of planting and harvesting, and performing the duties involved in a boarding-school system. With the help of these pupil-teachers, who often faced students older than themselves in the classroom, thousands of young people received an education that combined study and work; thus a means was provided of meeting the demand for teachers, while at the same time furthering economic plans, producing new wealth, and matching education to the society under construction in Cuba.

The transformation of the area and the fact that a settled population came to exist side by side with a fluctuating community of students gave the territory of Jagüey Grande a particular personality and style of life, influenced by its major agricultural resources, and giving rise to various cultural tendencies and movements reflecting concern for interaction and communication. The educational establishments are separated from each other by plantations, but their activities and objectives are similar and the system under which they operate is the same. As a result, many felt the urge to find ways and means of forging new links between the people living in the area. Among the many activities planned and implemented, the idea of starting a radio station that would base its services on the immediate socio-economic environment took shape. Various agencies and institutions were asked to support the plan. Cultural circles, the cinema, science and technology and the sporting world were all asked to play a role. The Cuban Radio and Television Institute backed the establishment of the broadcasting service and it was inaugurated on 8 September 1977, taking the name Radio Victoria de Girón.[2]

One of the policies and objectives of the country's national radio and television system is to cater to the interests of young people in its programming. The items transmitted by both media for young audiences include news broadcasts, cultural programmes, entertainment and competitions as well as discussions and various forms of guidance. In addition, radio and television have kept in close touch with the activities of young people in their political, social and student organizations, with their sports events, and with their achievements in national defence, education and the productive field.

The creation of the new radio station did not signify a further expansion of the general influence of radio, but represented rather an attempt to introduce a new dimension into radio work with and for young people on the basis of the new socio-economic phase that their total immersion in a study and work-plan had brought about. The creation of an instrument consistent with the type of education students were receiving was seen as a natural consequence of the contribution young people were making to the country's economy through such activities as those under way in Jagüey Grande. If young people were able to engage in productive work, fulfil targets, manage their affairs and organize their lives in the context of a combined enterprise of study and work, they were surely entitled to have instruments that they could handle according to their way of life and mode of action. And so the idea came about of putting young people in charge of programme planning and of the production of the programmes they selected. In short, young people in this case were the agents of socio-economic achievement and were making an important contribution to society through a new form of participation.

At the inaugural ceremony, the President of the Cuban Radio and Television Institute (ICRT), Nivaldo Herrera, outlined the objectives and characteristics of the radio station, announcing

> the birth of a young radio for the education of youth in the most fundamental values of the human conscience, for the dissemination of information regarding their concerns and achievements in the light of the education of the new generation, and in support of the self-sacrificing efforts of young people in the economic, political, ideological and cultural fields.

Relations between the broadcasting service and the Cuban national education system have never been so close as in the period of revolutionary reconstruction. Since 1959, strong links have been established at various times with schools and teachers. Primary, secondary and adult education have all made use of the resources of radio and television on many occasions to serve their aims. 'Radio classes' and 'teleclasses' became a commonplace of media jargon during the 1960s and played a very useful role until the country had a sufficient supply of teachers for the grades with the largest enrolments. But radio and television did not then relinquish their auxiliary role in education. They continue to provide instruction in music, dancing and languages, and special programmes are broadcast to help Cuban workers complete the ninth grade.

Another special link exists between the broadcasting service and the national education system. It consists in the provision of vocational guidance through so-called circles of interest. These circles, set up in some grades of primary education and at secondary level, bring together students engaged in similar activities with a view to identifying their inclinations towards specific branches of science, technology, art and other fields. There are, then, radio and television circles of interest in which students have an opportunity to get to know all the specialized branches of both media, for instance broadcasting, audio and video operations, script-writing, aspects of journalism, announcing, etc.

Preparatory work

The experiment described above provided an opportunity for the circles to work in the practical context of a radio station run by young people.

In the light of these possibilities, Radio Victoria de Girón began to set up circles of interest in the field of broadcasting in each of the establishments belonging to the Schools in the Countryside scheme. A committee of assessment was formed to pre-select students for the circles, which were to be composed of professional programme directors, journalists, technicians and announcers. A timetable was drawn up and the process of selection was initiated. At the same time, a number of specific technical criteria were established, for instance a good speaking voice, diction, reading, writing/editing and the ability to integrate into a working unit of the kind proposed. An opinion poll was conducted to discover aptitudes for radio work.

As soon as this process and that of selection had been completed, responsibilities were assigned as follows: (a) director of the circle; (b) writers and/or editors; (c) announcers; and (d) news correspondent.

It was recognized that selection did not in itself guarantee the proper functioning of the circle, and so a seminar on the various specialized fields was organized and students were coached in a variety of skills ranging from script-writing to news editing.

The success of the learning process depended on the quality

of the advisory services that could be offered, because the material studied and explained during seminars was not sufficiently comprehensive. The practical application of certain procedures helped to consolidate the theoretical knowledge acquired and test whether it had been correctly assimilated.

In this connection, two separate methods were employed, both of which proved effective:

1. Analysis of a script with the members of the corresponding circle prior to programme recording, so that the text can be corrected where necessary and the style adapted for radio. This first phase is followed by oral practice, covering aspects of elocution, dialogue, forms of presentation, tone of voice, modulation and inflexion. Once the form and content of the programme have been finalized, work can begin on the recording of voices in the studio.
2. Operation and control of the radio bases in the educational establishments through the local network. In this case, the students are given practical training for their future radio work under the effective guidance of a teacher specializing in a branch of the humanities, either Spanish or literature. The correspondent plays an important part in this activity, summarizing the principal events of the day in the school, such as information meetings, work in the citrus plantations, competitions, sports events, etc., and sending them to the station.

In planning the radio training scheme for young people, both the educational and radio and television authorities considered it advisable to keep membership of circles of interest stable, with students spending as much time as possible in contact with the station and making full use of the capacities that they develop with experience. The selection process takes place among students in the seventh grade, that is, the first year of secondary education. Successful candidates can therefore work in the field of broadcasting for six school years, until they have completed the twelfth grade. But this does not come about automatically. In order to remain a member of the circle and to continue working in the field of broadcasting, students have to achieve consistently satisfactory results from year to year.

When specific needs or unforeseen circumstances lead to transfers of students that may affect the membership of the circles, a further evaluation session is organized in addition to that carried out each year among seventh-grade pupils. Moreover, an assessment procedure similar to that for secondary students is conducted in pre-university and polytechnical establishments.

The studio managers, editors and sound technicians work with professional equipment that requires special care in order to keep it in good operating order and to ensure that it is used to full advantage.

It is therefore given very careful attention. Radio Victoria de Girón can count, then, on the services of experienced student managers, sound technicians and editors. Those who have shown the greatest skill and facility in applying radio techniques are made responsible for putting the station on the air, looking after the complex hook-ups or network operations and directing the live programmes.

The circles of interest clearly form the basis for this special type of work. Their major strength lies in the fact that the pupils' theoretical and technological studies find immediate application, being carried into practice through the radio base and the student broadcasting service. In this respect, the circles may be considered as a dependable source of manpower.

The fact that students have to be highly qualified and produce satisfactory results acts as an incentive and driving force in the educational field, since nobody wants to be deprived of his functions on account of laxity in his studies.

There are at present fifty-six circles of interest in all, one for each educational establishment. There are programmes with established student announcers who have built up three or more years of experience in broadcasting, a fact that bears witness to their enthusiasm and the interrelationship between their educational aspirations and their keenness on this kind of work.

It is interesting to see the resourceful way in which these 15- and 16-year-olds tackle the production of radio programmes of quite considerable complexity. They are helped in their task by the guidance provided by professionals who supervise every step taken by the members of the circles. Direction and guidance in educational terms must play an important role in a broadcasting service that forms an integral part of the educational system, since emphasis is laid on the acquiring of habits and the development of initiative and skills, as though it were an education unit within the broadcasting service. Well-qualified professionals must therefore be selected who will devote themselves fully to the task of guiding the members of the circles.

Programme planning

Cuban adolescents and young people as a whole are organized in the Union of Pioneers, the Federation of Secondary Students and the Union of Young Communists. Without the help of these organizations, ventures such as Radio Victoria de Girón would not meet with the same success in their work with young people. As organized forces, they provide backing for the achievement of objectives and targets in all kinds of fields.

All members of the circles of interest in the basic secondary schools are Pioneers, so that their programmes are used by the José Marti Organization of Pioneers in furthering its activities. In the case of the school, it promotes healthy rivalry between centres, citrus harvesting contests and the year-to-year struggle to achieve high results of outstanding quality. The broadcasting service is represented at all Pioneer ceremonies and events in the persons of its correspondents, who are responsible for providing information on political, recreational, cultural, historical and other activities.

In the pre-university establishments the Union of Young Communists has been carrying out similar work, with the support of the Federation of Secondary Students (FEEM).

This federation groups all students at pre-university level and those attending technical and vocational establishments.

The circles of interest at these levels provide information on their activities in the programmes they broadcast. Interviews with collectives that have achieved outstanding results in citrus production or in promoting cultural and sports events are a common feature.

Radio Victoria de Girón is also used as a means of developing awareness and it plays a part in the ideological struggle to protect our young people from deviationist and diversionist tendencies that are alien to our way of thinking and to the values of a new society attempting to construct a socialist system.

The Society for Patriotic and Military Education (SEPMI) has thousands of young members throughout the country and has advisory links with the Ministry of the Armed Forces. It has introduced a series of technical military sports activities that has aroused enthusiasm on the part of students at pre-university level in the context of the Schools in the Countryside scheme. SEPMI is given broadcasting time to publicize the activities of its leading units and the timetable of its training sessions. SEPMI's objectives provide the keynote for the radio programmes on this subject: education of youth in the highest patriotic values; preparation of youth to confront the enemy in the event of an invasion of our territory; helping them to occupy their leisure time by providing facilities for the pursuit of their recreational and other interests.

As far as free time and recreation are concerned, the student radio goes to great trouble to cater to young people's interests and succeeds in developing a close relationship between programme and listener, covering topics requested by the student body and offering suggestions on various issues.

Table 1 gives an idea of the various programmes transmitted by Radio Victoria de Girón in its six hours of daily broadcasts for students.

One of the factors that facilitates radio programme planning in Cuba is the close co-ordination between producers and

TABLE 1. Radio Victoria de Girón's student broadcasts

Type of programme	Hours per week
Information on the daily activities of the educational establishments: reports on progress and contests, sports, outstanding achievements in work on the citrus plantations, etc.	10[1]
General information on national and foreign affairs	4.25[2]
News and information on citrus cultivation, patriotic and military education, trends of youth organizations	9.45[1]
News bulletins	1.20[1]
Educational and methodological guidance	3[1]
Scientific and technical subjects	2[1]
Cultural, instructive and analytical programmes	1.30[2]
Music programmes including items of general interest	10[1]
TOTAL	42

1. Student presentation and production with advisory assistance.
2. Student presentation and student and professional production.

the institutions and bodies whose work has an impact on the radio message. Specialists in education and culture, for instance, play a direct role as consultants for programmes in these fields. Each year, the education authorities provide the materials used in the seminars, the teaching staff, methodologists and inspectors, and transport facilities for conveying students to the radio station. In the cultural field, an enormous amount of work has been done by the 'Twentieth Anniversary' Brigade of Art Instructors, whose specialists direct all cultural activities in the educational establishments belonging to the Schools in the Countryside scheme.

The cultural programmes broadcast on the student radio enjoy considerable prestige. Special mention should be made of an unprecedented experiment initiated and directed by the station itself. Part of the music broadcast is performed by the student members of an amateur movement that makes recordings each month in the studios of Radio Victoria de Girón.

This is a further aspect of the student radio that distinguishes it from the country's other broadcasting services.

The universal tendency to set up small local broadcasting units catering to the needs of smaller communities is everywhere the subject of penetrating analysis. The more relevant a radio service is to its socio-economic environment, the more likely it is to attract thousands of listeners who find their own specific interests reflected in the programmes.

However, the Cuban broadcasting system combines this approach with the stratification of programmes, differentiating between the municipal, provincial and national levels. Thus, the small stations have six to eight hours of their own programmes and link up with the provincial stations to which they feel most closely allied during the rest of their time on the air.

For twelve hours Radio Victoria de Girón relays the provincial programmes of its big sister, Radio 26, of Matanzas province. This leads to greater rationalization of content. In the case of news, provincial and national newsreels are relayed and the local station concentrates on preparing bulletins based on contributions from student correspondents in the schools. The correspondents vie with each other every month as regards the quantity and quality of their reports, which are communicated by telephone, telegraph or school transport.

Radio and production

Radio Victoria de Girón observes and monitors the progress of the plan through the students' work. It channels its own efforts in two directions: stimulation of educational activities and support for the achievement of economic targets. Its role is therefore based on the interaction between these two objectives.

Investment in school-building under the plan has exceeded 59,640,000 pesos, not including the state's investment in equipment for the centres. About 500 students are enrolled in each school. They are organized in brigades and are responsible for about 1,320 acres of citrus plants. Their work represents a considerable saving for the Cuban economy, and at the same time they are being prepared for life and imbued with a productive spirit.

The performance of the various districts in the plan is checked from time to time and the best brigades selected. Challenges are issued on the air, the winning collectives are given encouragement and daily production levels are publicized.

The information programmes go into great detail regarding technical questions. For thirty minutes each day they offer guidance on plant care, characteristics of varieties of citrus, ways of dealing with pests or vectors, the influence of climatic features on the spread of diseases, etc., and the results achieved in the eight districts into which the plan is divided. A very close link has been established in this connection with the management of the enterprise, which supplies the radio with useful scientific material and appoints technical experts to supervise the programmes and take part in them.

The manpower involved in implementing the plan at present includes 238 middle-level and 110 senior technicians—economists, agricultural engineers and mechanical engineers. Each year the technical and vocational education establishments in the same area produce hundreds of qualified specialists in citrus fruit cultivation who are incorporated in the plan or in those of other regions where their expertise is required. The scientific and technical programmes broadcast by Radio Victoria de Girón are presented by announcers, operators and producers from the polytechnical institutes specializing in citrus cultivation.

But the student radio in Jagüey Grande does not concentrate exclusively on favourable developments. Considerable importance is attached to criticism as an incentive to improve quality and output. Such criticism is usually levelled against collectives that are lagging behind or whose work is not up to the mark. But it is a method that requires careful handling on the air. A good deal of tact and skill is needed as well as rigorous control and reliable data. Criticism of this kind can be formative and constructive and exert a stimulating effect. A collective that is the target of criticism today may be singled out for praise tomorrow.

Sociology attributes to the media the role of organizer, teacher, guide, and habit-former, influencing social conduct and promoting a communal and united spirit. But each medium has been created for a specific aim and purpose, and one of the things that makes this Cuban experiment unique is the fact that it trains young people to perform practical tasks. It becomes clear, on analysis, that the phenomenon of a student-run radio station with student-produced programmes is closely bound up with the integrated educational approach that combines study and work—learning about a specific branch of agriculture and applying the theoretical knowledge thus acquired to practical cultivation.

This approach has yielded important results, which the national educational system considers to be highly positive, the use of radio having contributed to this achievement. We consider that, from the standpoint of national interest and the development of the country, the student radio scheme has fostered the all-round education of young people, providing them with vocational guidance in regard to their future development, training them to live together in harmony, inculcating awareness of their role as producers and cultivating work habits.

It has helped to raise the political and ideological level of young people in general, teaching them the principles of socialism and proletarian internationalism.

It has played a crucial role in achieving economic progress by showing young people their duties in terms of citrus cultivation and production, an important source of foreign exchange for the country. It has used information as a powerful vehicle for publicizing and organizing major economic tasks, providing evidence of the extent to which broadcasting can serve the purposes of development.

It has improved school performance and encouraged students to remain longer within the educational system. In addition, through its preventive campaigns, it has been a source of health education for young people and the population in general.

It has promoted and is promoting healthy rivalry as a motive force in education and economic development, turning it into an effective lever in the effort to expand production.

The Cuban state is extremely pleased with the experiment and plans have very recently been drawn up for two new stations, organized along similar lines and linked to agricultural development projects in the municipalities of Sola in Camagüey province and Sandino in Pinar de Río province.

Notes

1. The teaching detachments form an advance guard whose purpose is to back up the regular teaching staff in areas where the need is greatest, either in the national or international context. Manuel Ascunce Domenech was a young literacy teacher who was killed by bandits in the mountains of Escambray during the National Literacy Campaign organized in 1960 and 1961.
2. The radio took its name from the victory achieved in Playa Girón (Bay of Pigs) by the Cuban Armed Forces and Workers' Militia in 1961 when they repulsed an invasion of mercenaries trained in the United States, Nicaragua and Guatemala.

Japan: television for young children

Takashi Sakamoto

Television programmes for young children

Young children from 2 to 4 years watch television on average about three hours a weekday in Japan, according to a survey by the National Television Company (NHK) in November 1979. In summer, it is found that this figure is reduced by half an hour. Among children there are some viewers who watch television even eight hours a day.

Young children generally want to participate in games and plays on television programmes. Mothers and relatives are also very eager to see their own children playing on television. If someone appears on television, he can become a hero in his neighbourhood and in his nursery school. The waiting-list for participating in television programmes is now very long, sometimes at least three months.

In nursery schools and kindergartens, most young children watch educational television frequently. Many teachers recognize the educational effectiveness of educational (ETV) and some that of general television (GTV), and recommend that children watch these programmes. However, some parents worry about how negatively crime and violence on television affect children's habits, thought and language. The influence of television on a child's life is regarded as quite large both in terms of positive and negative aspects.

The most avid viewers are 3-year-old children; the next are 2- and 4-year-old children. The viewing hours of children over 5 are at the same level as those of primary school children. For 3-year-old children, a total of one hour and thirty-three minutes out of three hours and thirteen minutes is spent on viewing with other children. This kind of figure is usually reduced by about half an hour in a summer month such as June. According to a similar survey by NHK conducted at Osaka in June 1979, the most frequent viewers are also 3-year-old children.

The percentage of mothers who feel that their children watch television too much is 21 per cent of mothers of 1- to 3-year-olds, 28 per cent of 4- to 6-year-olds and 42 per cent of primary-school children. Children whose mothers control their viewing time watch television for a shorter length of time (the difference is approximately fifty minutes) and mothers who graduated with a higher level of schooling regulate their children more.

In effect, though children watch television for nearly three hours on a weekday, it is assumed that most mothers (70–80 per cent) do not feel this figure is too great. They seem to accept television for young children. Above all they themselves watch television for a great number of hours during the day. However, mothers who graduated with a higher level of schooling tend to emphasize the negative effects of television on child-rearing.

In pre-school education, children also frequently watch ETV in the classroom, mostly in the morning. In 1980, teachers in about 75 per cent of nursery schools and kindergartens utilized ETV in the classroom. ETV programmes are widely accepted and highly respected by both educators and mothers.

Kinds of broadcasts

The Forum of Children's Television, a voluntary group of mothers studying the effects of television on children, examined the television programmes produced for young children from pre-school to primary school and shown in the evening by five television stations in the Tokyo metropolitan area from 5 to 8 p.m. in one week of July 1981. They found that eighty-two programmes were broadcast, for a total of twenty-eight hours and fifty-five minutes, during that period. The components of the content are shown in Table 1. We find that comic animations are most popular. In the morning a few television programmes for young children are also broadcast. For example, there are *With Mothers* by NHK, *Open! Pong-ki-ki* and *Play with Mamma, Ping-Pong-Pang* by Ruji TV,

TABLE 1 Components of television programmes for young children transmitted by five television stations from 5 to 8 p.m. in one week in July 1981[1]

Kinds of programme	Number of shows	Total broadcasting time, in seconds
News	5	7 500
Documentary (nature, scenery)	5	728
Drama (except animation)		
Specially photographed:		
Metamorphosis	6	9 020
Puppet	5	4 375
Series:		
Japanese	6	9 175
Foreign	1	2 700
Classic:		
Foreign	1	1 510
Information on art and artist	5	5 625
Animation		
Action	12	17 234
Comic	21	24 255
Others	15	21 991
TOTAL (in one week)	82	104 113[1]
TOTAL (in one day)	11.7	14 873[2]

1. 28 h 55 min 13 s.
2. 4 h 7 min 53 s.
Source: Adapted from *The Data* by Forum of Children's Television, 1981.

Curricular Machine by NTV. The first three are omnibus programmes for young children composed of dance, song, physical exercise, puppet shows, story-telling, animation, and so on. *Open! Pong-ki-ki* is rather similar to *Sesame Street*. *Curricular Machine* is intended to develop concepts of number and words. Generally speaking, an omnibus programme in the morning and animation and puppet-show programmes in the evening are viewed extensively by young children, according to an audience survey.

In these kinds of television programmes, the target is young children from 4 to 12 years in the evening, while programmes presented in the morning are produced for 3- to 5-year-old children. However, 2-year-old children watch television for three hours a day. Also, in nursery schools, children aged 1 to 2 watch television. These phenomena suggest that mothers and nursery-school teachers would favour a good series of television programmes suitable for 2-year-old children.

A special project for developing television programmes for 2-year-old children started in 1979. The members of the team were composed of NHK television producers, child psychologists and educational psychologists of television. They cooperated to produce a new type of television programme for 2-year-old children. Television viewing by 2-year-old children was studied and educational objectives were set up. At the same time, some pilot television programmes were produced, evaluated by a microcomputer-based viewing behaviour analysis system, and have been improved by the results of evaluative studies. Some of them are already broadcast and frequently viewed by 2-year-old children and rated highly by mothers, educators and specialists in ETV.

NHK is producing and broadcasting six series of educational television programmes for nursery-school and kindergarten children. Table 2 shows the names and the rate of utilization of each series of programmes. *Kou-Kou, Son of River* is a programme of moral education, played by puppets; *Can We Make It?* is a programme in which a tall man makes various types of handicrafts and artworks set to music; *Our*

TABLE 2. Six series of ETV for young children in kindergartens and nursery schools broadcast by NHK

Name of series	Rate of utilization in 1980 (%)	
	Kindergartens	Nursery schools
Kou-Kou, Son of River	(Started in April 1981)	
Can We Make It?	50.8	48.2
Our Rhythm	48.4	55.8
Puppet Show	62.0	54.8
Our World	37.9	27.8
Bag of Mr Baku	26.9	25.6

Rhythm is a musical programme with dances and songs; *Puppet Show* is a programme of dramatic stories played by puppets; *Our World* is a science and social studies programme, and *Bag of Mr Baku* is a programme for developing cognitive ability. These programmes are broadcast three times a week on alternate days. *Puppet Show* is the most frequently watched series, followed by *Our Rhythm* and *Can We Make it?*

Younger children like to watch ETV programmes that include dance, music, movement, and artistic productions, such as *Our Rhythm* and *Can We Make it?* On the other hand, the older children in kindergartens and nursery schools like to watch drama programmes as well as programmes on the observation of nature and society.

Effects of television on young children

According to the above-mentioned survey by NHK of 1,481 mothers, babies are interested in sounds and images on television as soon as they begin to see the outside world. Children aged 1 to 2 begin to understand the content. Most 3-year-old children acquire the habit of watching their favourite programmes.

In terms of responses to television, various kinds of

imitative behaviour occur, as shown in Figure 1. The imitative behaviour of clapping hands and doing physical exercises begins in 1-year-old children, approximately one year earlier than that of singing songs and speaking, which starts with children of 2 or more.

In terms of the effects on the development of intellectual behaviour, Figure 2 demonstrates that 'interest in the same picture-books as viewed on television' gradually increases to include more than 80 per cent of $2\frac{1}{2}$-year-olds, 'questioning of things on television' also gradually increases to include more than 70 per cent of 3-year-olds, and 'remembering of numbers and words by television' gradually increases up to 70 per cent for 4-year-olds. These figures are reached by combining mothers' answers 'very often seen' and 'often seen' to questions on children's behaviour.

According to our evaluation studies on television programmes for 2-year-old children, 2-year-olds imitate physical movements much more than 4-year-olds, while 4-year-olds respond verbally to questions from television in a 'quiz' programme much more than 2-year-olds.

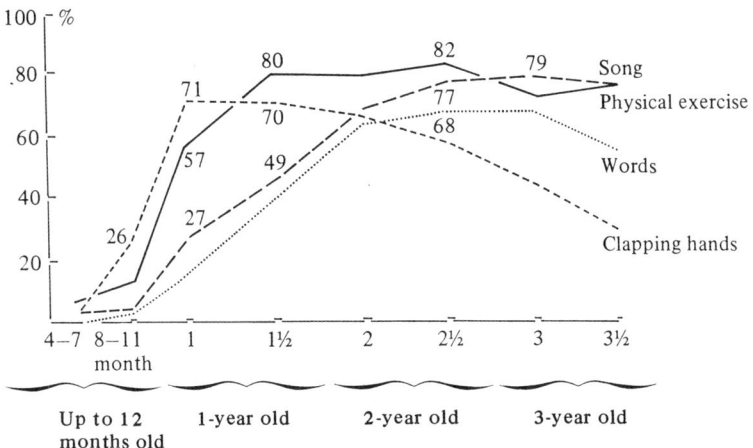

FIG. 1. Imitative behaviour stimulated by television (survey by NHK).

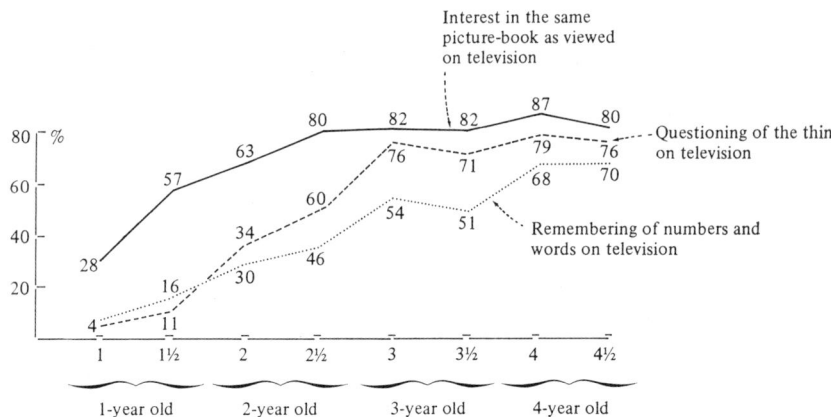

Fig. 2. Development of intellectual behaviour influenced by television (survey by NHK).

We can assume that drastic changes in the effects of television are found at various times in young children aged from 1 to 3 years, and also that television has a large educational impact on child development.

In terms of educational effectiveness, the following percentages indicate that of the mothers who answered 'yes' in the survey by NHK mentioned above, 43 per cent think that television enriches a child's knowledge; 38 per cent think that mutual empathy with other children is acquired by watching the same television programme; and 37 per cent believe that television enriches verbal expression in children.

On the other hand, some mothers feel that television has a negative influence on children: 35 per cent think that television teaches children more things than necessary; 28 per cent believe that it stimulates children to speak roughly and behave toughly; and 28 per cent think that it corrupts the Japanese language.

Above all, it is an interesting phenomenon that most mothers (73 per cent) evaluate television neither positively nor negatively. These figures are thought to represent a general climate among mothers about television for young children in Japan.

Concerning the negative effects of television on a child's behaviour, much information can be gained from another survey by NHK conducted on teachers from all nursery schools and kindergartens in Japan between September and November 1979. Generally speaking, more teachers from nursery schools than from kindergartens emphasize antisocial behaviour as one of the influences of television. A total of 23.4 per cent of teachers in nursery schools (17.0 per cent in kindergartens) feel that television affects the emotional equilibrium of young children, 31.4 per cent (29.5 per cent) that it encourages the use of rough language, and 28.2 per cent (23.8 per cent) that it stimulates violent behaviour.

Obviously, in most of these cases more teachers feel that there are no negative effects on a child's behaviour, as indicated by the figures above.

How are ETV programmes used?

ETV programmes for pre-school children are frequently utilized in kindergartens and nursery schools. In 16.7 per cent of kindergartens (10.3 per cent of nursery schools) teachers systematically use the series of ETV programmes by integrating all of them into the formal curriculum. In 39.4 per cent (35.8 per cent), of cases teachers use some series systematically but others not, according to the kinds of television programmes. Also in 26.4 per cent (32.9 per cent), ETV programmes are utilized differently, depending upon the teachers.

The statistics suggest that many teachers are utilizing the series of ETV programmes as a formal means of education.

In fact, some teachers put ETV into the daily, weekly, monthly or yearly teaching plan. The educational objectives of a series or a programme are clearly described and these are integrated with those of the ordinary teaching plan. Therefore, some teachers provide preparatory teaching on the content of the programme for children before letting them watch television. Also they help children to develop behaviour stimulated by the content of the programme after watching television. For example, after letting children view a programme in which songs and dances appear, teachers encourage children to continue to sing the same songs and dance the same dances. Later, new songs and dances can be created by the children themselves. After letting children view a programme in which handicrafts were made by a character on television, teachers show children pre-prepared materials and suggest that they make similar things. Making imitative products at first, children develop their activities to create new products. In these cases, ETV seems to provide cues for developing a child's creative behaviour. Certainly television programmes on the observation of nature and society give children much useful knowledge, and those with puppet shows stimulate children to talk about the story, empathize with the feelings of characters on television and imagine the future development of the story in the next show.

Improving ETV

In order to make better use of educational television, teachers should make continuous efforts to evaluate and improve their teaching with television. There are various ways of doing this. In the classroom situation, for example, the prescription sheet for improving teaching by ETV can be applied and also teaching simulations such as the desk-top teaching simulation game and microteaching can be undertaken. In the desk-top teaching simulation game, one of the teachers or student teachers takes the part of the teacher and the others play the role of students. They put a large paper board on a wide desk, which represents the classroom. On the paper board, they place puppets made of coloured paper representing the teacher, children, radio and television. Each child puppet has his or her own name and salient characteristics. By moving the puppets, they play the teaching simulation game. Those who play the role of students are expected to make their paper puppets behave badly. If someone feels there are problems, he or she can ask all the members to interrupt the game at any time and discuss how the teaching performance and lesson plan could be improved. These provide the kind of teacher-training methods for ETV education.

Meetings of teachers who utilize ETV in kindergartens and nursery schools also contribute to promoting the educational use of ETV.

First, there is the National Convention of the Japanese Association of Education by Radio and Television, which is held once a year. In 1981 more than 14,000 participants, including teachers at all school levels, producers, directors and researchers, got together to observe classroom teaching utilizing ETV and to discuss the effects of ETV and ways of improving teaching by ETV. There are also regional and local conventions of this type held throughout Japan. Teachers interested in education by broadcasting in the area where the National Convention is to be held have had many opportunities to learn and improve the methods for using ETV in class for one or two years prior to the conventions. Several local meetings are held and experienced teachers and leading scholars on education by broadcasting visit the area to advise teachers on how they should proceed with the activities in the preparatory period. Japan is divided into eight area blocks. Each block has the convention in turn. The impact of this sort of event seems to be very great.

Secondly, we have the Special Workshops for Studying Education by Broadcasting at each school level once a year. Experienced teachers, television producers and directors, and researchers get together to study theoretically as well as practically how to use and improve ETV, and how to improve education by broadcasting generally. Approximately 500 participants in total got together, who work at each school level in different places in 1981.

The cost of ETV

Television has a great deal of effect on children nationwide. As a vast number of young children watch television programmes and are influenced by them, the cost-effectiveness is assumed to be high. However, it is very difficult to calculate the actual cost of producing and broadcasting one ETV show.

A variety of costs are related. There are, for example, costs for facilities, personnel, planning, recording, producing, transmission, and so on. If we exclude the costs for establishing and using facilities and resources and the costs for salary of full-time personnel such as producers, directors, technicians, cameramen, artists, administrators, clerical and catering staff, we can calculate the direct costs for producing just one fifteen- to thirty-minute ETV show for young children. It is assumed to be no less than one million yen (US$4,500).

The role of adults

Television programmes for young children present a variety of songs, dances, plays, stories, puppet shows, pictures, forms, colours, motions, more skilfully and more attractively than teachers and mothers do for their own children. Moreover, television brings children to distant and dangerous places where teachers and mothers cannot take them.

In this connection, television can enrich a child's environment. However, television can neither diagnose children's responses to television nor give intellectual as well as affective knowledge of results (KR) to children. Television cannot change the speed of presentation and the degree of difficulty depending upon the child's responses. Television cannot evaluate behaviour in each child. It cannot transmit knowledge of results such as 'John, you are right, but Jack, you are wrong' to John and Jack respectively. Television cannot give each child an effective KR such as 'Wonderful!' or 'You are working very hard'. Teachers and mothers must diagnose each child's responses to television presentation, and they should give a suitable KR. If a child cannot understand the content of a television programme, it is a teacher or a mother who may explain it to him simply. If a child expresses incorrect responses to a television programme, a teacher or a mother may correct his errors, for example, by saying 'You are wrong'. By correction, he can absorb knowledge more strictly and reliably. When a child imitates the game presented on television, a teacher or a mother can accept his behaviour in a comfortable atmosphere. Supported by this affective acceptance of adults, a child is motivated to continue the game and finally he may create new games. If a child behaves in a violent way stimulated by a television programme, it is the mother herself who can scold him and instruct him that this sort of violent behaviour is not acceptable.

This means that three-way communication between adults and children is important for child development, that is, presentation of information by adults to children, diagnosis and evaluation of a child's behaviour by adults and presentation of KR information by adults to children. Though television expands only the first kind of communication such as presentation by adults to children, it cannot carry out the other two facets of communication. However, as the expansion of the presentation function by television is quite large, powerful and valuable, we should use television as much as possible, in so far as it has beneficial effects on young children. After that we can support and extend the educational function of television by diagnosing and evaluating a child's responses and behaviour to television and by giving them KR. Here we can achieve three-way communication mediated by television.

France: educating young television viewers

Évelyne Pierre

Instinctive caution often leads educators, whether teachers or parents, to fear any new device that captures and thus deprives them of their pupils' attention. This apprehension can be transformed, however, into creative ingenuity that will turn the threatening object into an educational instrument. As a result, by combining pleasure with the acquisition of knowledge, young people can become more confident in their discovery of the world.

As far as television is concerned, the truth of this statement has been put to the test since 1979 in France, in the context of an educational experiment known as 'Young Active Television Viewers'.

New educational theories

In 1979, acting on an initiative of the Cultural Intervention Fund, the various ministries involved in educational activities for young people—the Ministries of Agriculture, Education, the Family, Leisure, Youth and Sport—decided to conduct jointly, over a period of two years, a nationwide experiment in educating young television viewers. In a global approach to education, they urged all those who had a role to play in the learning process—the family, teachers, and organizers in the socio-educational and socio-cultural sectors—to take account in their educational activities of the part played by television in young people's daily lives. They encouraged voluntary education workers to organize educational activities with a view to enabling young people to turn this medium of communication to better account.

The educational programme is based on two premises. First, introducing young people to a new approach to television viewing and giving them an insight into the way in which the images of the world presented to them on the screen are programmed, produced and transmitted is going to make them more 'active', that is to say selective, critical, curious and receptive to information and the possibility of making new discoveries. Second, this training in independent thinking with respect to television will have an impact on the way young people approach other learning processes and on their relationship with the environment.

A complex, interministerial administrative scheme has been devised at the national level, involving, in addition, the social partners at the local level. It will help to protect the embryonic system against the sluggishness that bedevils even the most resolute innovators when their action is concentrated within a single institution. A further advantage of broadening the scope of discussions on education to take in a wide range of institutions is that it becomes easier to avoid the fragmentation of educational objectives that occurs when institutions operate separately, and to adopt an approach based on the interests of the child considered as a complete human being.

The experiment starts with a training period for the education workers who are going to act as innovators among groups of young people. Voluntary teachers, socio-cultural organizers and parents come together for a ten-day course to obtain information about television, and when they go back to the young people in their charge they devise learning situations involving that medium. For instance, they watch programmes recorded on video-tape, analyse television newscasts or discuss the programmes watched at home—activities that must be adapted to the ages, interests and reactions of the participants.

Exchanges of views between these educators are encouraged by local and national steering committees and foster a climate of mutual support conducive to a better knowledge of children and their relationship to television, and of creativity in education.

The steering committee has thus chosen to rely on the ability of educators to create their own educational tools. Rather than teaching standard exercise patterns, it proceeded on the assumption that by providing educators with the means of gaining an insight into the workings of television as a medium, they would be motivated and qualified to show young people how to do the same in their turn.

The programme is being conducted in various places in eleven of the country's administrative departments. It was introduced in 1979 in Dordogne, Hauts-de-Seine, Lozère, Maine et Loire, Pyrénées-Atlantiques, Seine Maritime, Eure and Tarn. Three new departments were added in October 1980, Haute-Garonne, Pas-de-Calais and Vaucluse. All in all, this represents about 25,000 young people and 2,000 educators, of whom 1,300 are teachers.

Testing the scheme's premises

After two years' experience, the Interministerial Committee commissioned an educational evaluation project to serve as a basis for decisions regarding the continuation of the programme and its expansion to include a larger number of young people. A team of three researchers was instructed to study the changes that had occurred in young people in the experiment areas.

The three researchers contacted 120 of these young people. They interviewed them before the experiment started, after three months, and then after seven months of educational activity. On the basis of these case-studies, they were able to establish a dynamic record of how the group related to television and their environment. The 120 young people were selected with a view to constituting a representative sample of French youth in the 9 to 18 age-group,[1] the operative variables being age, sex, parents' occupation and area of residence.

The information produced by this study, which is summarized below, provides greater insight into young French television viewers in the 9 to 18* age-group and encourages reflection on the possible formative impact of educational activities relating to television.

The following three sections will deal first with the results of observations made before the experiment started, which shed light on young people's behaviour and the way it is affected by the different variables, age in particular; consideration will then be given to the changes in this overall picture brought about by the educational experiment; and the author concludes with an appeal to teachers to use television for educational purposes.

Preliminary observations

TELEVISION IN CHILDREN'S LIVES

Behind the cold statistic of an average of two hours of television consumption daily, rising during the winter holidays and falling during the spring school term, is the warm affective universe of television viewing within the family circle. The pleasure derived from televison programmes, with the adventure, gimmicks and gags they present or from the thrill of fear when one is oneself safe and protected, is enhanced by the

---

* The experiment involved young people aged 4 to 18, but because of the limited time and resources available it was decided to concentrate on the 9 and over age-group. Information is, then, lacking in respect of an important period in the child-television relationship and the picture that has been compiled will have to be completed in due course.

ordered pattern of daily life. Television becomes part of the daily round. The child knows what to expect. He is familiar with the serials and the publicity and he derives pleasure from this familiarity.

Watching television always bears some relationship to other people. Either the child watches it because he is alone waiting for someone else to return and it acts as a substitute for someone else's presence, or he may watch it in the company of others, with the rest of the family.

Everyone has his own place around the set. The same ritual is followed in deciding which programme to watch. Alliances and conflicts among the members of a family are accentuated by television, which comes to occupy whatever place they assign to it: it accentuates the dialogue or lack of dialogue between parents and children or between father and mother, depending on whether it is the custom in the family to talk to one another or to remain silent.

The survey showed that children differ in terms of the benefit they derive from watching television. The extent to which they benefit seems to be closely related to a family variable, namely the active accompanying role played by some parents who offer their children reassurance and explanations and listen to what they have to say about television.

When the programme is over and the set has been switched off, the television is still present. The images are still there, assimilated by the child who proceeds to transform them and use them in his relations, games and conversation with his peers. The traces left by these programmes thus form a kind of shared cultural heritage in which children can recognize one another, confront one another and differentiate themselves from their elders. Among children in the 9 to 10 age-group, this interchange consists primarily in re-experiencing the pleasure of the actual viewing.

For adolescents, television tends rather to serve as a basis for discussion. It is their source of information about the world. Among themselves, they forge opinions and work out arguments and systems of proof.

For young people of all ages, television and the various activities and interchanges to which it gives rise are important factors in the process of their socialization.

THE WORLD ON THE SCREEN

How much do young people really know about this phenomenon of television which they sit watching for several hours a day and which figures so prominently in their conversation and play? How does it function? Who is behind it? How are the programmes made? How real is the world shown on the screen? The second research theme focuses on these questions. The replies obtained from young people reveal the predominant influence of age on the way in which the phenomenon of television is perceived. Taking the 9 to 18 age-group, we find two types of reaction among young people, the first characteristic of the 10 to 12 age-group and the second of adolescents; the transition from one to the other occurring gradually, through a series of discoveries made as the young person's experience of the world around him expands.

10- to 12-year-olds

How does television work? The 10- to 12-year-old child observes with curiosity the aspects of the technical world of television revealed to him: flickering, line crawl, picture break-up, the characteristic features of break-downs due to different causes. He draws analogies with the telephone to account for the technical functioning of television. His conception of the way images are transmitted derives from a comparison with networks of railway lines running in straight lines from the centre to the periphery. The child's reasoning processes are based on generally visible technical objects which he isolates from the system in which they occur, for example wires, spark-plugs or coils. Explaining things is a game and he is able to build up a logical argument, adding to it as new unknowns or new contradictions come to light.

His misguided notions about the technical functioning of television do not prevent him from having an intuitive grasp of the main implications of the process. For instance, he will have recently discovered that the same picture is transmitted to all sets at the same time. He knows that space and time in a television programme are different from the viewer's space and time. The location and duration of the events shown on the screen are determined somewhere in Paris. He knows what is meant by a live broadcast. It is none the less a fragile kind of knowledge and a few well-aimed questions can make him begin to have doubts and cut the ground from under his arguments.

Who is behind television? The world behind the screen, as children see it, is a world of actors and other persons who work with or for actors. They gather from the credits that a large number of people work together to put a programme on the air. These people are all in one place. They have others in charge of them, a director. To explain how the work is organized and how television operates financially, the child refers to the simple model of what he knows about his father's occupation or the jobs of other members of the family. The television buys films from the people who make them. It gets its money from what viewers pay for electricity.

In the child's view, the procedures for producing television programmes are much the same as those used for producing any other item of consumption. And it is the viewer who decides whether or not to watch such and such a programme.

A child's curiosity is attracted more than anything else by the way in which programmes are produced. It is the topic that elicits from him the most inventive observations and explanatory theories. The ideas he forges over the next two or three years about the real world and the world depicted through the media will stem from questions such as 'How are programmes made?'

Children tend to assume that the camera takes our place as a seeing eye and shows us what it has seen. Thanks to the camera, we see the object as it is. This idea is in keeping with the purpose of television, as the child sees it, which is to inform and educate viewers. Television backs up what it says with images. It shows us things and thus proves their existence. It is true because we see it.

If it wants to entertain us, television tells us stories. The stories are played by actors. The camera is placed in front of them and films them in order to show them to us.

Children begin to ask questions when the camera shows things too extraordinary to be done by actors without endangering their lives; for instance the man who can fly or who is cut in two. Children then talk about tricks and the kind of trick they usually suspect is that involving an object. The man cut in two was replaced by a wooden dummy. Thus, it was all done by conjuring, while the camera filmed the process, passively.

Later on children notice the visual effects produced by the camera itself. It moves, is positioned above the football field and follows the ball, showing the goal that has just been scored again in slow motion. The camera chooses what it is going to show. It may choose to turn in another direction, to show something else. The child has discovered the sequence. Many new questions arise: How does the cameraman manage to speed from the scene of the first sequence with the cowboy to that of the second with the cowboy's fiancée ten miles away? What is the cowboy doing when he is not on the screen?

The image is no longer a real object but neither is it yet a depicted object. Apparently, the notion of a recording medium which gives physical form to the 'representation', making it possible to cut and separate or join and juxtapose, is only just beginning to be grasped by most children in the 10 to 12 age-group, so that they still have difficulties in understanding the changes that may occur in the televized representation of an event.

In conclusion, children tend to make more and more observations regarding image-making processes in the 10 to 12 age-group. However, as they still enjoy the emotional security of their home and school environment, they do not fully exploit the implications of these observations and remain convinced that television is credible and demonstrates the reality of what it says by means of images.

Adolescents

If the camera exerts an impact on what it films and there is an intermediary between the object to be filmed and the viewer, the world on the screen is obviously not the real world and therefore calls for a vigilant and critical approach. The child has now become an adolescent who, actively endeavouring to achieve independence *vis-à-vis* his adult environment, is curious to know what is going on behind the screen and to find out about the intermediaries who transmit programmes to television audiences.

Young people of 14 or even 18 years of age are not very well informed about how television works in technical terms. Most of them are not particularly interested in having it explained to them and are content with a few unsystematic notions. On the other hand, their curiosity is considerably aroused, not so much by the activities involved in making television programmes as by the people who make them. Consequently, the world of television, which began and ended for children in the 10 to 12 age-group with the actors, becomes, for the adolescents, an environment peopled by professionals, each with his own field of specialization and mode of operation. Their explanations include certain economic phenomena borrowed from their immediate environment. The language of television comes into being as a result of these economic and human phenomena of production. The reporter is sent on an assignment, he travels, he decides to film this or that. The producer looks at the material and makes his choice. The length of the film depends on the amount of money available for filming and the space left by others in the transmission schedule. Thus, the language of television is formulated through a series of complex stages and negotiations. It expresses one point of view among others.

This awareness of the relativity of the language of television provides the setting in which the image is viewed. It is a man-made image, constructed purposely. People behind the camera—the cameraman, the producer, the director, the chairman—are trying to produce certain effects on the viewer. The world on the screen is not the real world but a representation of it which commands the viewer's attention and influences him in certain ways. On the basis of the data gathered from the sample of young people in the survey, it seems that between the ages of 14 and 18 there is an increasing tendency for adolescents to adopt a defensive attitude to the language of television, which they see as potentially dangerous for viewers who are not on their guard.

CAN TELEVISION PLAY AN EDUCATIONAL ROLE?

Young people's replies concerning what they have retained from television programmes open up a very interesting field of investigation for teachers. They reveal the meaning that young people attach to the word 'learning' and the attitude they attempt to adopt in a learning situation. In general, the replies do not differ greatly between the age of 12 and adolescence.

Children feel that in a visual context they miss a great deal and that they have no hold on what they see. The images flash past in swift succession and they claim to remember only what has moved them. When they cannot call to mind or rehearse orally what they have seen, they think they have lost all trace of it. They take voluntary recall as the sign of memorization. If something has been committed to memory, one should be able to recount what has occurred in the exact terms in which it occurred.

This conception of memory is not unrelated to their conception of learning: Learning means drumming something into one's head by repetition so as to be able to reproduce it word for word in the form of a recitation. This idea of learning, based on the model generally prevailing in education systems, which concentrates on rote learning and verbal exercises, affects their attitudes to television as a source of knowledge. It gives children the impression that television with its constant succession of images is not a valid medium for learning purposes.

These views are contradicted by two facts. When children relate what they have seen on television for their peers or an adult audience, they rely for the most part on memorized images. And in order to involve their audience in what they are relating, they tend to concentrate on the description of images.

The second fact to be noted is that attentive listeners are usually astonished at the variety and breadth of information about the world, both far and near, that even a child of 10 is capable of reproducing. All this contact is established through the television screen, whether or not it is processed by the family or peer group. Television is undeniably a source of learning, even if their school environment leads children to think otherwise. But, as teachers may well ask, what is the nature of the knowledge imparted by television? How is it to be integrated with that derived from other, more institutionalized sources of knowledge?

What are ambivalent attitudes produced in children, as spontaneous consumers of images, by our culture's denial of the role of images in memorizing and learning?

Three months and then seven months after the start of the experiment, the same children were asked the same questions and an attempt was made to see, through their replies, how the general picture of young people's relationship with television, as described above, had been changed by the educational activities carried out in the context of the Young Active Television Viewers experiment.

Findings of the experiment

The observations made prior to the experiment showed that children's replies tend to evolve, frequently in accordance with their age. It was found that children gradually become more independent in their attitude to television. This occurs in a series of stages, like periods of receptiveness during which they are interested in a specific problem and seek explanations which bring them closer, little by little, to the correct answer. At this point, they are receptive to whatever teachers may do to facilitate the process of understanding.

To begin with, it was ascertained that the Young Active Television Viewers experiment speeded up the transition from one period of receptiveness to the next. These activities, then, when adapted to one of these phases, made it easier for children to grasp the notions towards which they had been groping. As a result, after the experiment had been under way for seven months, the replies of some children were similar to those of children in the age-group above them.

The teachers contributed in several ways to this process of acceleration.

Children's observation capacities were developed by watching video-recorded programmes and making a joint effort to provide answers. They saw and heard things that they had not seen or heard under the usual family viewing conditions, discovering, for instance, film sequences, camera effects or the role of music. Moreover, they found that they were able to make discoveries on their own.

Supplying a child with vocabulary when he needs to describe what he has just discovered—close-up, zoom, voice off—helps him to understand things and makes the process of observation more interesting.

Explanatory comments bringing into relationship certain phenomena of direct relevance to what the child is exploring is another way in which the teacher can facilitate understanding and make new ideas more accessible. For instance, a teaching session on the 'jump cut' and its uses, many of which are already familiar to the child without his knowing it, makes it easier to understand subsequently what is meant by a sequence.

But the most important findings concern something more than the mere acceleration of development. In some instances, where there had been a large number of sessions, a high level of creativity among teachers and a strong spirit of co-operation among other adults, the reactions of young people indicated that they had adopted a new attitude to television and, by transference, to their environment. These reactions are indicative of development and encourage teachers to undertake further research.

One of the most important findings was that television can help teachers understand what motivates young people to learn. An adult, for example, accepts the idea of the pleasure that a child derives from television. He agrees to join him in studying the effects of these fleeting images and in investigating how television can be educational. This open-minded attitude gives him access to the world of the child, who is then more willing to engage in dialogue. The first step, that of motivating the child to learn, has been taken. The child's reaction to television indicates the stage he has reached in his questioning and the point at which contact can be made between him and the adult.

The child talks and the adult sees how the child has constructed his own picture of the world about him on the basis of all the information at his disposal. This self-directed intellectual process of construction for which television has supplied the widest range of material is thus revealed to the teacher. And it is his job to reorganize the elements of knowledge used in the process and to provide a foundation for them.

As far as history is concerned, viewers are offered programmes covering various periods of history, which are not in chronological order, and teachers tend to worry about the effects of this disorder. But it has been confirmed through the experiment that children take technological progress as their guide for re-establishing the sequence of history. The history of tools provides the framework for the human time-scale.

The survey thus brought to light some fragments of the world-views constructed by children and their organization. But it opened up a whole new field of investigation and of possible educational applications: for instance, how does a child of 10 or 14 perceive geographical space, the marine world or interplanetary space? And how should teachers set about grafting new material on to young people's conceptions of the world so as to give them access to a structured body of knowledge?

How should television be used?

The diaglogue about television between young people and adults that has been set in motion by the Young Active Television Viewers experiment has rekindled interest in the basic role of education, and television seems best equipped to deal with this subject.

Two themes for reflection are proposed.

First, television, with its representations of the world, is a good starting-point for investigating the phenomena of communication and the mediating of reality. Reality is presented to us from various sources through the juxtaposition of different points of view. Every description and transmission of reality proceeds by way of a channel which codes it. For instance, some groups of children participating in the experiment discovered, by analogy, that language is a code and that the relationship between an object and the name of the object is coded, just as the relationship between an object and the televized image of the object is coded.

A process of reflection may thus be set in motion. Who does the coding? How do they do it? What games can be played with codes? What is a jump cut? And what of the poetic dimension?

Television as a way of making children understand what learning means is a second basic theme for teachers to think about. In the process of analysing their difficulties in memorizing images, children are led to reflect on the concepts of memory and learning. Several types of observation may be of assistance in this task: a child discovers that he remembers the things that move him, and thus becomes aware of the important role of emotions in memorization. Or a child may attempt to explain the mechanism of intuition, for instance, by analysing the dynamics of a television narrative. But the idea of learning he has acquired at school prevents him from being able to co-ordinate this information without the teacher's help. He thinks that nothing exists save what is explicit or what can be made so.

It seems clear that the conventional approach of educationists in describing the learning process as the reproduction of external models supplied by a competent adult designated to perform that function, may impede and undermine a child's efforts to construct his own view of reality, efforts which are fostered to a very considerable extent by the material he sees on television. Moreover, the findings of the Young Active Television Viewers experiment justify the assumption that the best way of furthering a child's self-reliance and of giving him greater control over his environment is by teaching him how to control his own learning processes through personal observation enriched by appropriate inputs of knowledge by the teacher.

With a view to reassuring teachers who still feel cautious and encouraging those who are willing to take the risk of rethinking their role, the author wishes to put forward the idea that it is a more promising approach for teachers to act as guides for young people engaged in building up their own intellectual and social identity than to confine themselves to inculcating existing models.

The United States: visual literacy

Howard Hitchens

The study of the modern communications media has been a long-standing concern in education programmes in universities and colleges around the world. Social scientists and artists have evolved a language of film and television and are hard at work seeking the appropriate resting place for these media in our societies and cultures.

The growth of our ability to transmit information electronically all around the globe used in combination with fixed orbital satellites and increasing numbers of cable systems in many countries is a phenomenon that is causing concern in most countries of the world. For example, in the United States television has become the most pervasive and influential medium of communication.

Most of the population is served by broadcast or cable television. There are 270 public broadcasting stations, 720 commercial broadcast stations, and 25 per cent of the United States population is served by cable television (and that grows every day). The number of dollars involved with television broadcasting and reception in the United States is truly overwhelming. Television programming is available in the American home twenty-four hours a day, every day of the year. Is there any doubt that such a pervasive medium must be studied? Does not the citizen of a soceity so inundated with electronic information deserve to know more about it and how to cope with it?

Visual literacy

From the context of media education the need to cope with today's technological world in which we are inundated with information, particularly in visual form with the advent of television, has given rise to a movement in the United States scholarly community which has been labelled the visual literacy movement. 'Visual literacy' is a term that has been coined to describe a variety of theoretical constructs and practical considerations relating to communicating with visual signs.

The members of the newly formed National Conference on Visual Literacy in the late 1960s agreed on a definition of the term as follows:

Visual literacy refers to a group of vision-competencies a human being can develop by seeing and at the same time having and integrating other sensory experiences. The development of these competencies is fundamental to normal human learning. When developed, they enable a visually literate person to discriminate and interpret the visible actions, objects, and symbols natural or man-made, that he encounters in his environment. Through the creative use of these competencies, he is able to communicate with others. Through the appreciative use of these competencies, he is able to comprehend and enjoy the masterworks of visual communications.

That definition has evolved in the dozen years since its promulgation. Until today, the best definition is that visual literacy comprises at least four components: (a) competencies in visual languaging; (b) the ability to appreciate visual symbols and signs; (c) a process of developing competencies in visual languaging and appreciation; and (d) a movement, formal or informal, fostering the development of competencies in visual languaging and appreciation.

The framers of that original definition have enlarged their notion of visual literacy to include several general categories of activity, which deserve some discussion. Those categories are: teaching about visuals, relationships between visual learning/literacy and verbal learning/literacy, visuals in classroom teaching, and influence of the media.

Teaching about visuals

This area has traditionally been the domain of art teachers concerned with developing the skill to produce still pictorial images as well as the skill to analyse and to make judgments about the quality of such images. The teaching of the elements of design has come to be included in the curricula not only of art studies but of languaging arts studies and, as the audio-visual specialization has increased in the last three decades, as a part of the audio-visual curriculum in post-secondary institutions.

For example, four years ago a major curriculum project was instituted at Salisbury College of Advanced Education in Australia to develop a curriculum and materials used by hundreds of teachers in thirty schools. The project crossed over traditional disciplines in the development of its curriculum for teacher education, thus becoming inter-disciplinary. The project director, Deane Hutton, said 'A teacher may have practical skills is using the visual without the accompanying theory; but to have the theory without practice would leave him ill-equipped for the classroom.'

Visual and verbal learning

Television's pervasive influence has provided a strong reason for teachers to look carefully at the relationships between visual and verbal learning. In addition there is growing research evidence that visual languaging ability may occur earlier than verbal languaging ability in human development. Research at the Massachusetts Institute of Technology leads to that conclusion. One specific piece of research by Dr Phyllis Myers in 1980 led her to the conclusion that visual language abilities occurred developmentally prior to and serve as the foundation for verbal languaging. This growing research evidence supports the inclusion of the study of visual languaging as it applies to the development of learners in our teacher training programmes as well as in our elementary and secondary school curricula.

Several projects to develop a visual literacy curriculum have been undertaken in the United States in the last decade. In Milford, Ohio, an outstanding kindergarten-through-twelfth grade programme was developed in English language arts.

As early as 1967 in Greece (New York) Central School, four teachers addressed the problems of visual sequencing and written sequencing, major tools in developing adequate language skills. After working through a visual/verbal approach in their schools, the teachers concluded that the camera is a vital tool in written and oral communication with primary children. Mrs Ruth LaPolt, supervisor of language arts, concluded: 'evidence gathered during the regional summer school also clearly indicated that when youngsters planned to take a series of photographs, took the photographs, sequenced the photographs, and wrote or told a story with the photographs, the number of ideas they could successfully order doubled, or tripled. Further pedagogical practice indicates that in training visualization and sequential memory, the pupil should begin with visual cues which are then progressively removed as performance improves.'

A demonstration project in the Green Chimneys School in Brewster, New York, in 1966, concluded that 'children with reading or writing disabilities could develop communications skills through practice in photosequencing and through learning visual/verbal parallels.'

Other programmes have been developed in public schools throughout the United States in classes for both gifted and handicapped children. Both the research evidence and the results of curriculum development practice in the United States point to the importance of development of visual skills both in the schools and classrooms, and in our teacher training institutions.

The use of visuals

The use of visual material in our classrooms has been growing through the middle of this century. Again, research has demonstrated repeatedly the effectiveness of the use of such materials. In a summary of research findings in 1977 on the value of still pictures Brown concluded:
Pictures stimulate student interest.
Properly selected and adapted, pictures help readers to understand and remember the content of accompanying verbal materials.
Simple line drawings can often be more effective as information transmitters than either shaded drawings or real-life photographs; full realism pictures that flood the viewer with too much visual information are less good as learning stimuli than simplified pictures or drawings.
Colour in still pictures usually poses a problem. Although coloured pictures appear to interest students more than black-and-white ones, they may not always be the best choice for teaching or learning. One study suggests that if colour is to be added to an otherwise black-and-white picture, the teaching value may be reduced. But if what is to be taught actually involves colour concepts, pictures in realistic colour are preferred.
When attempting to teach concepts involving motion, a single still picture (including those in film-strips) is likely to be considerably less effective than motion picture footage of the same action. Yet a sequence of still pictures, such as might be shot with an automatic 35 mm still camera, might reduce flooding brought about by the too-fast flow of live

action portrayed in some motion pictures and thus improve the viewer's grasp of concepts involved.

Verbal and/or symbolic cueing of still pictures through use of arrows or other marks can clarify, or possibly change, the message intended to be communicated by them.

Although there has been considerable research on message variables and perceptual preferences of learners, little of this affects the development of typical classroom materials. Verbal elements are frequently overused, legibility standards are ignored and visual quality suffers when compared with creative images viewed on television.

However, there have been great strides in the use of visuals in classroom teaching in the past three decades, not only in the United States but in most of the industrialized countries of the world.

Influences of the media

Visual images are used extensively in magazines, on billboards, on television and in other media to influence our thoughts and actions. The most pervasive medium is, of course, television, with 98 per cent of the United States' households owning television sets. In the average home in the United States the television set is on for six hours per day. The influence of the television medium in the United States has grown over the past twenty-five years to the point that most people get their news from television rather than the newspaper. For example, recent evidence indicates that daily newspaper readership is in a real decline. The proportion of adults who claim to read a newspaper every day has declined from 73 per cent in 1967 to 66 per cent in 1975 and to only 57 per cent in 1978. Among children the preference is for television over newspapers as a source of information during the elementary-school years, the high-school years and on into adulthood.

One of the leading research organizations on television, the Annenberg School of Communication at the University of

Pennsylvania, holds that the television medium cultivates one's beliefs. Researchers there flatly assert: 'Television is a central cultural arm of American society.'

The effects on children that are of general concern are responses to advertising, anti-social behaviour, and pro-social behaviour. In American society, children's understanding of the nature of television publicity increases with age, and they are influenced significantly by this.

The major anti-social behaviour that has been studied is violence and aggression. The report of the Surgeon General of the United States in 1972 on television violence concluded: 'A modest relationship exists between the viewing of violence on television and aggressive tendencies.' While not as much attention has been given it, the development of pro-social behaviour by the medium is on the increase. The same principles that underlie learning and performance of television-mediated anti-social behaviour seems to operate for more positive behaviour.

Concern with the ability of citizens to cope with the television medium has given rise to a great deal of effort in the past decade. A report of the House of Representatives of the United States Congress in 1977 concluded that

> parents are the most powerful agents in curbing this problem. Three ways are suggested: Parents should (1) monitor more closely the viewing habits of their children, (2) participate in a positive and active way in their children's television viewing, and (3) write to local broadcasters and networks to register complaints about offensive programs.

This and other efforts has given rise to such activities as Action for Children's Television and Television Awareness Training Program, as well as major research efforts in such institutions as the University of Michigan's Institute for Social Research. We are daily becoming more aware of the influence of the television medium in our culture, reinforcing the need to develop a true visual literacy.

Training of teachers

What does this visual literacy movement portend for the teacher training efforts in our various institutions? As you can see from the evidence above, we must recognize that visual learning seems to precede verbal learning in the very young child. The logic systems that developing youngsters have are based originally in visual cognition. There have been several developments in the past few years in teacher training which both reflect the growth of the visual media in education and point the way for us.

The microteaching movement began approximately twenty years ago and has developed as a method of allowing a teacher to perceive himself, from the days of using only an audio-tape machine to the complete classroom simulations that are available today using video equipment and allowing a complete audio-visual record and playback of a teacher's mini-performance.

Ten years ago the Associated Organization for Teacher Education (AOTE) of the United States developed a description of a teacher education programme which incorporates instructional technology to its fullest capabilities. Among those characteristics were: (a) the use of instructional media as inquiring, discovery and reporting modes, in addition to usual expository uses; (b) the collection of data about learner reactions to media and to the effectiveness of technological applications to learning problems; and (c) the differentiation of roles for teachers including diagnostician, programmer, evaluator, and manager. The report concluded with the following sentence: 'Both teacher trainee and students will use electronic and mechanical devices for documenting and reporting phenomena and processes.'

But, more important for a specific visual literacy programme in a school, a brief description of the teacher's role might help us envision what the teacher training programme should include. Recognizing that the crucial first step for a child is the self-selection of experience, the teacher should try to offer new, potentially beneficial, opportunities from which the child can select. Secondly, the teacher, recognizing that no experience offered a child is nearly so appealing as the opportunity to do something himself, of his own choosing, the teacher should give the child the opportunity to draw, to act out, to collect pictures, to arrange visuals, to link visuals with sound, to create montages or collages, to contrive multi-image events with visual flow and sound, etc. This will guarantee a highly involved learner. Thirdly, the teacher should then encourage evaluation of the new analogue the child has acquired and encourage the youngster to create new materials and experiences. Essentially, the role of the teacher is to make the child create—not to create things him or herself.

This review of the status of the visual languaging or visual literacy movement in the United States leads to the conclusion that more emphasis is needed in this area, particularly in the teacher-training programme throughout the country. We must make good use of the research results surfacing in our professional literature. Today's highly visual society with its prevalent television medium demands that our citizens be trained to be visually literate. The visual literacy movement and the training programme for teachers are gradually coming together, but a great deal more work needs to be accomplished.

Bibliography

An Assessment of Parent Education and General Needs That Can Be Served by Educational Programming for Television. Silver Spring, Md., Applied Management Sciences, 1977. (Executive Summary, G–98.)
Audiovisual Instruction, Washington, D.C., Association for Educational Communications and Technology, 1971. (Special issue of *Teacher Education*.)
Basic Guidelines for Media and Technology in Teacher Education. Washington, D.C., Association for Educational Communications and Technology, 1971.
CHU, Godwin C.; SCHRAMM, Wilbur. *Learning from Television*. Washington, D.C., National Association of Educational Broadcasters, 1967.

COMSTOCK, George. *Trends in the Study of Incidental Learning from Television Viewing*. Syracuse University, New York, ERIC Clearinghouse of Information Resources, 1978.

CURETON, Jan; COCHRAN, Lee. *Visual Literacy (The Last Word)*. Iowa City, Iowa, Lake Okoboji Educational Media Leadership Conference, August 1976.

DEBES, John L.; WILLIAMS, Clarence. *Visual Literacy, Languaging and Learning. Provocative Paper Series 1.* Washington, D.C., The Visual Literacy Center, 1978.

FRANSECKY, Roger; DEBES, John. *Visual Literacy: A Way to Learn—A Way to Teach.* Washington, D.C., Association for Educational Communications and Technology, 1972.

FRANSECKY, Roger; FERGUSON, Roy. New ways of Seeing: The Milford Visual Communications Project. *Audio Visual Instruction.* Washington, D.C., Association for Educational Communications and Technology, 1973.

GERBNER, George; et al. The Demonstration of Power: Violence Profile No. 10. *Journal of Communication.* Vol. 29, 1979.

HELLER, Melvin S.; POLSKY, Samuel. *Studies in Violence and Television.* New York, American Broadcasting Company, 1976.

HITCHENS, Howard. Discussion of Visual Literacy. *Educational Media International* (Paris, International Council for Educational Media), 1981.

LOCKARD, James. Computer Blossoms at a Small School in Iowa. *Instructional Innovator* (Washington, D.C., Association for Educational Communications and Technology), September 1980.

MYERS, Phyllis Reynolds. *Developmental Aspects of Four, Ten and Sixteen Year Olds' Recognition and Reconstruction of Sequentially Presented Words and Pictures.* Doctoral Dissertation, University of Toledo, Ohio, August 1980.

OXFORD, Jacqueline; MOORE, David. Can Teachers Learn to Cope with Our Visual Society? *Audiovisual Instruction* (Washington, D.C., Association for Educational Communications and Technology), May 1979.

PETT, Dennis W. Visual Literacy...Theory and Practice. *Indiana Media Journal,* Summer 1980. (Reprinted.)

ROBERTS, Donald F.; BACHEN, Christine M. Mass Communication Effects. *Annual Review of Psychology*, No. 32, 1981, pp. 307–56.

SPRING, Jack. *Report of Field Research Using Technology.* Rochester, N.Y., Society for the Study of Technology in Education, June 1968.

Third world:
images and reality

Do mass media reach the masses? The Indian experience

G. N. S. Raghavan

In any country, education for citizenship, or social education, goes on well beyond the stage of formal schooling. The process continues in a variety of ways: through the mass media, through participation in the political system and through religious, neighbourhood and vocational associations.

In a developing country, where social education must have a development orientation, both formal schooling and the reach of the mass media are limited. The modes of social education mentioned above have therefore to be supplemented by organized non-formal education: by wide networks of agricultural, health and other extension services, and by the traditional media that have served for centuries as carriers of a community's cultural values from one generation to the next.

This article attempts a critical survey of the process of formal and non-formal efforts in India to educate citizens in their rights and duties, and to mobilize them for economic development and the attainment of equality of opportunity. Some aspects—both positive and negative—of the Indian experience are likely to be of interest to other developing countries, even though they differ from India in size and in their political and social structure.

Limited reach and role of mass media

Like the economy, which is a mix of private and public ownership, the modern mass media in India are partly in the public and partly in the private domain. Newspapers and feature films are in the private sector; on the other hand, radio and television are operated exclusively by the central government. The Films Division of the Central Government has a virtual monopoly on documentaries and newsreels.

Communication planning is undoubtedly difficult, but is inescapable for rapid progress in a country of continental dimensions and diversity—religious, linguistic and ethnic—whose population of about 650 million (548 million at the 1971 census) is spread over 575,936 villages and 2,643 urban centres, which include nine cities with a population of more than a million each.

The need for decentralized, two-way communication in support of development—as distinct from mere publicity for the government's achievements and intentions—was recognized very early. The document on the First Five Year Plan (December 1952) said:

It is only in terms of local programmes that local leadership and enthusiasm can plan their part. The Plan has to be carried into every home in the language and symbols of the people and expressed in terms of their common needs and problems with the assistance of creative writers and artists, which has to be specially enlisted. If obstacles are encountered, and things go wrong anywhere, it would be helpful in every sense if information is imparted candidly and the people are acquainted with the steps being taken to set things right.

The 1969 document on the Fourth Plan acknowledged the problem of a serious information imbalance within the country:

In the spread of information facilities, the imbalance in favour of urban concentrations and prosperous areas continues. There is need for a deliberate attempt to inform the people in the rural areas, and in particular those in backward regions, about the specific schemes in agriculture, forestry, road construction, marketing, the supply of credit and other inputs, so that the benefits of these programmes are more widely spread.

Unlike the Minister of Railways, who receives policy advice from a Railway Board consisting of railway officials with long experience of construction, traffic, finance and other aspects of work of the railways, or the Minister of External Affairs, who is advised by permanent officials who are experienced diplomats, the successive Ministers of Information and Broadcasting since independence have followed the system of relying for policy advice on generalist administrators rather than communication professionals. Liable as the generalist officers of the Indian Administrative Service are to frequent transfer from one central ministry to another, or from the centre to the states, their rate of turnover in the Ministry of Information and Broadcasting has been even higher than that of the ministers, who are subject to the vicissitudes of political fortune.

As for the communication professionals, they tend to ask in each successive Five Year Plan for expansion of the activities and staff of the particular organization they run. There has been, as a result, an indiscriminate and incremental growth of each communication medium, and not a truly planned development based on studies of relative cost-effectiveness of the different media *vis-à-vis* different sections of the population.

Hence, scarce resources are wasted. Two examples are the misplaced emphasis on print material and the persistence of mobile film vans to screen documentaries of little local relevance in rural areas, notwithstanding the escalation of petroleum prices since 1973.

There has been no experimentation with small-gauge, portable, low-cost film and video technology for local production and dissemination of locally relevant and useful messages or to promote participation in place of one-way, top-down communication.

In the absence of any communication planning worthy of the name, the modern mass media have developed mainly as purveyors of information and entertainment for the urban population and the rural well-to-do; their role as vehicles of non-formal education for improving the material conditions and quality of life of the rural masses has been marginal.

This could not perhaps have been avoided in the case of newspapers, since they are published by diverse interest groups in the private sector, ranging from big business houses to the communist parties. Daily newspapers increased in numbers and circulation from 330 and 2.5 million respectively in 1954 to 875 and 9.3 million in 1976. But the consumption of newspapers has remained overwhelmingly urban, for the reason that literacy and purchasing power are concentrated in the cities and towns.

Although the clientele of the press are necessarily concentrated in the urban centres, the major Indian newspapers evince considerable interest in the problems of farmers, agricultural workers, artisans, tribal groups and other sections of the rural population. Commending this, the Second Commission says in its report (1982):

Though judged by readership or by ownership, it is not necessary for most of our newspapers to highlight the issues of poverty, the Press has made a major contribution by reminding readers of those who live below the poverty line and giving the ruling middle and upper classes a feeling of guilt. Many newspapers have from time to time drawn attention to such matters concerning the weaker sections of society as the non-enforcement of minimum wages and the failure to revise them to keep pace with the fall in the purchasing power of the rupee; the persistence of bonded labour despite its abolition by law, or its emergence in a new guise as contract labour; the generation of black money and its use, frequently entailing the involvement of corrupt officials and politicians, etc.

The Commission urges the Press to contribute further to social betterment along these lines through the two-step flow of information from the newspaper-reading literate to the non-literate.

Radio and television, which are not constrained by the literacy barrier, are publicly owned and their growth has been funded in the name of social education. It is the urban dwellers who own 80 per cent of the estimated 25 million radio receivers in the country (the last precise figure of licensed receiving sets, as at the end of December 1977, was 20,091,450). The actual access of rural people to radio is far behind radio's technical reach: the signals from All India Radio's eighty-four broadcasting centres now cover 80 per cent of the area and 90 per cent of the population. The spectacle of the farmer carrying a transistor set to his field—what has been called the transistor revolution—is confined to areas like Punjab and Haryana, where there has been a Green Revolution. Elsewhere, radio listening in rural areas is negligible.

Yet the electronic media do not in fact reach the masses directly. The reason is that widespread social consumption of radio and television programmes has not been made an integral part of the plans for investment in the expansion and strengthening of radio and television stations and transmitters. They market their entertainment and information to those who can afford to buy receiving sets. Their educative role in relation to the masses is minimal.

There are about 576,000 villages in India and almost as many schools, but rural community listening sets number less than 50,000—and more than half of them might be out of commission at a given time—and radio sets in schools numbered 30,766 at the end of 1977. This being the case, the educational and rural broadcasts have made a token rather than substantial contribution to non-formal education. Most of the school sets are located in secondary schools in cities and towns, whereas primary schools in rural areas need help the most. The effort to popularize new high-yielding varieties of seeds through rural broadcasts has had some success, as for example in the well-irrigated Tanjore district of South India, where, in the 1960s, farmers took to what they called 'radio rice'. But the total number of rural listening-cum discussion groups organized so far is less than 45,000 and only a small percentage of them are active.

In an attempt to widen access to radio, an experiment has taken place concerning the provision of a community listening facility. But it has been a half-hearted experiment. Part of the reason is that radio, like other modes of communication, can play a development role only at the grassroot level whereas the electronic media have developed on a top-down and centre-to-periphery pattern in India's federal democracy.

The experiment of community listening was introduced on the basis of a central subsidy. But following the 1967 general elections, which brought in wider party participation, there was an assertion of state autonomy for need-based local planning. This caused a number of centrally sponsored plan schemes, including community listening, to be scrapped.

Since then, the provision of community radio listening has been a responsibility of the state governments, which have differed in their perception of its usefulness and importance in their scheme of priorities. As a result, there have never been more than 90,000 community listening sets as against the 576,000 villages in which the bulk of India's population live.

Radio has been operated primarily for urban listeners, most of them literate and readers of newspapers, for whom it is a carrier of entertainment—mainly film music—and of spot news and sports coverage. Its role in promoting economic growth or social change is marginal, but significant enough where programmers imbued with social commitment have made imaginative use of the medium.

Such programmes which contribute to development must necessarily be localized and area-specific. This requires a decentralized broadcasting system with stations at district level whose managers should be responsible not only for programme origination but also for arranging wide listening and promoting two-way communication between radio and audience. Local stations with their requirement for locally recruited staff will serve to bridge the cultural distance that now separates the radio programmer, typically an urbanite, from the rural audience.

This decentralized broadcasting system is precisely what was recommended by a working group on the broadcast media, headed by George Verghese, which was formed by the Government in 1977 and gave its report the following year. It said:

Decentralized and participative development from below suggests the need for decentralized messages through local radio and television. We would envisage the Station as something more than a single studio-transmission complex, distant and seemingly exclusive, or even inaccessible to the people it is intended to serve. Instead, we envisage at the local level a small and relatively simply equipped 'mother station' with a cluster around it of small recording units and programming facilities which will help bring broadcasting to the people and people to broadcasting. This consideration applies both to radio and television.[1]

Yet, in 1983, district-level sound broadcasting remains an experiment to be tried out in a few districts during the Sixth Five Year Plan (1980–85).

Secondly, the Verghese Group recommended that priority be given to the densification of radio listening before the expansion of television. This was in the light of the resource constraint and the need to democratize communication within the country at the least cost. But in fact the television network is being expanded for the benefit of the upper crust of Indian society even while radio remains beyond the common man's hearing.

Before turning from radio to television, it will be useful to consider the state of the use of short films (documentaries and newsreels) for social education, since it shares some common problems with television.

The 9,000 cinema houses in the country are required under law to show one or two short educational films along with each screening of a feature film. The documentaries and newsreels supplied by the Films Division to this commercial theatrical circuit are mostly made in urban locations. The same short films are used by audio-visual vans of the central and state governments for free screening in villages, though few of the films have relevance in rural areas. A documentary on family planning, for instance, shows a father of six children standing while the kids pester him for school fees and pocket money. When such a film is screened in a village, the audience is likely to regard the father not as the harassed head of an unduly large family but as a rather lucky urbanite, draped in several yards of white clothing, who can afford cigarettes in contrast to the *beedi* or cheroot of the rural poor.

Again, a film made in one part of rural India cannot evoke audience identification in another region. I once met a group of extension workers engaged in fertilizer promotion in the state of Andhra-Pradesh. I asked them whether they had audio-visual vans for screening films on fertilizer use to villagers with little or no access to cinema houses. But, they said, the films were made in locations in Maharashtra and therefore did not click with Andhra Pradesh audiences. Maharashtra and Andhra-Pradesh are not widely separated parts of the Indian Union but are adjacent states.

Linguistic problems

The language of the commentaries in the documentaries is often not followed by villagers, because the short films are dubbed in the correct literary form of the major languages of India as spoken by the urban educated. Villagers, on the other hand, use the locally prevalent dialectical variant of an Indian language. Take for example Hindi, which is the most widely spoken language of India. It is not one language except in its literary usage. Spoken Hindi has many dialects and languages, such as Garhwali, Haryanvi, Rajasthani and Braj Bhasha.

In some areas where qualified personnel are not locally available for recruitment, the language barrier affects also the person-to-person communication of extension workers in the field. On a visit to Rajasthan as member of a study team on family planning communication, I found that a large percentage of the female extension workers (known as Auxiliary Nurse Midwives) were drawn from the far-way Kerala state. These young women knew Hindi but not the distinctive local variant, which is Rajasthani. They could make themselves understood, but could not follow what the local women said. In family planning, as in other spheres of development communication, it is necessary to relax educational standards to the extent necessary to ensure the recruitment of local personnel for work at the grassroots level. The lag in formal education can be made good through intensive functional training. A beginning has been made in strictly local recruitment in the Community Health Workers scheme, which was launched in 1977.

Television

The higher costs of programme production and receiver sets required that, even more than in the case of radio, television should be organized as a medium of social education for social consumption on a wide scale. This has not been the case.

The first television centre was established in Delhi in 1959. Though the next centre was not set up till 1972, the die had been cast in 1969, when the government entered into an agreement with the National Aeronautics and Space Administration (NASA) of the United States for a Satellite Instructional Television Experiment (SITE). After 1972, terrestrial television centres were set up in rapid succession in six cities: Amritsar, Bombay, Calcutta, Lucknow, Madras and Srinagar. New centres were to be opened during the Sixth Plan (1978—83) in three more cities: Ahmedabad, Bangalore and Trivandrum.

There were 676,618 licensed television receivers in the country at the end of 1977. Most of them are in the four metropolitan cities of Delhi, Bombay, Calcutta and Madras. There is no question of private ownership of television in rural areas except by a few wealthy families.

The other non-SITE city-based stations also put out some programmes on improved agriculture and other aspects of rural development. But they account for a small percentage of total transmission time, the bulk of which is applied to entertainment, news and discussions of current affairs. The most popular television programmes are feature films. Many among the middle class and the rich who own sets have undertaken the investment as a wholesale purchase of movie entertainment; it is cheaper in the long run to see films on television, and it saves the discomfort of queuing for tickets.

There are 921 television sets in schools, 538 of them in Delhi and 272 in and around Bombay. Educational television thus augments the already high level of information and education in the urban areas, instead of benefiting those whose need for non-formal education is greatest.

It will be evident from this survey of the four modern mass media that, except for SITE, they have been in no position to reach the rural masses directly. The social education messages carried by them can travel only indirectly to the weaker sections of the population, who constitute the majority, through extension workers and opinion leaders such as the village teacher, chairman of the Panchayat (village council), organizers of industrial trade unions and unions of agricultural workers, teachers at adult education centres and other social workers.

An exception to the above generalization is the Srinagar television centre in Kashmir. Unlike the other fully-fledged television centres, Srinagar has more than 550 community viewing sets in villages within its range. Moreover, the urban-rural divide in terms of speech and life-style is very little in the Kashmir valley. These factors make for socially relevant programming.

The modern mass media can play their largely indirect role in social education more effectively if they disseminate information of relevance to the poor more systematically. Many information officials and extension workers are recruited from an urban middle class background, and have inadequate knowledge of various agricultural and industrial occupations and the lower rates which actually prevail in many areas, or the availability of bank credit at concessional interest rates for the poor.

Assessing SITE

The Satellite Instructional Television Experiment (SITE), which was conducted for a year from 1 August 1975, was the first occasion on which the government concerned itself not only with the production of rural-interest television programmes and their transmission, but also with their widescale social consumption.

Direct reception sets with 24-inch screens were installed in 2,330 villages in backward districts of six states with programmes in four languages: Oriya for Orissa; Hindi for the states of Bihar, Rajasthan and Madhya Pradesh; Telugu for Andhra Pradesh; and Kannada for Karnataka.

SITE utilized ATS-6, which was made available and put into geostationary orbit by NASA. The Indian Space Research Organization (ISRO) was responsible for all technical operations of the ground segment, including the maintenance of the direct reception sets. Doordarshan, as the Indian television organization is known, was responsible for the software.

There was a morning transmission for school children of one and a half hours, with programmes of twenty-two and a half minutes each in the four languages. The programmes covered science education, biographies of great Indians, health education, current affairs and entertainment. The evening transmission of two and a half hours was intended for the rural adult public (though children turned up in the evening too and accounted for well over a third of the audience). It carried news; entertainment programmes, many of which served also to portray the unity underlying India's cultural diversity; and instructional programmes on agricultural improvement, animal husbandry, health, hygiene and nutrition, and family planning. A 'national segment' in Hindi was also telecast in all the six clusters of villages.

In addition to the six clusters served via satellite, a low-power terrestrial television transmitter at Pij in Gujarat telecast a one-hour programme each evening. About 500 conventional television sets were installed in 355 villages of Kheda district, with more than one set in several villages. The Pij transmission comprised the half-hour national programme of SITE in Hindi, telecast through rediffusion, and a half-hour Gujarati programme prepared at Ahmedabad under the auspices of ISRO. In several programmes the Charantari dialect prevalent in Kheda district, instead of standard Gujarati, was employed.

While the experiment was an unqualified success in terms of hardware and technical operations, SITE was only a qualified success as an exercise in social education for the rural population.

The software operations presented a more varied and continuous challenge during SITE than the installation and operation of hardware. The main reason for the limited social impact of SITE was that there were only three base production centres (BPCs) to make the bulk of the programmes for villages with varied agro-economic and cultural backgrounds, many of them more than a thousand kilometres apart. Area-specific programmes were therefore minimal. And it is a truth apparent to common sense that decentralized and area-specific programmes, employing the local dialect and depicting the local agro-economic and human landscape, are necessary in any attempt to persuade people to change their attitudes and practices in agriculture or hygiene or, even more so, in family planning.

The commonsense view on the need for area-specificity and the employment of local speech in development communication is borne out by the findings of a research study undertaken by ISRO. It entailed holistic studies by anthropologists in seven villages: one each in the six clusters served by the satellite and, in addition, one village served by the Pij terrestrial transmitter. The anthropologists lived for about a year and a half in the respective villages for data collection and continuous observation prior to, during and after the conclusion of SITE. Their findings have been written up by Dr Binod Agrawal in a report as follows:

> The linguistic profile of these villages shows a higher use of dialects than the standard language of the region... None of the languages spoken in the villages were used on TV except in Dadusar where Charautari was utilized to some extent. Furthermore, the use of English-sounding technical names (in programmes on agriculture and animal husbandry) compounded the problem... If the programmes were entertaining enough in terms of songs and dances, language did not become a barrier. Due to this reason, recreational programmes of other clusters were viewed with enthusiasm in all the villages... The Hindi common news was almost ineffective in all villages... The problem of lip synchronization affected the credibility of the TV medium to an extent (in Andhra Pradesh and Karnataka which used one video and two audio channels).[2]

The last observation is at variance with the claim made in the foreword of a report[3] based on a study in the two states that 'our experiment conducted in the Andhra Pradesh and Karnataka clusters has had encouraging results. This finding has wide potential for application in most of the developing countries.'

Opposite opinions on the efficacy of SITE as a communication exercise (as distinct from the success of the hardware operation) have been expressed by the authors of the reports on the in-house survey[4] conducted by ISRO and of the Planning Commission survey that has been referred to already. The first entailed the interview of about 6,500 respondents in twelve experimental and six control villages in each cluster. They were interviewed three times: for base-line survey prior to, and for assessing impact during and on the conclusion of SITE. The Planning Commission survey, also in three rounds, covered a smaller sample of 1,600 divided between five experimental and five control villages from each of the six clusters.

The two surveys differ not so much in the actual findings of positive and negative changes in levels of information or in attitude—both cite some instances of greater gain in the control villages!—as in the interpretation of the data, and in the resulting verdict on SITE. Whereas the ISRO survey tends to be self-congratulatory, the Planning Commission survey is sceptical.

Impediments to research

Unfortunately, all the research studies conducted during SITE, including the above two, were vitiated by the prevailing atmosphere of fear of the government on the part of Indian citizens. SITE began a little over a month after the establishment of a state of emergency by the government.

Even in normal times Indian villages are suspicious of all strangers—officials or researchers—who approach them for information on the extent of their landholding or income, or their attitude towards government-sponsored programmes. It was unrealistic to expect them to respond candidly to questions put to them, especially by interviewers identified with the government, during the emergency.

In the circumstances, the holistic study appears to be the most reliable guide to the social impact of SITE. The anthropologists—unlike the visiting interviewers—lived for a year and a half in their villages and could continuously observe at close range the nature and extent of impact of television viewing in the seven villages.

The impact of the telecasts from the terrestrial transmitter at Pij, which put out part of the programmes in the local speech, comes through more impressively from the holistic study than that of the telecasts via satellite. However, interesting cases are also reported of the adoption of improved agricultural and health practices—but not of family planning—as the result of television viewing in villages in the six SITE clusters.

INSAT 1–A

The next big spurt in Indian television after SITE came in 1982. A domestic satellite, INSAT 1–A, fabricated to Indian specifications by the Ford Aerospace Corporation of the United States, was launched in April. It enabled the inauguration of nationwide television networking, partly through micro-wave and partly through satellite links, on the Independence anniversary (August 15). Another landmark was the introduction of colour transmission. However, INSAT 1–A failed and became non-operational early in September 1982.

Policy unmatched by performance

The initiatives described above are laudable but the follow-up action has not been impressive. An example of administrative slackness is the easy and lazy prescription of the availability of electricity as a condition for the installation of community viewing television sets in the coverage area even of the post-SITE terrestrial stations, though SITE has demonstrated the workability of battery-operated television receivers.

A second example is the failure to provide local studio facilities for post-SITE telecasting. The six post-SITE 'rural stations' are—except in the case of Hyderabad—merely transmitters, which are fed by the same three Base Production Centres of SITE. The Delhi BPC continues to prepare programmes in Hindi for transmission to the three widely separated states of Bihar, Rajasthan and Madhya Pradesh. All three BPCs have extremely limited facilities by way of outside broadcasting vans and portapacks.

Out of the six post-SITE 'rural' stations, two—Jaipur and Hyderabad—are state capitals. There, a large number of middle and upper class residents acquired television sets in the hope of adding this latest amenity to the range of their entertainment. However, these stations are required to put out programmes of predominantly rural interest. This has left the well-to-do television families disappointed and angry. Ironically, it has brought negligible benefit to the intended beneficiaries because of the lack of viewing facilities on any large scale in villages. About 1,800 of the SITE direct reception sets have so far been converted for terrestrial reception and installed in the area covered by the post-SITE transmitters. The central government is handing over to the states the responsibility for community viewing, which it had undertaken during SITE. It will hereafter be for the state governments to maintain the community viewing sets and augment their number. This implies the likelihood of the rural population in the backward states, who need television most for adult education and agricultural extension, having the least exposure to it.

In respect of sound broadcasting the 1978–83 Plan provided, for the first time, for the establishment of five low-power radio stations for operation at district level on an experimental basis, each station broadcasting in the locally prevalent dialect instead of the literary form of the regional language. This radical experiment in local broadcasting is yet to be launched.

Again, from all accounts available so far, the National Adult Education Programme has got off to a feeble start both quantitatively in terms of the number of adult education centres that have started work, and qualitatively in terms of the social education they provide. The programme has worked well only where it has been taken up by dedicated voluntary workers.

Altogether, the performance has thus been poor in follow-up of the promise held out in 1977 of new beginnings in the multiple directions of formal schooling, adult education, decentralized and participatory broadcasting, and improved political participation.

Though this has caused disappointment, it is clear that

there can be no better strategy of social education for the 1980s. The response to the challenges previously discussed will be a measure of the earnestness of the Indian authorities who are applying public funds to develop the mass media—and television, in particular—for the professed purpose of promoting social education.

Notes

1. *Akash Bharati: National Broadcast Trust*, New Delhi, Ministry of Information and Broadcasting, February 1978.
2. Binod C. Agrawal, *Television Comes to a Village: An Evaluation of SITE*, Ahmedabad, ISRO, October 1978. (Mimeo.)
3. *One Video—Two Audio Transmission in SITE*, Hyderabad Audience Research Unit, All India Radio, November 1976. (Mimeo.)
4. Binod C. Agrawal, J. K. Doshi, Victor Jusudason and K. K. Verma, *Social Impact of SITE on Adults*, Ahmedabad, ISRO, September 1977. (Mimeo.)

Mass media and the transmission of values

Rita Cruise O'Brien

The rise in the number of radio and television stations in the Third World in the past two decades has been staggering. Many of the television programmes shown by these new broadcasting systems are foreign. Therefore, one principal question might begin: What is the power of the media in the transmission of foreign values to school-age children? And our second question: Are these values in conflict with those that are fostered in the systems of education? The questions are simple, but the answers are necessarily complex.

Through the transfer of media systems and worldwide sale of programmes are we really becoming a global village, as Marshall McLuhan suggested some years ago? Or, in consideration of the importance of the power of commercialism in television, are we becoming a corporate village, as some writers on the media would have it? Looking at the transnational ownership structures of the media and considering the absorptive capacity of newly established media systems for foreign material, a simple answer might be affirmative and raise the concern of educators and parents throughout the world.

Programmes, values and impact

We have a basic problem trying to get underneath some of the ephemeral tendencies of the global media. While it may be startling to turn on *Kojak* in places as culturally diverse as India, Jordan or Brazil, we really have no comparative studies to guide us as to the effects of such programmes and the values they contain on people of diverse cultures and social backgrounds within those cultures. And without such studies we cannot judge the transfer of values to any group in the population. We do not know, for example, what is the potential conflict of values contained in programmes of foreign origin compared with those of local origin. In television particularly it is tempting to argue that the conflict is not so great because of the imitative nature of many programmes made in the Third World, which follow the skilful technical formats in terms of sequence, timing and characterization that were developed particularly in American media. Sometimes programmes on national cultural history are even directly derivative of the formula of the American Western, a formula that is popular and will be understood and appreciated by audiences. Directors know that and proceed accordingly.

Whenever one tries to argue that television reaches a very small minority of the largely urban affluent population in developing countries, the image of television serials in the shanty towns of Latin America (and elsewhere) returns to trouble one's knowledge of the real statistics. Broadly speaking, however, the impact of the values of television programmes on middle-class children who have an opportunity also to read comic books and magazines and buy records from similar foreign sources would only serve to reinforce a set of influences with which those of television would not seriously conflict.

The impact of television and therefore its capacity to change the values of impressionable young people could, in the absence of surveys in different cultures and different groups, be partially enlightened by the results of surveys in Western countries. Early work focused on the impact of violence on television on the attitudes of children.[1] More recently, surveys on the adult population seek to examine its important impact in social and political terms.[2] We have derived two important lessons from this work. First, the direct impact of television is minimal unless the values it contains are reinforced by other forms of learning in the society—socialization in the family, the peer group and at school. It can safely be assumed that if the values implicit in television programmes are seriously at odds with other cultural and social influences, it may first be regarded as an unusual spectacle. Take, for example, the different impact of American serials on Latin America's urban youth, who are influenced by the dominant culture of North America in so many other ways, and compare it with the impact of *Mission Impossible* on a Sudanese audience, for which this imported cultural artefact must be much more exotic. In the programme context itself, Latin American television contains a high proportion of American material and locally made programmes that fit into a similar cultural mode. In the Sudan, by contrast, the rapid pace of an American serial might be followed by a long programme of Arabic poetry with the performer sitting still in front of the camera. The impact of each must be different. Thus, while it is possible to dissect the values implicit and explicit in such programmes, their effective transfer will be different in cultural terms, and also according to the age, education and life-style of the viewer, as well as the regular television diet.

Second, television as an influential medium is directly related to the frequency of viewing. In high-density television cultures in North America and Western Europe, we do have studies that indicate that some children (usually of low-income groups) spend more hours watching television than going to school and that school performance is low.[3] Apart from Latin America, where there is a greater number of broadcast hours on television than anywhere else in the Third World, this kind of high-density viewing would not be possible. Most television stations in developing countries broadcast only a few hours in the evening, which cannot begin to replicate the potential effects of continued viewing among children in rich countries. This, combined with cultural differences, must necessarily minimize its effectiveness. We cannot ignore, however, the impact on material values fostered by commercialism in the media and its potential effects on life-style and buying patterns. This particular feature may be considered under the rubric of taste transfer. There are two forms of influence: the first is the commercial itself, which is selling a given product, the second is the influence of clothing, material objects, and the general life-style in the programmes themselves. Most American programmes reflect a very high standard of living largely beyond the capacity of the potential viewing audiences, especially in the Third World. One must carefully differentiate between this form of materialism, however, and its effect on a more coherent, deeply held value system. The danger is obvious: it encourages people to emulate standards that may be beyond their capacity to fulfil, thus generating personal frustration. But in social terms the revolution of rising expectations may only partially be attributed to material values derived from television or radio. Many other forms of influence contribute to it.

Structures and global television flows

We have dealt thus far with personal impact. It is perhaps important to underline some of the structural factors that have contributed to foreign media influence in the Third World. The largest international market for worldwide sale of television programmes was developed by United States exporters.[4] On domestic network programming and content advertising agencies are pre-eminent. Sufficient profits are made on the domestic market so that programmes are sold internationally at 'what the market will bear'. Based on the number of receivers in each country, programmes are sold very cheaply to developing countries at a fraction of the cost of making local equivalents. In the early years of the establishment of television stations in many Third World countries, in the 1960s, few of them had a sufficient stock of programmes to fill even the few hours of broadcast time they had. The problem was resolved by importing programmes of any kind. This situation was further exacerbated by the demand for more and more hours of programme time from those who had television receivers (the more affluent and articulate members of the urban population). Thus, further imports were the obvious answer.

In the early 1970s, several countries in Africa and the Middle East adopted policies of reducing foreign imports by establishing a percentage ceiling, largely owing to a consciousness of cultural imperialism. The Arab states, in particular, objected to sex and violence, which they felt were at odds with the values of Muslim society. Pressed to produce programmes as rapidly as possible, overworked production staffs tried with great difficulty to comply with quantitative norms established often for political reasons. One means of defraying the cost of local productions was to invite advertising even in many state-run broadcasting systems, the executives being only too happy to see a sufficient rise in the number of receivers in order to attract advertising agencies.

Television is a complicated, costly and somewhat brittle medium for adaptation to different forms of cultural expression. The growing rise in cost was further complicated in the early 1970s by the move to colour equipment and the phasing out of black-and-white production and transmission equipment by the larger transnational firms. The promise of many broadcasting stations was high: their charters raised many high-minded aims about national, developmental and cultural goals. Performance has been much more disappointing.[5] One is tempted to ask, with all the will to the contrary, will television in the Third World become just like television elsewhere?

Whither radio?

Radio remains a much more powerful mass instrument of information, entertainment, and education. It is much less influenced by foreign material, apart from music, than is television. The reason is simple: radio programmes are much easier and cheaper to make. They have for a long time been well within the professional capacity of local staff, and many programmes in the Third World are in vernacular languages. This, combined with the ubiquity of the cheap transistor receiver, means that it reaches a much larger audience and, above all, those of limited income and far from major cities. So obvious, yet in statistical terms the estimation of its importance per capita of the population eludes even the most assiduous quantifiers at national and international level.

Radio has been used very effectively for educational campaigns.[6] Radio may be used to explain rather than promote debate on the parameters of national development policy. Radio is an effective way of reaching illiterate groups in the population. It has been used successfully for school broadcasting in different contexts. Yet two cardinal problems arise: the relationship between radio programming and school curriculum has often been very formalistic. First of all, while great strides have been made and exceptional examples may be cited,[7] there remains much to be done by both educators and broadcasters to share the experiences of other developing countries in formal and non-formal educational programming and to rely less on the traditional models of school broadcasting developed in rich countries. I sometimes wonder if knowledge and evaluation of these systems is not more effectively shared on the international circuit of specialists rather than getting to those on the spot who must develop and enlarge this important area.[8] Secondly, although radio is so important, it has in recent years been starved for professional and financial reasons by television. For young professionals it has had a less exciting and glamorous image in comparison to jobs in television, and despite its renewed vocation and importance in the rich countries, the reverse is true in much of the Third World. Partly for reasons of prestige and partly because of the sheer cost involved in making programmes for new television stations, radio is constrained by its more attractive sister medium. This particular problem is one for planners and professionals: in practical terms it is sometimes necessary to resist political pressures for the expansion of television for prestige reasons, perhaps most evident in the least developed countries, which need most to try to marshall all available resources for education.

Professionalism under scrutiny

Optimism about the contribution of the media to education and development, which was pervasive in the 1960s, has now given way to consideration of the inequality of access to information and communication, which reinforces other growing inequalities in developing countries.[9] Optimism has also been tempered by the transfer of values herein discussed. The process of re-evaluation is based on a consideration of the effects of transnational ownership in the media and programme flows, and on the transfers of models of professionalism in broadcasting. Each of these trends has created a hiatus between national broadcasting and the experimental use of the media in formal and non-formal education, literacy or development campaigns. Thus, while 'small is beautiful' perhaps and is relevant to appropriate circumstances, big media became dominant in institutional terms, using considerable resources yet raising questions about their cultural or developmental relevance.

All questions of this kind are based on an underlying, perhaps prejudicial, assumption that the maintenance of cultural identity (or identities) in developing countries is a means of containing transnational influence and of promoting economic and social policies more relevant to the needs of those countries. The transnational influences carried through the mass media operate at two distinct levels: first, the direct influence on consumption patterns and life-styles of foreign programmes and advertising: second, the influence on standards and norms of training, professionalism, models of organization and media production, which causes various occupations to identify with their metropolitan counterparts, and ultimately draws the media away from the cultural base and resources of a poor country.

For an electrical engineer trained in a metropolitan university and with close professional contacts with his counterparts throughout the world (through professional meetings, journals and, above all, a positive attitude towards the most sophisticated technology that is most important to his 'transnational community'), the system he would most like to have installed in his country reflects not necessarily local needs but reference to outside standards and norms. Engineers in broadcasting are as impressed as other members of the scientific and technical élite in developing countries with the ingenuity and sophistication of very expensive 'gadgets'. In addition, a source of their claim to authority as an occupation or profession may be based precisely on the sophistication of the equipment with which they work, and on which they have become dependent because of certain objectives of training or socialization in the wider sense. Considerations of this kind engender the choice of complex system design and costly equipment while placing a heavy burden on the local service, which may have originally been intended to achieve low-cost national coverage. Such a problem is indicative of the fact that the reorientation of cognitive categories achieved in the process of socialization may be at odds with the realities of local economic capacity.

It is, on the whole, much easier to focus on the external features of dependence and cultural imperialism, about which there has been much discussion in recent years, particularly by politicians and government ministers from the Third World. These pronouncements have served to call attention to some of the apparent characteristics of dependence—television programme imports, dependence on a few Western agencies for the circulation of news and information. More subtle processes that are essentially structural and technological, however, are hardly questioned. Such processes are, of course, less apparent, but no less penetrating. So while the percentage of locally produced programmes in proportion to imported television series is improving in many countries, thus satisfying at least the ephemeral characteristics of the battle against cultural imperialism, the quality and relevance of local production remains heavily constrained by the organization, technology and professional assumptions that go into it. In many instances the percentage improvement in local production is just a reflection of a form of 'cultural import substitution' or imitating the formula of the imported programme locally. A critical attempt to confront the tendencies of the 'global villager' begins at home with a much more serious reconsideration of the aims of broadcasting, its integration with other sectors in planning, management and programming terms, a critical evaluation of finance and new expenditure in this traditionally high-technology sector. The form of sterile materialism contained in the consumer values circulated by television programmes and commercials is a genuine 'culture of poverty' compared to the richness and variety of values contained in local cultures in developing countries.

Schools and screens: texts and alienation

Having made some progress towards answering the first question set out in the introduction about the transmission of values through the media, I now tread somewhat more hesitantly into the professional territory of most of the readers *prospects* in trying to relate these tendencies to the educational process. First, in most of the Third World the school will remain for several decades to come a much more powerful instrument of socialization and therefore transmission of values than the media. Although some emphases may conflict, it can be fairly safely assumed that the school environment will remain paramount.

Second, even in the high television-viewing cultures that I described, there are and will remain serious limitations on changes in values being promoted solely by the media. Measuring the effects of the media in diverse cultures and among different social groups is something we can anticipate in social analysis in the years to come.

In this last section, however, I wish to draw attention to the cultural values contained in a particular textbook published in 1975 and now fairly widely used for teaching French to African schoolchildren at the primary level. The authors of the text claim in the note for teachers that they have 'adapted it to African needs'. The analysis of its content is necessarily limited since it is abstracted from the educational context in which the book is used, mediated naturally by the curriculum, teaching methods and teachers' interpretations.[10] Yet the values it contains are very dramatically outlined, making implicit assumptions about the superiority and inferiority of cultures, the promotion of Western values, particularly consumerism, and above all raising concern in the mind of a sceptical observer about the vehicle of language teaching and alienation.

The preface tells the children that they will be presented with the daily life of French people (cooking, school, song, etc.) and urges that they make a comparison of this with what happens in their own countries. They are told: 'Reflect carefully on the differences, which will show that which is characteristic of your culture and those of the French.' Another rubric covered by the text is languages, in which the child is urged to reflect on the use of French and African languages. The next phrase refers to the importance of the use of a dictionary, a clear oversight by authors who must be aware that there was until very recently no transcription for vernacular languages in francophone Africa. It is precisely the primacy given to French in the language policies of these countries that has until now precluded this possibility. Dictionaries of African languages would not be available to schoolchildren.

The layout of the book is skilful while inexpensive, but there is a striking difference in the use of illustrative material. All the grammar lessons are illustrated with block drawings of instances of African life, wherein the boy or girl visibly grows in situational use of French, emphasizing in part the difficulties of studying in Africa. Each section of the book has an excerpt of an African story, including Sembène Ousmane, Camara Laye and other well-known authors. The illustrations for these stories are exceptionally dreary and stylized. Contrasted with each of these stilted representations of 'authenticity', the information about France or French culture is presented through cartoons, well reproduced photographs and attractive line drawings.

The content conveys an even stronger meaning. Articles on the circulation and world translations of *Tintin* and *Asterix* (most well-known French strip cartoons), the competition between them for international popularity encourages a positive identification with French-centred youth culture. A small culturally-specific quote from the very upper middle-class education of Simone de Beauvoir, taken from the first volume of her autobiography, is followed by a few lines of dialogue from *Zazie dans le métro* (Raymond Queneau), a highly sophisticated Parisian play on words. It would be hard to know how most African teachers would put this into context. It is followed by a quote of exceptional misery from *The Black Docker*, by Sembène, entitled 'The Illiterate Woman'. The cultural contrast is so remarkable, the difference in life-styles and use of language so marked that the effect on a child must be very peculiar.

A section on music and instruments is highly culturally specific, with the traditional African drum presented in stark contrast to the range of classical instruments and forms of music in European society. Nowhere is a cora (an African string instrument of considerable sophistication) or a flute apparent. And some space is devoted to a Greek singer of enormous popularity in Europe with reviews of her performances from French dailies. This seems more a reflection of current urban European tastes exported to francophone African cities for those young people who can afford her records than of traditional French culture.

A section on shops and markets uses an African woman to describe the 'decline' of use of the traditional market, and even of small shopkeepers, in favour of supermarkets: 'Larger surface areas sell products cheaper than elsewhere...' While true in Europe, the opposite is the case in Africa, where supermarkets are a luxury of the urban middle class. The traditional market, for economic and cultural reasons, is still used by the large majority. The section on housing portrays a distinct historical evolution from thatched hut to large apartment block as a natural feature of modern development. The accompanying grammar lesson is presented with a four-sequence line drawing in which a young African builds a cement house and in the last drawing of the sequence closes himself inside by building himself into it. (What does this suggest—the stupidity of Africans, their incapacity to deal with modern life, despite its desirability?)

The geographical and artistic reality of the provinces of France are contrasted with the romantic 'placelessness' of African locations; travel to Timbuktu, a place that presumably has a school that might even use this book, is presented by the historic unreality of a nineteenth-century French explorer (René Caillié). And in the final sequence, the children are told of Tibet by the recent travels of a Parisian writer, whose interpretation of this exotic place is done with typical Western urban sophistication.

Looking at this startling material, its 'adaptation' and its obvious cultivation of values, one is tempted to pose a dramatic suggestion. When African children repeated to the tapping of a ruler in French colonial schools. '*Nos ancêtres, les Gaulois*', the clarity and absurdity of that phenomenon must naturally have generated a much more strident reaction of national and cultural pride. The dialectic has become more fuzzy now, and the result a much more penetrating form of cultural alienation. How many other textbooks still contain such material?

By drawing attention to the difficulties of interpreting the transmission of value through the media and outlining some of the structural and professional influences that underline external media influences in the local context in developing countries, suggestions for changes go much further than limiting foreign exports. Measuring the impact of the media in relation to the cultural or social differences found throughout the Third World may serve as a catalyst, by drawing attention to some of the political and planning changes that are necessary. But the manner in which individual young people are able to observe with an open and questioning spirit messages and influences from the media and other cultures depends directly on the integrity of the educational system in promoting genuine motivation and self-fulfilment and a pride in local culture and values.

Notes

1. H. L. Himmelweit et al., *Television and the Child: An Empirical Study of the Effects of Television on the Young*, London, Oxford University Press, 1958.
2. G. Gerbner and L. Gross, 'Living with Television: The Violence Profile', *Journal of Communication*, Vol. 26, No. 2, Spring 1976.
3. P. J. Arenas, *Learning from Non-Educational Television*, Cambridge, Mass., Harvard University Graduate School of Education, 1971.
4. K. Nordenstreng and T. Varis, 'Television Traffic—a One-Way Street?' Unesco Reports and Papers on Mass Communication, No. 70, 1974.
5. E. Katz and G. Wedell (eds.), *Broadcasting in the Third World*, Cambridge, Mass., Harvard University Press, 1977.
6. The Tanzania 'Man is Health' campaign and rural educational radio in Senegal stand out.
7. D. T. Jamison and E. McAnany (eds.), *Radio for Education and Development*, 2 Vols., Washington, D.C., The World Bank, 1978.
8. See, for example, the Unesco report, Division of Methods, Materials, Structures, Techniques; and R. Postgate et al., *Low-Cost Communication Systems for Education and Development Purposes in Third World Countries*, April, 1979.
9. See several articles in W. Schramm and D. Lerner, *Communication and Change: The Last Ten Years and the Next*, Honolulu, University Press of Hawaii, 1976.
10. I shall not cite the specific text in question, for I do not wish to single it out for criticism but to raise questions contained in it that may appear in other texts of the kind.

Transnational advertising and education in the developing countries

Rafael Roncagliolo and Noreene Z. Janus

It has become common practice to look upon the relationship between education and the mass media as being a question that is confined to determining ways and means of using the media to extend the scope of formal education. Discussions on the subject have accordingly centred on the planning and cost-effectiveness problems involved in using the mass media to transmit educational messages. A vast amount of research has been conducted into such variables as audience profiles (age, sex, geographical location, etc.), the media themselves (type, the range and duration of broadcasts, etc.) and the operational aspects of teaching (use of the medium alone, with teachers, or with written supporting materials, etc.).

Even in instances where such research, and the experiments that usually go with it, may be instrumental in significantly raising standards of education and training, the fact is that relations between mass communication and formal education range over problems of far greater complexity and importance than those involved in the mere use of certain media slots or time for educational purposes.

As Ivan Illich has said, 'the relationship of schooling to education is like that of the church to religion'.[1] Like the church, the school is merely the institution that by general consensus is formally responsible for education. The school can hardly be said to be one of the media capable of being used for educational purposes. Moreover, the school as an institution displays anachronistic features and shortcomings that stem from what Paolo Freire calls 'banking educational'[2], a vertical, passive process whereby teachers deposit knowledge in the student without any give-and-take relationship being established.

The criticisms which Illich and Freire have levelled against the school system—and which also partly apply to the mass media—are widespread in Latin American thinking and can be regarded as one of the starting-points or premises of this article, although this is not the place to deal with them at length.

The parallel school

The crisis of the school as an institution is certainly not entirely due to the intrinsic limitations of present-day schools, nor can it be solved by bringing the mass media into the school system. What has happened, in fact, is that the media—which share some of the features of schools but also evolve forms of communication of their own—have come to display a high degree of socializing efficiency and have partly supplanted the functional hegemony of the school. This is due, among other things, to the extent of the penetration by the mass media into private life,[3] to the illusion of freedom they produce (for it is possible to change newspapers or television stations), the variety of programmes they offer, their entertainment rather than pedagogical function, and their permanent character—since their influence extends throughout life instead of being confined to the period of schooling.

In view of these and other factors, there is no doubt that the whole mass of messages delivered by the media represents an effective form of instruction. It is indeed so effective that it is easily capable of undoing the results that may be achieved through a few hours' educational broadcasting on radio or television. It is for that reason that the mass media are now regarded as being literally a 'parallel school',[4] and for the same reason that a factor of greater importance than the educational use of the media is their educational nature—in other words the educational impact achieved by their transmissions every day. It is this aspect which it is absolutely essential to take into consideration in establishing national education systems and policies.[5]

The universal existence of such a parallel school would not be a source of concern to educators if the contents of the two schools, and above all the results obtained, were similar or convergent. However, such concern exists, and it derives from the fact that, in most countries and particularly in the developing countries, the mass media are introducing a model of education of values, behaviour patterns and personal and collective aspirations that bears little relation to the goals explicitly laid down for national education systems. As a result, a 'Cain and Abel' relationship[6] grows up between school and the mass media. In the hostility between them, there is always a danger of the mass media emerging as the victor and thus of educational policies being effectively and systematically sabotaged.

Whenever societies and countries are faced with these two 'parallel schools' and the growing antagonism between them, the response they make is fraught with contradiction. On the one hand, no one nowadays questions the need to draw up educational policies, or the right to do so. In mass communication, on the other hand, resistance is still opposed to any attempt to spell out explicit communication policies.

Nevertheless, in practice every country has a national communication policy of some kind, but whereas education policy is formulated by society as a whole and there are authorities and officials who have to report on its application and results, communication policy is a private matter that is decided on and applied exclusively by those who exercise a monopoly over the media, that is, the ruling classes and transnational forces that have become deeply involved in the communication systems of the developing countries, especially in Latin America.[7]

These privately controlled communication policies are frankly incompatible with educational policies. The declared humanist goals of education are national development and the affirmation of national sovereignty and culture. Privately controlled communication, on the other hand, is interested more in the sale of goods than in human beings. It sets out to boost compulsive consumption, without any regard for the rational needs of development, and it disseminates a transnational culture that threatens and undermines all native cultural traditions. In the name of the 'global village' postulated by McLuhan, present-day commercial communication aims at creating a 'global supermarket'. This approach is diametrically opposed to the principles and objectives on which national education systems and policies are founded.

Advertising as the dominant cultural speech-form

The mass media themselves cannot be blamed for this outcome. The media do not function independently of a social context and do not have the freedom of action to decide for themselves what their content will be. In point of fact, the mass media everywhere reflect differences that have always existed and still do today. Indeed, the struggle against the existing state of affairs is largely being waged by alternative media—in the form of journalistic ventures which, with surprisingly limited resources and at some sacrifice, sprout up in one place or another and set out to restore the true cultural, educational and consciousness-raising functions of mass communication. The fact that, in the conditions of monopoly capitalism, the mass media have fallen into private hands, has caused them to be enlisted in the service of alien causes that run counter to true mass education.

The origins of this phenomenon can be traced back to the

middle years of the last century, when the alliance between the press and advertising was established.⁸

From that time onwards, the mass media became increasingly commercially oriented. Actual communication and news itself have now become commodities governed by the laws of supply and demand and by the maximum utility factor, which determines the guidelines for communication policies at the corporate and national levels. Furthermore, the media have been turned into producers of potential audiences and markets that are sold as commodities to advertisers when they conclude publicity contracts. As the media are drawn into this mercenary process and ally themselves with advertising, they become increasingly divorced from the objectives of education.

The subordination of the media to advertising is immediately apparent from the media content. In Latin America, for instance, the leading daily newspapers contain more advertising than news features. The space bought for advertising purposes accounts for between 50 and 70 per cent of the total space.⁹

However, the growing presence of advertising in the mass media plainly cannot be reduced to a problem of apportionment of space, which is only a symptom or indicator. Underlying the problem is the control which the financial power of the advertising agencies and their clients wield over the media. As Alex Schmid points out, since as much as 80 per cent of newspaper income is obtained from advertising rather than from sales, advertising agencies and advertisers are in a position to make or break newspapers. The history of the press in Latin America is rich in examples that illustrate pressures and power of this kind. The situation is even more serious in the case of commercial radio and television, since they are totally financed by advertising. As far as advertising is concerned, the media are nothing more than vending machines, which are good when they attract large numbers of readers with sufficient purchasing power, and bad when their news content interferes with the status quo in which business and sales expand. The leading private newspapers are therefore as free as the main advertisers and their advertising agencies allow them to be;[10] and the universally accepted principle of freedom of expression eventually becomes, in practice, a mere appendage of the freedom to do business, in other words the freedom to be used exclusively for the purposes of the major economic interests.

The fact that advertising has succeeded in subjugating so powerful an instrument as the media, and in enlisting the so-called 'Fourth Estate' to work for it, is due to the pull exerted by advertising in the conditions of monopoly capatalism. We are completely immersed in advertising; advertisements invade every sphere of life and are a fundamental part of everyday culture. Advertising has succeeded in penetrating people's lives to such an extent that, even if they do not buy the product advertised or do not pay attention to a particular advertisement, they cannot escape its overall impact.

Advertising has taken on a dimension of its own that marks it out completely from the commercial publicity of the last century in which its origins lie. Present-day advertisements bear no relation to the standard which Émile de Girardin suggested be set a hundred and thirty-five years ago, when he said: 'Advertisements should be concise, straightforward and frank, should never be of a covert nature, and should not be ashamed of driving home their point.'[11]

Nowadays, there is no semblance of frankness, concision or objectivity in advertising. It has evolved its own language and its own linguistic and iconographic codes. It has no effect unless the messages it generates reflect imaginary psychological values and are incorporated in complex symbologies of the social statuses at which the products are directed, regardless of their actual utilitarian value. Since advertising has become an essential link in the workings of the economy, the problems it generates extend far beyond the ethical criticisms that have quite rightly been levelled against it. Advertising has become so overwhelming a feature of contemporary capitalism that it has been regarded as being the 'dominant cultural speech-form', the economically based cultural effusion superseding manifestations of the past whose sources lay in mysticism, philosophy or science.[12]

Advertising and education

The strength which our system of economic organization has conferred on advertising is so great that the interests it represents and the styles it has developed are succeeding in influencing the actual formal education system to a marked degree. Advertising is even penetrating into schools and, with the support of the mass media, is capable of successfully renovating styles of schooling.

A good example of the penetration of advertising interests into schools is provided by the education programmes on nutrition sponsored by the leading food manufacturers in the United States for classroom use. In 1978, one Congressional subcommittee stated that these programmes were nothing more than 'product promotions', in other words, they consisted of advertising directed at children who, as a result, were turned into captive audiences for such messages. The chairman of the subcommittee gave a warning that 'there is a distinct danger that classrooms will become the new frontier of advertising'.[13]

At the same time, however, advertising has managed to introduce new forms and styles of education, and well-known examples of these are *Sesame Street* and *The Electric Company* in the United States. *Sesame Street* has been translated into several languages and is broadcast in more than seventy countries. Joan Ganz Cooney, the president of the Children's Television Workshop and producer of the programme, has explained that it was designed after the manner of advertising 'spots', with the specific aim of using the attention-holding devices developed by advertisers. According to Kenneth O'Bryan, the child psychologist, these devices are so powerful that they make a thirty-second commercial advertisement the most effective teaching tool ever invented for instilling into children's minds any relatively simple idea, including the idea that a particular product is desirable. It has also been pointed out that television advertising is especially effective among children who are still too young to understand the sales purpose of advertisements.[14] Other research has confirmed that children become loyal to specific product brands from a very early age.[15] All this points to the existence of an advertising culture in the socialization of children alongside school, and sometimes prior to school. Against this background, programmes like *Sesame Street* condition children, among other things, to be receptive to the hundreds of thousands of commercials to which they are exposed throughout their lives.[16] We have reached the stage where, instead of educational policies and instruments being designed to help children develop 'cognitive filters' to protect them from the distortions of advertising, the reverse is the case and the way is being opened up for the penetration of advertising culture as an acceptable and desirable form of education.

The situation in the developing countries

These complex relationships between advertising and education are even more alarming in the developing countries, in which, as a result of the low school attendance rates, the educational role of the media and advertising is even more overwhelming. Suffice it to say that for a very large proportion of the population of Latin America, radio is virtually the only medium and at the same time the only school to which it has access. Not only are the media in those countries under the control of advertising, but that advertising is becoming increasingly transnationalized. This pattern started to emerge in the 1960s, when the advertising markets in developed countries, and particularly in the United States, were relatively saturated and were showing signs of sluggishness. The widespread transnationalization of economies that took place over that period was accompanied by the incipient mass penetration of transnational advertising agencies into the countries of the Third World.[17]

As a result of the presence of advertising, the developed countries have to content with problems of national sovereignty and the survival of national cultures. Transnational advertising[18] has succeeded in gaining control over national communication systems. In Mexico, out of the 270 commercials which the popular XEW radio station broadcast daily in 1971, 84 per cent advertised transnational products. Furthermore, out of the 647 commercials broadcast daily by the five Mexican television channels, 77 per cent were also for transnational products.[19]

In regional terms, some thirty transnational companies, most of them from North America, control almost two-thirds of the advertising revenue for the Latin American press.[20] Close on 60 per cent of the advertising in the women's magazines circulating in the region is transnational,[21] and the same can be said of every one of the media. All the evidence suggests that the private control of the mass media in the developing countries works to the direct advantage of the transnational corporations, not only in terms of growth in sales[22] but also of the penetration of a transnational ideology which lays claim to being a contemporary universal culture.

Admittedly, this purported universal culture is the natural outcome of the market-oriented style of thinking rather than the product of a deliberately subversive strategy towards native cultures. Standardization of production demands standardization of consumption and cultures. Global marketing techniques are a reflection of the need to create a universal consumer community that drinks, eats, smokes and uses the same products. Global marketing accordingly creates global advertising, as expressed in the image of one brand of perfume, the population of Latin America being presented with the same picture of a blond American woman strolling down Fifth Avenue in New York as is used for viewers in the United States. The message is the same in every case: 'Consumption is the key to happiness and the global corporation has the products that make life worth living.'[23] Thus, the image of the perfume in any developing country has the effect of associating it in viewers' minds with its relevance to the universal consumer society already mentioned, even though such relevance is only imaginary and is unattainable, and even though it implies standing aloof from one's own country. The educational impact of the imposition of such a culture on people cannot be underestimated, since it is diametrically opposed to the objectives of any national education policy. Such basic ideas underlying the development of national education systems in the underprivileged countries as the assertion of national culture and sovereignty, the linking of education with the development process, and the affirmation of democratic awareness, are all directly undermined by the values, ideas and behaviour patterns disseminated and inculcated by such transnational advertising.

There is abundant evidence to show how the inroads made by transnational advertising sap people's sense of national identity and esteem for their own culture. Eduardo Santoro, for example, analysed the representative content of programmes and commercials on Venezuelan television and then put a questionnaire on them to a broad sample of schoolchildren, in which he asked them what had taken place, where and for what reason, and who the 'goodies' and 'baddies' were. The following stereotypes repeatedly emerged from the children's replies:

The 'goodies' are from the United States, while the 'baddies' are from other countries, chiefly from Germany and then from China.

The 'goodies' are whites who are rich and are usually policemen, detectives or soldiers.

The 'baddies' are black and poor, and they work chiefly as labourers or peasants, or in offices.

Santoro's conclusion is that 'the hero is a rich, elegant white American, who goes about the world dispensing peace and justice'.[24]

In terms of national development, whatever the political leanings of the regimes in power in the developing countries, there is general agreement as to the need to encourage collective and private savings and to gear production to the social needs of each country. The fact is that transnational advertising runs directly counter to those aims. It need only be observed that the products most widely advertised, in developing and developed countries alike, are perfumes and cosmetics, cereals and processed foods, soap, beer, mineral waters and tobacco.

Similarly, consumer culture, individual rivalry, the unification of the international consumer community at the expense of the eradication of national realities, in short the whole set of values which advertising promotes, have in practice, an antidemocratic content. Values such as these are the very antithesis of a sense of common purpose, participation, criticism, tolerance and indeed of all the qualities that go to make up the democratic ideal. Furthermore, the brainwashing and psychological compulsion characteristic of advertising motivation techniques are the reflection of an authoritarian outlook which is opposed to the democratization of communication and societies.

Countless other examples could be cited of the contradiction between educational goals and the consequences of surrendering control to transnational advertising. However, the instances already mentioned are sufficient to bear out and illustrate the existence of such contradictions and the need to resolve them if the undermining of education systems and policies in the developing countries is to be avoided.

How can we contend with advertising?

The purpose of this article is not to outline a programme of action for coping with the educational—or rather the anti-educational—impact of the mass media and present-day advertising. However, the seriousness of the problems involved, their proven ability to wreak havoc with educational programmes, and the enormous amounts spent on advertising are all such as to call for urgent action, both nationally and internationally. Individual countries are becoming increasingly conscious of the need to switch existing inexplicit communication policies, in which control of the mass media is in private hands, to explicit policies, in which the views of all sectors of society are elicited and rational and social use can be made of the power of mass communication. It is with this in mind that a variety of forms of grassroots participation in media management has been tried out in Latin America—particularly in Mexico, Chile and Peru—which could serve as a precedent for embarking on a more systematic effort to democratize mass communication. The authorities responsible for educational and cultural policies in every country would necessarily be expected to play an important part in drawing up such policies and in setting standards aimed at protecting the public from the anti-educational effects of advertising. The state should likewise give financial support to the media in systems that are not under government control—for which there are precedents in a number of European countries—so as to ensure that advertisers do not take them over completely.

At the international level, Unesco's action in setting up two special commissions in recent years has been of the utmost significance. The first of these was the Faure Commission on the problems of education, while the other is the MacBride Commission on communication issues. With the findings of these two commissions, the international community will be well equipped to participate in a special conference, convened under the auspices of Unesco, with a view to analysing the existing conflicts between education and advertising and to seeking an answer to them and to the serious prejudice being caused to national cultures by the growing invasion of transnational advertising. This idea has been put forward on other occasions[25] and appears to be an excellent way of channelling and responding to the concerns that are now so widely felt by educators and parents and by all those who are committed to the task of culture and education.*

Notes

1. Ivan Illich, *Alternativas*, p. 113, Mexico City, Editorial Joaquin Mortiz, 1977.
2. Paolo Freire, *Pedagogy of the Oppressed*, New York, Herder & Herder, 1970.
3. There exists a considerable amount of research demonstrating the considerable time given up to the media. In Europe alone, for instance, more than half the total number of children watch television every day; in the United States, children in the 4- to 8-year age-group watch it on average for two and a half hours a day and those in the 10- to 16-year age-group for four hours a day. See George Comstock, et al., *Television and Human Behavior*, p. 178, New York, Columbia University Press, 1978.
4. Louis Porcher, *L'école parallèle*, Paris, Librairie Larousse, 1974.
5. This subject of the mass media and the role they play in the field of education is discussed at length in Fernando Reyes Matta, *Communicación masiva: la escuela paralela*, Mexico City, ILET.
6. Max Ferrero, 'L'École et la Télévision: les Soeurs Ennemies?', *Éducation 2000* (Paris), No. 7, September 1977.
7. Of the thirty-one in the world with private commercial television networks, sixteen, more than half, are in Latin America. This is the result of imitating and importing the communication system of the United States. See Elihu Katz and George Wedell, *Broadcasting in the Third World*, Cambridge, Mass., Harvard University Press, 1977.
8. Bernard Cathelat, *Publicité et société*, p. 33–7, Paris, Petite Bibliothèque Payot, 1976.
9. However, studies in which this type of measurement is included show significant variations. In Costa Rica, four newspapers were analysed and were found to consist, on average, of 42 per cent of advertisements, while the figure for one of them was as high as 66 per cent (José M. Fonseca, *Communication Policies in Costa Rica*, Paris, Unesco, 1976). In Peru, in 1968, 'a morphological analysis of newspapers with the largest circulation figures... showed that the seven leading newspapers included no less than 35.5 per cent of advertisements and that the newspaper devoting most space to advertising included as much as 58.4 per cent' (Pontificia

---

* This is, of course, the authors' opinion and does not commit Unesco.—Ed.

Universidad Catolica de Peru, *Investigación de los medios de comunicación colectiva*, Lima, 1961). Even higher figures are quoted in Alex Schmid, *The North American Penetration of the Latin American Knowledge Sector—Some Aspects of Communication and Information Dependence*, a document presented to the Seventh Conference of the International Peace Research Association, Oaxtepec, Mexico, 1978 (mimeo.), pp. 13 and 14. On this question, see also Noreene Janus and Rafael Roncagliolo, 'Advertising, Mass Media and Dependency', *Development Dialogue* (Uppsala, Sweden), No. 1, 1979.

10. Schmid, op. cit.
11. Quoted in Cathelat, op. cit., p. 36.
12. Ibid.
13. *Advertising Age*, 6 February 1978, p. 2.
14. *Federal Trade Commission Staff Report on TV Advertising to Children*, Federal Trade Commission, Washington, D.C., 1978.
15. Scott Ward, Daniel B. Wackman and Ellen Wartella, *How Children Learn to Buy*, p. 189, Beverly Hills, Sage Publications, 1977.
16. Armand Mattelart, 'El imperialismo en busca de la contrarevolución cultural, Plaza Sésamo; Prologo a la telerepresion del año 2,000', *Comunicación y cultura*, p. 146–223 (Santiago de Chile), No. 1, July 1973.
17. Janus and Roncagliolo, op. cit.
18. The term 'transnational advertising' as used here refers to advertising contracted out by corporations that are owned or controlled by foreign interests, for the purpose of promoting their own products. With regard to the transnational concept in the communication field, see Juan Somavia, 'La estructura transnacional de poder y la información internacional', in Fernando Reyes Matta (ed.), *La información en el Nuevo Orden Internacional*, Mexico City, ILET, 1977.
19. Quoted in Victor Bernal Sahagún, *Anatomía de la publicidad en México*, p. 117, Mexico City, Editorial Nuestro Tiempo, 1974.
20. Schmid, op. cit. See also Magdalena Brockmann, *La publicidad y la prensa: análisis quantitativo de una semana en los diarios latinoamericanos*, Mexico City, ILET, 1979.
21. Adriana Santa Cruz and Viviana Erazo, *Compropolitan: el orden transnacional y su modelo informativo femenino*, Mexico City, ILET, 1979.
22. A sample of television viewers in Indonesia, who were asked which advertisements they remembered from the previous week's broadcasts, mentioned only transnational brands in their replies. Alfian, 'Some Observations on Television in Indonesia', in Jim Richstad (ed.), *New Perspectives in International Communication*, p. 58–9, Honolulu, East-West Centre, 1979.
23. Richard Barnett and Ronald E. Muller, *Global Reach*, p. 33, New York, Simon and Schuster, 1974.

24. Eduardo Santoro, *La televisión venezolana y la formación de estereo-tipos en el niño*, p. 279, Caracas, Ediciones de la Biblioteca, 1975.
25. Juan Somavía, *How to Go about Basic Needs: the International Perspective*, address to the Plenary Session at the International Development Conference, Washington, D.C., 8 February 1978 (mimeo.); Janus and Roncagliolo, op. cit.

A tentative conclusion

Education and the mass media: where they differ, where they converge

Michel Souchon

The media and education: from the past to the present

All the major mass communication media had their origins outside education. Schools have always thought them as competitors as regards their influence on society and ways of thinking, which explains the constant desire to make use of mass communication techniques in schools and the illusion about their ability to solve the major problems of education.

Educational institutions and the mass media are essentially rivals. Throughout the world, teachers make virtually the same criticisms of them. The mass media are reproached with placing such emphasis on entertainment and spectacle that whatever information they may convey is drowned in a flood of empty words. Education and the media rest on two irreconcilable principles: on the one hand the spectacle, with its facility, superficiality, passivity and illusion of effortless learning, and on the other the training process, which implies effort, depth, the solidity of real learning and activity. Lastly, the most fundamental clash is between two orders of faculties: the school gives priority to reason and logic, while in the media imagination and the senses reign supreme.

Teachers do indeed admit that benefit may be derived from media men's attempts to present educational topics—as, for example, in popular science programmes. They are quick to point out, however, that such programmes cannot supply the coherent, structured knowledge that only schools can provide, and therefore give the illusion rather than the substance of knowledge. They also condemn what they see as the excessive amount of media time taken up by fiction: modern children may spend more time engrossed in imaginary adventures seen on films, television or cartoons than in their own history.

In the developing countries, it is pointed out that the ideology or values that the school seeks to impart differ from—and often contradict—the ideology and value-system conveyed by the media: the school is to some degree explicitly expected to keep children on the land by teaching them more efficient farming methods, while at the same time the media put out formidably effective messages highlighting the town and urban models. It may be objected that there are similar contradictions within the messages put out by each system: the school should help the peasant to farm his land more efficiently, yet it often encourages him to leave for the town, while media programmes aimed at slowing down the flight from the land often conflict with advertisements that glamorize urban life-styles. It must, however, be admitted that teachers have good grounds for pointing critically to the contradictions between the two basic contemporary systems for moulding the mind.

A study of the greater part of the media's content is enough to show that it calls into question schools as institutions, emphasizing their often outdated curricula, their failure to keep abreast of the latest knowledge and their often boring teaching methods, etc.

So the two institutions are competitors and rivals. But it must be confessed that the media exert a kind of fascination over teachers. Whenever a new communication medium appears, schools want to know what use it might be to them. In many cases, this is prompted not by a thorough correlation of educational objectives with the potential of the media, but by a wish to adapt modern techniques for use in education as audio-visual aids. The list is endless—school radio and television, educational films, sequences and slides with spoken commentaries or explanatory notes, language courses on records or cassettes and more sophisticated uses of tape-recorders in language laboratories, etc.

Without in any way denying the benefits and many successful applications of such techniques (monographs could usefully be written to catalogue and describe the most productive experiments), it should be noted that there are three limitations on the use of the media in education. The first is the imbalance between those fields that lend themselves to visual techniques or spectacular presentation and are thus popular media topics, and the underrepresented fields that are based on ideas rather than images. Catalogues of audio-visual aids show the same tendency as television newscasts to emphasize topics for which pictures are available rather than more abstract topics—how can the problems of inflation or fluctuating exchange rates be 'illustrated'?

The next limitation lies in the inflexibility and unwieldiness of both institutions, which make co-operation difficult. The most typical example is that of school television broadcasts: it is very difficult to correlate the timetable of any class and the broadcasts designed for it. The rigidity of school timetables matches that of television schedules.

Third, the use of modern audio-visual techniques tends to separate the two functions of education—to pass on information and to mould the mind. The first may be performed, subject to the foregoing provisos, by technical means: the second, conversely, implies physical contact—real education can only be won by close combat. The really important things, Nietzsche used to say, can only be taught person to person. So that while these techniques may be useful, it is misguided to think that they can be self-sufficient. In the language of communications theory, it may be said that there is no education without feedback—and in that respect, one example is illuminating. All experiments in educational television, whether with children or with adults, show that there can be no genuine feedback with groups of more than twenty. If that number is to be exceeded, properly organized audience groups must be arranged, each with its leader—an organizer or teacher—within which the message may be 'reactivated'. The reactions to educational messages depend largely on the quality of the audience network and the training of the group leaders. The economic consequences of such observations are plain: it is generally hoped that the mass media will be a panacea providing cheap education for large numbers of children or adults. Such expectations overlook the importance of providing a suitable context, without which media messages remain a dead letter. This illusion is persistent, and it would be surprising if it did not re-emerge periodically in the future.

But schools have not only attempted to use media techniques as audio-visual aids: they have also grappled with the problem of teaching young people how to use the media, which take up a large proportion of their free time. Here again, there is a long list of attempts to teach critical reading of the press, or intelligent viewing of films and television. Just as the school taught people in oral civilizations how to speak and listen, or to read and write when the written word held sway, should it not now teach them how to watch and show? The many experiments such as 'screen education', or the more recent 'training of the active young viewer', were attempts to answer this question affirmatively.

There may, then, be said to be 'tangential encounters' between the schools and the media: attempts to use media-style techniques to assimilate the two different languages that pupils hear, or to establish training in the discerning use of the mass media. But the geographical distribution of those encounters is very uneven: frequent in the industrialized countries, where sufficient resources are provided to give them some chance of success, but far rarer in the developing countries—and when they do occur, they possess only limited resources.

Lastly, should it not be acknowledged that in comparison with the hopes awakened by the enormous capacity of cinema, radio and television for disseminating knowledge, the results as a whole seem disappointing? The proportion of educational and informative programmes is slight in comparison with that of entertainments such as serials, series, films, games, variety, sport, etc. And if, rather than the structure of messages broadcast, we take as our criterion the structure of messages received, the structure of viewing or listening time, the proportion of educational and cultural programmes declines even further. The mass media do not to any great extent serve the cause of education, and teachers consequently feel that they should either teach pupils the discerning use of the media, or else divert some of the fascination of cinema and television to their own account by using them as audio-visual aids.

The education of tomorrow: the major challenges

Only the naïve could hope to break new ground on the major problems for tomorrow's education, and no more than a cursory list will be presented.

One prior remark should be made: the situation differs widely from region to region. In what are called the industrialized countries, the number of pupils in primary education is now static, while in the developing countries it is rising very rapidly. Many countries have fairly uniform education systems, while in others different models coexist—a traditional oral-based sector, a modern sector for mass literacy and the written word, and a modern élitist sector using up-to-date educational techniques, for instance. And most important, of course, the resources vary enormously from rich to poor countries. These differences between countries and regions create a serious problem for the future: how to prevent them giving rise to disparities in the quality of the education systems which could not but have cumulative effects?

Two major educational problems will be the number of people to be educated and the number of subjects to be taught. The number of adults and young people seeking admission to educational instututions will rise greatly: more children will require primary and secondary education in countries with fast-growing populations, more young people will be kept at school by the raising of the school-leaving age, and more adults will rejoin the education system through the development of lifelong education. Of course, the problem will be most acute wherever the shortage of funds and manpower is greatest.

At the same time, the amount of knowledge to be taught is growing constantly. The advance of technological and scientific discovery is such that curricula require constant updating. If education is effectively to prepare young people and adults for life in this technological age, new subjects or at least the latest developments in traditional disciplines must be included. Several countries feel it necessary to provide, for instance, basic training in data-processing and computer languages. This adds another 'stratum' of education: which traditional disciplines must be sacrificed to make room for it? Might not education, which reproaches the media with disseminating superficial and incoherent knowledge, expose itself one day, and possibly soon, to a similar grievance?

The decline of the egalitarian ideal seems to me to be one of the major challenges ahead for education. During the nineteenth and the first half of the twentieth centuries, school systems inspired by the ideal of maximum equality of educational opportunity were established everywhere: free and compulsory primary education, the extension of public education through 'common cores' at secondary level, and extremely generous access to higher education. But alongside this there is now a trend towards commercial, voluntary and élitist sectors whose purpose is to give their clientele a distinctive brand of education. At times they are established in response to a crisis in the public sector, which is accused of inefficiency or 'holding back the best' by lavishing excessive care on all. Elsewhere the commercial sector confines itself to providing extra services, thereby enabling the few to gain maximum advantage from the free and compulsory system for all. Typical examples might be the evening classes in Japan, residential language courses abroad, the serially published encyclopedias which ambitious parents purchase for their children, and all the systems of 'tutoring', 'coaching', etc.

Another major challenge: will the future bring adequate educational solutions to the enormous problems of poverty, hunger and large-scale technological change? It is too often felt today that we cannot design or set up education systems that might help—slowly, since lasting educational solutions cannot be quick—to solve the problems of rural development or health in the developing countries: coping with these countries' increased problems over the coming decades will be doubly difficult. At a time of ever faster technological change, the unwieldiness of educational institutions makes it hard for them to make the necessary adjustments.

These problems outlined rather than described or analysed, are those that education systems will have to face in coming decades. How will the media evolve in that same period?

The media: looking ahead

It is no easy exercise to attempt to predict the future of the media. Admittedly, it is not difficult to provide a list of foreseeable technological innovations—but the technologically and industrially possible is not always commercially or socially probable. Yet social probability is governed less by 'needs' or prior 'expectations' than by the demands of the market or the commercial policies of industrial managers. Those policies are based on calculated risks, and their success is judged in terms of wars, in which each company seeks to win predominance for its own products and standards.

A further point is that the media as a body are so structured that any change in the place or function of any one of them—or the introduction of a new element—alters the place and function of all the others. Neither finance nor time-resources are infinite: no matter what additional factors need to be added to so oversimplified a model of causal relationships, television has clearly altered the place and function of the cinema by providing a large number of fictional programmes and taking up a large proportion of the public's time (box-office sales have fallen sharply, the audiences are structurally different and younger, the content of films has changed, etc.). And since the geography of the media is changed completely by a shifting border or the emergence of new territory, it is difficult to make forecasts in this area. The best solution is to start from the simplest aspect, the description of new technologies.

No substantial technological improvements to the cinema seem likely, with the possible exception of three-dimensional picture techniques.

Television techniques, conversely, are changing rapidly, both for production and in respect of transmission and reception. Technological advances and the use of smaller equipment—such as one-inch instead of two-inch lenses—make lower production costs likely. Light-weight viewfinding cameras (ENG) will make for faster operations that will put television on a par with radio in news gathering. The replacement of analogue methods by digital techniques for processing audio-visual signals should improve the quality of transmission and enable a single channel to be used for television, radio and telephone signals, communication with data banks and reception of teletext systems, etc.

Programme transmission by direct broadcasting satellites will induce countries that have not yet installed ground transmission networks to save themselves the cost. Such satellites will extend the range of cross-border overspill, thereby improving opportunities for receiving programmes from neighbouring countries. Another possible use of satellites with important educational implications is 'radiovision': the equivalent of a satellite television channel is used to carry fifty programmes of still pictures each with its own sound-track. Also known as 'still-picture television', this system was tested in Japan during trials of the experimental communications satellite.

Messages will reach the television sets either by private aerials, different from and more expensive than the present models, or by community aerials and cable networks. This latter system, known in various countries as 'tele-distribution' or 'cable distribution', enables more programmes to be broadcast to the consumer than the overcrowded Hertzian system. A particular advantage is that it makes it easier to establish strictly local news and communication stations. Another application, still unusual but likely to become less so with the growing use of optical fibres, is in 'interactive systems', in which the user may converse with the broadcaster and participate more fully in the programme. Where optical fibres are concerned, it also brings closer the single network of which we spoke earlier.

The structure of messages received on television sets will also change profoundly. More programmes will be available, as we have said, via satellites and/or cable networks. Additionally, the television set will be the core of a range of equipment and services that is starting to be called 'video technology'. The video-recorder, which is to the audio-visual media and television what the tape-recorder is to sound and radio, will be used to record programmes for screening whenever desired, and will be programmable several days ahead. It can also be used with pre-recorded video cassettes and home productions made with a video camera. With an appropriate reading head, private or family television sets will be able to show programmes recorded on video discs (here the user cannot himself record). Lastly, the set will serve as a display screen for teletexts, either broadcast or carried by the telephone network from data banks. This is known as telematics.

A further foreseeable development is the system of pay television, or 'toll television' as the Canadians call it. In these systems the user receives both channels financed by advertisements or licence fees and programmes for which he pays either a flat-rate fee (monthly or yearly subscription to a channel) or a fee per programme watched, in the same way that he pays for telephone calls.

All this equipment will make two radical changes to the

system of the media. By sharply increasing the number of channels and accessible sources of messages, it will first of all bring about fragmented audiences and specialization of contents: the 'big media' will give way to the 'little media', 'broadcasting' to 'narrowcasting', and broadcasters, editors and producers of all kinds will appeal more directly to particular audiences, or will provide a greater quantity of messages designed to meet a single function or demand (sport, information, fiction, etc.). Secondly, the more advanced of these systems will be interactive, enabling the user to intervene more and more in the course of the programme. For instance, the possibility of producing interactive video discs is being studied: they would include pauses for users' questions and the messages would be recapitulated, made more detailed or repeated in the light of the answers.

Such are, in brief, the major audio-visual techniques now available, or shortly to become so, that will become widespread over the next two decades. Such a list can be drawn up without too much difficulty. But as a forecast of media developments it will not suffice: it must include the dates by which the equipment will be in general use and the impact of each upon the media system. The video-recorder, for instance, is sure to become a part of many households, since sets are already on the market and are selling. But who can forecast when the numbers bought in any given country or group of countries will reach the critical threshold that forces television companies to review the now-prevailing rules for programming, such as the distinction between 'off-peak' and 'peak' times? And who, furthermore, can foretell where that critical threshold will lie?

To complicate matters even more, it should be added that all the evidence points to wide variations from country to country or region to region in the pace of development of the new audio-visual techniques. In California, fifty-five television channels are available thanks to cables and satellites, and ownership of video-recorders and cameras is among the highest in the world, yet several African countries have no television network and, even when there is a station in the capital, broadcasts can only be received within a radius of a few kilometres. Putting these differences in chronological terms, one might talk of a delay of thirty to forty years. But that supposes a linear and isomorphic form of development, while there are several reasons to fear that the gap will progressively widen: growth in communications media is slow in the developing countries, but explosive in many industrialized countries.

The countries which until the end of the century will progress no further than the major mass media—radio and television as now understood, without peripheral television services—seem unlikely to catch up with those that invest heavily in equipment for highly diversified content and specific programmes as well as mass messages.

In the latter, a rapid proliferation of video-recorders can be foreseen. Six to seven per cent of households already have them in Japan, some 3 per cent in the United States and 1.5 per cent in Western Europe. In a dozen years or so, the rate may well be 25 to 50 per cent. Where video-disc reading heads are concerned, the suggested price—or the actual price in the case of RCA—is about half that for video-recorders, and this in many specialists' view should lead to an even more rapid penetration of the equipment. Connection to cable networks should also become common, giving as it does access to more television channels, and to various telematic services. Here, however, it is extremely difficult to suggest even very approximate figures, since the situation is likely to vary greatly from country to country.

The other group, the developing countries, is more or less certain to catch up rapidly in television, since direct broadcasting satellites will make it possible to do so without terrestrial transmission networks. These satellites should become commonplace in the second half of the 1980s. As a result, households will doubtless soon be equipped with sets, and sales graphs will resemble those in the industrialized countries in the 1950s and 1960s, with market saturation in some fifteen years. Only an urban minority, on the other hand, will be equipped for video technology, mainly with video-recorders and video-disc reading heads.

The big difference between the two groups of countries is that only the second will have the new generation equipment giving access to personalized messages and interactive systems. The others will remain at the stage of mass communication, with messages designed for vast audiences and so for the 'average viewer', without opportunities for genuine feedback.

Media forecasts often overlook the programmes, forgetting that unless the revolutionary growth in communication channels is matched by the development of productions, there is a risk of programme shortage—or at least of a serious imbalance between channels and messages, 'hardware' and 'software'. It may be argued that the production of messages always lags behind communication techniques, and that each new technique begins by transmitting programmes borrowed from its predecessors. The cinema films theatre plays, the radio broadcasts concerts and music-hall, and television draws heavily on the repertoire of the cinema. But a technique comes of age when it finds its own repertoire of messages.

Two phenomena may be adduced to illustrate the tendency towards imbalance between 'hardware' and 'software'. Although the statistics are hard to ascertain, it has been estimated that, in many countries, the ratio of television transmission and household equipment costs to programme production costs is of the order of three to one—and, of course, the imbalance is greater in some developing countries which lean heavily on cheap foreign programmes. The second illustration, also from the world of television: several countries have calculated the finance available per programme hour in constant figures, and have observed a decline: finance stagnates or grows slowly, while the increase in airtime continues because of the establishment of new channels or increased daily broadcasting hours for old ones.

International exchanges—buying and selling, co-production and exchanges proper—will increase. The relationships will be as unequal as they are today, and involve the same dangers: the first influence of foreign products, that exerted on local producers through the imposition of models of international commercial success, is probably at least as important as their impact on the users of products that convey—implicitly in fiction, explicitly in the case of news and commentaries—stereotypes and models, standards and values.

The shortage of programmes will be made good by other methods, including the systematic use of archives, recourse to all the existing audio-visual collections, production rationalization procedures such as the re-use of 'stock shots', and frequent retransmissions. The promoters of new services or media will probably wish to include educational documents in their catalogues.

Interaction between the media and education

If the enormous growth of educational needs is compared with the prodigious development of the media, the multiplication of channels and carriers, the correspondence may appear to be pre-ordained. To resume the principal points made above, the mass media can meet the challenge of the growing numbers of people to be educated, since they can transmit the same message millions of times. The problems arising from the number of subjects to be taught are offset by the opportunity of consulting the best specialists in every field, those abreast of the latest knowledge, or constantly updated data banks, and by the ability to store, catalogue and distribute audio-visual products designed for teachers and their pupils. Even the problem of economic disparities seems soluble: while techniques such as radio and television for schools are costly, the size of audience reached results in a very low cost per pupil.

This argument is admittedly not new. Although challenged by several experiments, it is constantly resorted to, and the safest prediction in this study is that it will be used again in future. When confronted with the magnitude of the educational problems of the future, the temptation will yet again be to place excessive hopes on the old or new media. An essay on the illusions of the future is neither hard nor hazardous to write.

But perhaps the observation that in the past the appearance of new media has complicated teachers' problems rather than helping to solve them is insufficient ground for declaring hopes for the future vain. In support of these somewhat pessimistic views, a few powerful tendencies should be recalled that will in all probability leave a lasting imprint on the history of relations between the world of education and the media.

The first of them is that the media are used predominantly for entertainment purposes. Each new medium is presented as an instrument for disseminating knowledge and information or promoting culture. No new television or radio station is launched that is not claimed to be different, to meet the thirst for knowledge that is not satisfied elsewhere. But in the vast majority of cases, subsequent achievements do not match up to ambitions.

In Tokyo I had the opportunity of visiting the headquarters of the 'Captain' system, which links homes to data banks by telephone and could produce around 80,000 pages of text on home television screens: by the end of 1981 the figure was 200,000. It carries political, economic and social information, administrative information, weather forecasts and road reports, train and aircraft timetables, entertainment programmes, lessons in various subjects are various levels, games, especially quizzes, and horoscopes, etc. The educational potential of an interactive system that makes programmed education possible is clear. When I asked for accurate fugures giving the most popular pages, I was told they were those containing horoscopes and quizzes.

This majority use of the mass media and the new, more personalized techniques cannot fail to give them an image that will rebuff teachers and make them doubt the educational potential of these instruments. All teachers are willing to concede that television can in theory provide education and culture, but all are convinced that in fact its main purpose is to entertain.

The mistrust which the dominant use of the mass media arouses may of course be dispelled. But there is a further consideration which more effectively banishes dreams of the media solving tomorrow's educational problems: the state of the available financial resources. These are very unevenly distributed, and are not co-extensive with the greatest educational needs. This can only entrench existing inequalities: rich media in rich countries—and, incidentally, benefiting more especially the education of the richest—and in the poor countries, poor media that will still be mass media, with their cumbersome institutions reinforcing the inherent inflexibility of one-way transmission technology.

The new media are theoretically more centred on news, the search for information and the dissemination of knowledge (even if there are surprises here, as we said above in connection with the 'Captain' scheme), while the old media, cinema, radio and television, are clearly more concerned with entertainment. Yet the latter will probably be the only ones within the grasp of the developing countries, where educational needs are greatest.

The conditions that educational television has to meet must once more be stressed in order to shatter the illusion that it can provide a cheap solution to the developing countries' educational problems. Everyone feels that it is not enough to broadcast programmes, no matter how good, regardless of the educational standards of the target audience or of the reactions and environment which will make or break their impact—as is confirmed by every serious experiment. It is realized everywhere that the needs, knowledge and motivation of the target audience must first be studied. Similarly, an audience network must be established, and its quality is more important to the success of operations than is that of the television programmes themselves. Again, television is often no more than the centre-piece of a 'multimedia' system. Radio, for instance, can correct the unwieldiness of television: while television programmes must generally be prepared well in advance and are very costly, radio programmes can be improvised quickly and more cheaply in response to questions and to recapitulate points which have been misunderstood. In short, there is and can be no genuine educational television that merely puts out courses, even good ones, at fixed times. Television is only a cog in a machine, a machine that makes it work and without which it is nothing but a voice crying in the wilderness or, worse, an instrument that widens cultural gaps.

At this point in the argument, the two dominant tendencies in modern teaching practice should be recalled: the first is the trend towards maximum rationalization, in which education becomes a technique (teaching by objective, programmed instruction, etc.), while the second emphasizes individual motivations (non-directive teaching, freedom to learn, etc.). Both reject the massive use of broadcasting techniques to swamp entire regions with educational programmes, much as vast areas are sprayed with fertilizers (while the comparison is left unspoken, such projects are often spelled out: doubters are referred to the many statements concerning 'educational satellites').

Rational educationists insist that teaching methods must be closely aligned to specific objectives and that the results of education must be monitored at every stage. If we inquire which of the old or new media can meet these requirements, traditional radio and television must be ruled out in favour of more flexible techniques that enable programmes to be interrupted on the spot in order to repeat sections and slow down or speed up the course (sound records or cassettes, combined sound and images, films, video discs or video cassettes, interactive teletext systems, etc.).

For its part, non-directive teaching reminds us that the pupil genuinely masters only the things to which his personal interest guides him and that he discovers for himself. To help him in this process, he should be given the documentation he needs for his research and be helped to produce his own lesson—the teacher serving to help him formulate his ideas rather than as a repository of knowledge to be dispensed in a pre-ordained way. For this purpose, particular use should be made of media that enable audio-visual archives to be stored and consulted in documentation centres: series of slides with spoken commentaries, films, sound cassettes and records, video cassettes and video discs.

Whichever attitude is adopted, educational preferences clearly go to the new or future media with their capacity for flexible use, decentralized consultation and a personalized approach—in other words, those whose penetration seems likely to be slow in the developing countries or the deprived areas or communities in the industrialized countries. It was noted earlier that a parallel, commercial educational sector had in many countries emerged alongside the free and compulsory public sector: it seems probable that the most sophisticated and educationally advantageous of the new media will be used above all in commercial institutes that train élites.

Finally, we should mention one last dominant tendency that together with the restrictions on financial resources will very probably leave its mark on the future: the limitations imposed by the habits of teaching staff. The news media create a need for technical instruction courses—in itself no easy matter—but above all for an often radical rethink of traditional teaching methods. I do not consider the teaching profession more attached to its traditions and habits than any other social group. But it is as much so, and it would be naïve to expect it to show more than the usual adaptability. It must be repeated that educational reforms will not fall from a sky full of satellites. They will only come about through changes in the attitudes of teachers.

Consideration of these powerful tendencies (predominance of entertainment in the media, restricted and unequal resources and the weight of inertia) leads to a vision of the future in which the school and the media are still competitors and rivals, with 'tangential encounters' whose impact on educational habits and media operations is slight. But such views may be valid only for the relatively near future of the next six to ten years, the 'future of the present' which John McHall said was contained in the past since it reflected outworn habits and was shaped by past decisions. However, he added that the future of the future was contained in the present. The more distant future will probably be fashioned by the attitudes of today; it is prefigured by micro-decisions that hold the seeds of a closer relationship and possible co-operation.

Attempts at a closer relationship and prospects for collaboration

These new attitudes will doubtless be brought closer by certain developments that can even now be glimpsed: a renewed emphasis on low-cost techniques, the rediscovery of the resources of audio-visual archives, some of which are now being catalogued, the gradual separation of the publishing, manufacture, storage and carrying of messages, and lastly, the potential combination of large-scale and small-scale media in more flexible systems than the current mass media.

The first path towards a closer relationship between the worlds of school and the media lies in the renewed interest in simpler technology. While the most sophisticated technical media exert a kind of fascination over teachers, a more objective appraisal shows that simpler techniques can bring important educational results because they are closer to the user and his daily concerns: witness some Latin American school radios which played a major role in the literacy and conscientization campaigns, or the use of the mobile cinema in India.

The second contemporary trend that opens new vistas of co-operation is the discovery of the potential that lies in the systematic exploitation of cinema and television libraries, both those that are now available and those now being constituted. Just one example: the Centre National de Documentation Pédagogique (National Centre for Educational Documentation) has calculated that in France alone there are 200,000 scientific, technical or industrial films ranging from the birth of the cinema until the present day. There are similar resources in many countries, and when the different problems of teacher access have been solved, they will be a virtually inexhaustible source of educational documents. The circumstances surrounding those problems are now more favourable, and solutions appear more imminent.

Admittedly these libraries must be sifted to find the technically and educationally suitable material. There are also problems over the physical conservation of documents. None of this is new, and solutions should be found when the benefits of the exercise are fully realized. Computer techniques will be very useful for cataloguing and indexing the libraries. For carriage, transmission and reception, two conceivable solutions are satellites linked to storage video-recorders and the publishing of video discs.

The programmes will more usually be presented as collections of short documents rather than ready-made lessons, which leave nothing for the teacher to do. The latter will thus look for short programmes which he can develop in his own lesson. To use an analogy with the written word, textbooks will be less sought after than dictionary or encyclopedia articles.

Several systems will be available to carry the programmes, and cost/benefit calculations must be used in choosing them. One thing is certain: the present barriers and misunderstandings between message-carrying techniques, mass content designed for virtually everyone—for the audience in general and nobody in particular—and the giant organizations must be broken down if the entire process is to be managed. The idea of separating the publishing, producing, programming, storing and carrying of educational products is gaining ground. It is slowly being realized that the infrequent use of audio-visual media in educational institutions and the frequent failure or half-success of such use as is made of them might well stem from the antagonism between unwieldy bodies managing the media and unwieldly bodies managing education systems. A more human dimension must be found—and that cannot be done if message-carrying and publishing continue to be combined, and if satellites are matched by production organizations on a similar scale.

Technology is clearly advancing in two directions: one

towards 'gigantism', with satellites creating reception areas the size of entire subcontinents, and the other towards a measure of decentralization, with private media for audio-visual recording and storage, and local cable services. If these two directions are regarded as opposites, then two incompatible audio-visual systems will increasingly take shape with, on the one hand, satellites broadcasting mass messages produced by giant entertainment companies and, on the other, a reaction in the shape of a myriad of enterprises, attractive in that they satisfy the operators' needs for self-expression, but often insignificant in comparison with the major mass media, even when they do not merely repeat the same logic and idiom on a smaller scale. Yet the two might conceivably complement each other by combining more flexibly than today's ossified media. Such flexible combinations would certainly be very useful to education.

Once again, the example of the educational satellite may serve. Used to pour out complete and polished educational messages compiled by cumbersome, remote institutions, its failure is certain. But that will not be so if it is given its proper role to play in message-carrying, transmitting short programmes that can be received, stored and made available to teachers for classroom use as illustration and demonstration.

Lastly, it should not be overlooked that the dynamism of the major audio-visual and telecommunications enterprises will weigh heavily on the future of the relationship between the media and education. They will impose their products and programmes on the world market. But without wishing to minimize their penetrative power, I think that systems and programmes attuned to the tendencies we have observed have greater chances of success in both educational and commercial terms.

You will not be bored at the end of the twentieth century, Malraux once told a young friend. And he added: Prepare for the unforeseeable. An easy jest, perhaps, since the future is always surprising. But it is well to recall such banal remarks to give these notes a seal of unfeigned modesty. Not that self-

Education and the mass media: where they differ, where they converge

confidence is their biggest fault: it is, rather, excessive doubt and the provision of more questions than answers. Let us hope at least that the questions are the right ones, and that this paper will help to frame them correctly. As the Muslim sage would have it, the first half of knowledge lies in the question. The other half is the reply.

It remains for me to go back and correct whatever element of excessive, technologically-inspired optimism the previous section may contain as to the *leitmotiv* of this study, inequality. The media are the mirror of a non-egalitarian world: the communication and information media are unfairly distributed throughout the world; the market forces are unequal and power in the communication networks is unequally divided among individuals, groups and productions. Unless inequality is to be made a virtue, it must be recognized that there is a profoundly immoral situation for which the future guarantees no remedy—indeed, a widening of the gap is possible if not probable. In that other world this study has discussed, the world of education, the inequalities are no less flagrant: on the one hand, there are enormous quantitative and qualitative needs with very restricted resources, and on the other, lesser needs, particularly in terms of quality, and large resources. To hope that educational problems may be cured by use of the media is, it must be repeated, vain: it is to forget that the two orders of inequality are cumulative, not compensatory.

About the authors

YURI BABANSKI (USSR).
Vice-President of the Academy of Pedagogical Sciences, and professor of educational sciences. Author of more than 200 works on theoretical aspects of education, in particular monographs on perfecting the contemporary school, which have been translated into several languages.

GASPARE BARBIELLINI AMIDEI (Italy).
Professor of the Sociology of Knowledge at the Faculty of Political Science at the University of Turin. Vice-director of *Corriere della sera*. Author of several publications, including *I labirinti della sociologia* (with Ulderico Bernardi) and *La carovana di carta*.

THOMAS A. BAUER (Austria).
Senior lecturer in the science of mass communication and media education in the department of mass communication at the University of Salzburg. Director of the Institut für Kommunikationswissenchaft at Graz. Advisor for research in media education in the provinces of Styria and Tyrol. Numerous publications in media education including teacher-training manuals for in-service courses in media education.

GÉRALD BERGER (Switzerland).
Director of the Centre Fribourgeois d'Initiation aux Mass-Médias, Chairman of the Groupe Romand en Matière d'Audiovisuel à

About the authors

l'Ecole, and author of a study on Robert Desnos (*Robert Desnos et le cinéma surréaliste*) and of several works dealing with media education.

RITA CRUISE O'BRIEN (United States).
Mainly interested in French-speaking Africa, and recently in problems of mass communication in developing countries. Teacher in the Development Planning Unit at University College, London. Among her publications are: *White Society in Black Africa: the French Senegal; The Political Economy of Underdevelopment: Dependence in Senegal.*

ASLE GIRE DAHL (Norway).
Senior scholar at the Norwegian Council of Research in Science and the Humanities (NAVF). Former primary school teacher and lecturer in media pedagogy.

HENRI DIEUZEIDE (France).
Director of the Unesco Division of Structures, Content, Methods and Techniques of Education. Former Director of the Department of School Radio and Television in the French Ministry of Education. Author of *Les techniques audiovisuelles dans l'enseignment.*

DONALD P. ELY (United States).
Professor of Education at Syracuse University. Director, ERIC Clearinghouse on Information Resources. Co-author of *Teaching and Media: A Systematic Approach* and *Media Personnel in Education: A Competency Approach.*

FERENC GENZWEIN (Hungary).
General Director of the National Centre for Educational Technology (Budapest). Member of the Presidium of the Hungarian Pedagogical Society. Former director of a school for in-service teacher training and head of department at the Ministry of Education. Author of several studies on educational innovation and mathematics teaching.

HOWARD HITCHENS (United States).
Consultant to the United States Information Agency and the United States Department of Education. Until recently, Executive Director of the Association for Educational Communications and Techno-

logy. United States representative to the International Council for Educational Media.

NOREENE Z. JANUS (United States).
Specialist in communications problems. Currently research co-ordinator at the Instituto Latinoamericano de Estudios Transnacionales (ILET). Author of several studies on women and mass media and on transnational structures of mass communications.

DYMAS JOSEPH (Brazil).
Graduate in philosophy and psychology, journalist, lecturer in the philosophy of education, founder of the Education Department of the *Jornal do Brasil*.

MIRCEA MALITZA (Romania).
Former Minister of Education. Professor at the Faculty of Mathematics at the University of Bucharest. Has lectured on international affairs at academic centres in Asia, Europe and the United States. Author of books on education and mathematics: *The Chronicle of the Year 2000*, *The Grey Gold*; co-author of the report to the Club of Rome entitled *No Limits to Learning*.

LEN MASTERMAN (United Kingdom).
Lecturer in Education at the University of Nottingham. Participated in national media conferences in the United Kingdom, Sweden and Australia. Consultant in media education for Unesco and the Council of Europe. Author of *Teaching about Television*.

SIRKKA MINKKINEN (Finland).
Acting head of programmes for the Finnish Broadcasting Company TV 1. Has worked as mass media researcher and consultant to the state committee which formulated the curriculum of media education for Finland's comprehensive school system. Co-author of *Lapsi ja joukkotiedotus* (The Child and the Mass Media) and *Joukkotiedotus* (Mass Communication), and author of the Unesco publication *A General Curricular Model for Mass Media Education*.

ABRAHAM MOLES (France).
Founder and now Director of the Institute of Social Psychology of the University of Strasbourg, former scientific director of the

Electronic Studio Scherchen in Switzerland. Among his many books, of which most have been translated into various languages, are: *La création scientifique, Théorie de l'information et perception esthétique, Sociodynamics of culture, Art and Computer,* and *Handbook of Communication* (editor and principal author).

KAARLE NORDENSTRENG (Finland).
Professor and Chairman of the Department of Journalism and Mass Communication at the University of Tampere. Consultant to Unesco since the Meeting of Experts on the Mass Media and Society (1969), participating in the preparation of the Proposals for an International Programme on Communication Research (1971). Co-author of *Joukkotiedotus* (Mass Communication) a textbook on mass media education for teachers.

ÉVELYNE PIERRE (France).
Psychologist. Researcher at the French Ministry of Culture concerned with young people, culture and technology. Has undertaken several evaluations and studies of audio-visual educational projects. Co-author with Jean Chaguiboff and Brigitte Chapelain of *Les nouveaux téléspectateurs de 9 à 18 ans—Entretiens et analyses.*

G. N. S. RAGHAVAN (India).
Teaches development communication at the Indian Institute of Mass Communication in New Delhi and is a member of a working group, formed by the government, on software planning for Indian television. Has worked on newspapers and in government information organizations, and served as Secretary of India's Second Press Commission which gave its report in 1982.

RAFAEL RONCAGLIOLO (Peru).
Researcher at the Centro de Estudios y Promoción del Desarrollo (DESCO) in Lima and at the Instituto Latinoamericano de Estudios Transnacionales (ILET), which has its headquarters in Mexico City. Has taught in several Peruvian universities and has written on education and communication.

TAKASHI SAKAMOTO (JAPAN).
A specialist in educational technology and educational psychology, in particular instructional design and evaluation. Professor of

About the authors

Educational Methods, Head of the Teacher Training Division and Chief of the Research Laboratory of Science Education at the Tokyo Institute of Education. He is the author of many studies on various aspects of educational technology in Japan.

ANA MARIA SANDI (Romania).
Senior Researcher, International Centre of Methodology for Future and Development Studies, University of Bucharest.

PIERRE SCHAEFFER (France).
Professor at the National Music Conservatory and Member of the Audiovisual High Council. Researcher in the audio-visual field, writer and composer. Among his works are: *Machines à communiquer* and *Traité des objets musicaux*.

MICHEL SOUCHON (France).
Director of studies in the Department of Futures Research at the National Audio-visual Institute. Has written on the sociology of communication and of the media: *La télévision et son public, 1947–1977; Petit écran, grand public;* and *L'enfant devant la télévision* (co-author).

RENALDO INFANTE URIVAZO (Cuba).
Degree in journalism and political science (Havana University). Awarded a Unesco fellowship to attend a course in mass communication sciences in Quito, Ecuador, in 1971. At present, Programme Planning Director at the Cuban Radio and Television Institute (ICRT).

Note
The articles by Yuri Babansky, Thomas A. Bauer, Howard Hitchens and Mircea Malitza have not been previously published.
  The other texts are reprinted from *Prospects, Quarterly Review of Education*:
Abraham Moles: Vol. V, No. 2, 1975;
Rita Cruise O'Brien; Henri Dieuzeide; Donald P. Ely; G. N. S. Raghavan; Rafael Roncagliolo and Noreene Z. Janus; Ana Maria Sandi: Vol. X, No. 1, 1980;
Pierre Schaeffer: Vol. X, No. 4, 1980;

About the authors

Michel Souchon: Vol. XII, No. 1, 1982;
Takashi Sakamoto; Renaldo Infante Urivazo: Vol. XII, No. 3, 1982;
Dymas Joseph: Vol. XII, No. 4, 1982;
Gaspare Barbiellini Amidei; Gérald Berger; Asle Gire Dahl; Ferenc Genzwein; Len Masterman; Sirkka Minkkinen and Kaarle Nordenstreng; Évelyne Pierre: Vol. XIII, No. 2, 1983.

LB 1043.2 .F8 M43

FEB 15 1991

JUL 12 1993

[I]ED.83/XXXV.2/A